Contents

Chapter 1

One week in Paris – "Is your heart free?"

Alfred Nobel came to meet Bertha Kinsky at the Gare du Nord railway station an autumn day in 1875, and took her to Le Grand Hotel. His stylish reception of her must have impressed Bertha. For a secretary to be met by her employer in his new vehicle with rubber tyres and accommodated in one of the grandest luxury hotels in Paris was far from customary practice in the 19th century. Or, actually, in any century. But, in fact, Bertha was far from any woman. When she replied to the advertisement placed by a perfect stranger, a businessman, and travelled to Paris on her own, these were exceptional acts at a time when unmarried gentlewomen would hardly step outside the house without an escort.

True, Bertha and Alfred had learnt something about each other during the few months leading up to their first encounter. The mail carriage on the railway line linking Vienna and Paris had regularly carried their letters, written in German, French or English. Bertha's missives were verbose, running into several pages with much underlining, many exclamation and question marks. His letters were shorter, the pen-strokes thicker and the characters squashed more closely together. [7] She noted that the tone of Nobel's writing suggested that he was "...although intelligent and witty, a melancholic man. Indeed, he seemed unhappy, a misanthropist, but with a broad education and holding deeply felt philosophical views." Bertha discovers that her letters "seemed to have a stimulating effect on him, never mind what exactly might have been the cause." [8]

The inventor and businessman had handled his own correspondence for the last decade, but by now the sheer volume of letters was overwhelming him. Nobel was writing between 20-40 letters every day and received as many. It was normal practice at the time to employ secretarial help. His French partner, Paul Barbe, surrounded himself with secretaries and assistants, and so did his Swedish friend and colleague Alarik Liedbeck.

In his letters to Miss Kinsky, Nobel had interrogated her about her skills. Did she have any experience of typing, using a Remington typewriter? Was she familiar with shorthand? How many languages did she speak? For his part, Nobel spoke five languages with equal correctness and elegance: In addition to his native tongue, he knew Russian, German, English and French. He soon learned that his new secretary was competent in as many languages, but in her case, Italian had taken the place of Russian.

Alfred Nobel was a demanding employer, as one of his letters shows: "My requirements are terribly high, in that I want perfect English, French, German and Swedish, familiarity with the use of the Remington typewriter etc., but I don't ask for the impossible. Should I like the person in question, my demands would very probably collapse like a house of cards." [9]

He had received many replies to his advertisement. After an extensive exchange of letters, Miss Kinsky slipped through the eye of the needle, at least initially.

Would she meet her new employer's grand expectations?

The new Paris

Alfred and Bertha were driving to Le Grand Hôtel. What was the morning like? Did bright autumnal sunlight illuminate the red and yellow leaves on the chestnut trees along the boulevard? Or was it a grey, cloudy day that lent the grand buildings calm and mass?

The pavements in front of the new great fashion houses and stores were crowded with people. The city had been changed when the architectural plans by the architect Baron Haussmann were completed in 1870. Old Paris, with its narrow passages and tumble-down buildings, had disappeared and been replaced by wide boulevards, straight streets and fresh parks. The visions of Emperor Louis Napoleon III were being brought to life: Paris was to be the center of Europe and its capital of culture.

Bertha allows her eyes to stray and look at the luxurious shops. She cannot afford to buy any of the goods in the tempting displays - as a matter of fact, she has hardly a *sou* to spare. [10] She possesses nothing of value except a piece of jewelry set with diamonds, inherited from her guardian Friedrich Fürstenberg. Her only other adornment is her title: Countess.

Alfred turns left into Rue Royale, and then right for Boulevard des Capucines and the hotel. In the two years since he moved to the great metropolis, he has become familiar with the city. Paris, with its central location in Europe, is well placed to function as the center for his network of contacts in the dynamite trade. The entire continent was busy, welding and hammering, demolishing and building; factories were founded, railways and harbors constructed, canals dug and waterways spanned by new bridges. All of which required dynamite. Nobel's patent on the world's most powerful explosive meant that the list of his customers was lengthening rapidly. At the age of 40, he could invest in the first home of his own - a luxury villa in Avenue Malakoff.

He enjoyed the French capital with its wealth of historic buildings, grandiose monuments and green oases. The man who had grown up in the deprived areas of north Stockholm wrote in a letter home: "Here, at every street corner, you can practically smell civilization." [11] On the other hand, he was less delighted with the French, whose "chauvinism" irritated him. He thought them vain and that their tone of conversation was characterized by "tastelessness". [12] As for French women, he rarely encountered anyone who could speak any language other than her own. Was this the reason why he advertised for a secretary in Austria?

Nobel's brothers could not see the point. His older brother, Ludvig, wrote to him:

We can't stop discussing the fact that you advertised in Vienna. There is no lack of women here who would have accepted the position and become housekeeper in your home, women with all the education, language skills and talents you require – and since you do not include youth and beauty in your demands, many are indeed qualified for the work. [13]

Vienna, its people as well as its culture, occupied a special place in Alfred's heart. Since 1873, when he started up a factory in Pressburg (today's Bratislava), he had been visiting Austria regularly. Was it during one of his business travels that it occurred to him that advertising for a secretary here might be a promising idea? It was important that she should have good German, since a large part of his correspondence was conducted in that language. In addition, Austria adhered strongly to the *Bildung* concept of German humanism; an educational ideal that entailed not only acquiring knowledge but also the formation of character. [14] Did Alfred think it easier to find a secretary who was both well trained and highly educated in Austria?

Alfred stops in front of number 12, Boulevard des Capucines: Le Grand Hotel. He could hardly have found more fashionable quarters for his new secretary, with six floors and occupying two blocks. The vision of Emperor Napoleon III included a unique Parisian hotel to demonstrate to the travelling international elite what impressive progress the country had made under the rule of the Second Empire. Members of the city's high society, its famous artists, authors and politicians – all strolled in and out through the hotel's swing doors.

They agree to meet in the hotel restaurant a couple of hours later. Bertha goes to the reception desk to pick up her keys. Surrounded by marble columns and fine wood paneling, she telegraphs home to Vienna. Then she goes to her hotel room, which turns out to be a sumptuously decorated suite. Her first impression of Alfred Nobel is sober: "[He] made a good impression. I had assumed that he would be old, but he wasn't – only 43. Dark beard, average height, neither handsome nor ugly, with a grim expression softened by his kind, bright eyes." [15]

"Lily-white hands"

No one had foreseen that the well-educated Countess Kinsky would travel alone to Paris to work for a foreign businessman. Bertha had been given the upbringing proper to a "blue-blooded young lady with lily-white hands." [16] Blue blood signified aristocratic or clerical origins, while lily-white hands were acquired only by staying out of strong sunlight and away from physical work outdoors. A young noble lady's hands should be employed with sewing, embroidery and piano playing. The Swedish nobleman Fritz von Dardel was scarcely alone in holding the opinion that his fiancée Augusta Silfverschiöld's hands should "ideally never touch anything but flowers" and her thoughts should "dwell on nothing but love and poetry." [17]

The Countess's full name was Bertha Sophia Felicita, born Countess Kinsky von Chinic und Tettau. It sounds like a name straight out of an old-style society novel, full of mysterious connections, forbidden love affairs and castle towers hiding secret chambers. The sense of fantasy is certainly fed by the home of the Kinsky family: The gorgeous Kinsky Palace in Prague, one of the most beautiful rococo buildings in the Bohemian capital and the main home of the princely branch of the family. This is where Bertha first saw the light of day on the 9th June 1843. She was baptized in the beautiful small monastery church of Maria Snezna. [18]

The Kinskys were one of the most important noble families in Bohemia, and given to parading their blue-blooded arrogance. The family tree was adorned by a lengthy line of counts and princes, generals and ambassadors, and they were proud of their reputation, including the many stories about the "wild Kinskys" that circulated around Prague. Several of their earlier relatives had become known for their rebellious personalities. [19]

Bertha's father, Franz Joseph Kinsky, was a count, lieutenant and later field marshal. Portraits of him and his three brothers, all generals, show four straight-backed gentlemen with sideburns and plumed hats. They wear colorful uniforms with gold buttons and glossy black boots. [20] Like many aristocrats, they had the tendency to believe that they were exempt from the rules governing society. The nobility's credo was "I am above the law."

Although the aristocrats had lost much of their power and status by the beginning of the 19th century, they were still influential in many areas. Their huge land and property holdings had been handed down within the family for generations. Their castles loomed over the landscapes. In the saddle, they literally *looked down* on the people on foot. As the German author Karl Leberecht Immermann expressed it: "They [members of the nobility] move from their grand houses to the Court, to the spas and to the various meeting places of fashionable society, like warlike winged gods or demi-gods they pass through the lines of subordinates – indeed, even tread on their heads." [21]

It would seem to follow that the future looked promising for young Countess Kinsky. But even her baptismal ceremony sent out the message that she was not quite at home in the high society setting: No member of the Bohemian nobility had ever been baptized in the small church of Maria Snezna, and that included her close relatives. What's more, neither the princes nor the counts in the family were included among her godparents when the priest anointed her forehead. Already at the moment of her birth, Bertha's record had acquired a blemish: She did not have a sufficient number of blood-relations of the proper kind. Not only was there a wide gap between the upper class and the other social classes at this time, but distinctions existed also *within* the nobility: Eight noble ancestors were essential if one were to count oneself as belonging to the uppermost order. Bertha's mother, Sophie Wilhelmine von Körner, came from the middle class, which at a stroke reduced her daughter's claim to nobility to just four.

At the age of 18, Sophie had married Count Franz Joseph Kinsky, 50 years older than herself, with the hope of gaining social status and financial security. At the time, such age differences were not unusual. However, the 75-year-old Count died during her second pregnancy – and little Bertha was fatherless from birth. Sophie took her newborn daughter and her 6-year-old son Arthur with her and moved to live with the children's guardian, Landgrave Friedrich Fürstenberg in Brno, the largest town in Moravia.

Here Bertha had a happy, secure childhood. Her upbringing befitted an aristocratic young lady and included private tuition in languages and music. Nothing suggested anything other than that, when the time came, she would have all the right qualifications for attracting a suitable husband, preferably an officer. What mattered was that he should be wealthy, to secure for her a comfortable life and ensure that her thoughts would "dwell on nothing but love and poetry," as Fritz von Dardel had put it. [22]

However, this was not what life had in store for her.

Avenue Malakoff

Bertha and Alfred meet for lunch in Le Grand Hotel's elegant restaurant, Café de la Paix, all tall ceilings and huge wall mirrors. Waiters wearing long, white aprons glide soundlessly between the tables, carrying gleaming silver dishes.

What did they talk about during the meal? Perhaps the employer outlined his new secretary's various tasks? Above all, Bertha was to help him to deal with his correspondence with his many business partners, such as the Banque Lyonnaise in France, the Krümmel-based factory in Germany, a chemical plant at Lysaker near Oslo in Norway and the British Dynamite Company. Alfred sorted his incoming mail into *Letters from Men* and *Letters from Women* – unless they went into what is always the biggest pile: *Begging Letters*. [23] In addition to assisting with the deskwork, Bertha was to be the housekeeper in his home.

They finish their lunch and leave the hotel. Alfred wants to show Bertha his home and her new place of work. They turn left in Avenue Foch, lined with chestnut trees and home to many grand palaces. They continue into one of the most exclusive districts in Paris, the 16th *arrondissement*, where they stop outside the wrought-iron gate of number 53, Avenue Malakoff.

Bertha walks into the house and looks around. Built on four floors, her employer's home is spacious but not excessively large. Elegant, but not too pretentious. The interior seems to speak of the style of the past in the French tradition. The paintings hung on the walls were changed every fortnight by an agreement he had made with a gallery. [24]

For Nobel, it is his first ever experience of living in such a classy setting. Years of demanding work had eventually brought fruit. Many members of the Nobel family were gifted, however several of them struggled financially. Among his ancestors from the southern province of Skåne were several inventors and men with scientific interests. The most famous was his great-great grandfather, Olof Rudbeck (1630–1702), a natural scientist who had so many and varied talents that he was given the epithet "the Nordic Leonardo da Vinci" at the University of Uppsala, where he taught astronomy, mathematics, physics, chemistry and anatomy. Rudbeck's outstanding contribution to anatomy was his discovery of the lymphatic system (1653). His descendants included several remarkable people with both scientific and artistic abilities, though no one acquired actual academic qualifications.

Alfred's father, Immanuel Nobel (1801–1872), was a case in point. His enthusiasm for inventing was nearly unstoppable. As early as in 1825, three of his patents were granted by the collegiate committee of the Technical Institute. As an inventor, Immanuel's life was a series of economic ups and downs. For years, his Stockholm-based construction firm had full order books. During that period, one of his projects was to build Sweden's first rubber manufacturing plant. It produced elastic materials, which went into equipment for surgical, military and industrial use. One of his innovative concepts was a combined rucksack, mattress, life-jacket – and float – intended for the army.

However, in 1833, the year of Alfred's birth, his father went bankrupt. The family had to confront many other misfortunes that year, including the loss of their home in a ruinous fire. Only a few things remained, according to the tax authorities: "A couple of tables and beds; some chairs in poor condition; 6 sets of sheets; 3 pillowcases; copper- and ironware worth 20 Swedish thalers in all; glass and china worth 10 thalers in all." [25]

Alfred's mother, Andriette Ahlsell Nobel (1805–1889), only just managed to rescue herself and the children from the sea of flames. Andriette came from a hard-working farming family in the southern province of Småland. She was a tough, good-humored woman who contributed more than anyone else to keeping the family together during this difficult period.

After the fire, the family moved into a flat in a block dating back to the 16th century and built around a courtyard at Norrlands Street 9, in the outskirts of Stockholm. Alfred Bernhard Nobel was born here on the 21st October 1833. The new arrival was far from robust – in fact, Alfred was so weak that he almost died during the delivery. Without the loving care of his mother, he might not have survived his first year of life. The little boy grew very close to Andriette, a bond that would endure throughout life.

Alfred's formal schooling was three terms at Jakob's School, which was attended by the poor children in northern Stockholm. During the breaks, the pupils fought among the barrels and carts in the yard outside. The teachers kept order by physical means. According to his great contemporary, August Strindberg, who attended the same school, the pupils felt that a day when they got away without a beating was an exception. [26]

Little Alfred escaped punishment. He was small for his age and avoided scuffles with the other boys. He made himself invisible in the playground, but excelled in the classroom. Alfred was given top marks in every subject. Immanuel, who was usually slow to praise, would boast about his youngest son. [27] During these years, the family was constantly on the move within the suburban area of northern Stockholm, where the rents were the lowest. A new child was born in every home: Robert in 1829, Ludvig in 1831 and Alfred in 1833. When in 1836 they had moved into new lodgings at Riddare Street 20, a baby girl, Henrietta, arrived.

Little Alfred had moved to a new house five times before he was six years old. The poor living conditions did nothing to improve the boy's health. In the winters, the cold seeped in through ill-fitting windows and the smoking paraffin lamps made the children cough. He was to fear and detest cold for the rest of his life. In the backyard, rats were running around.

Early on, Alfred became determined never to go bankrupt like his father.

A booklover

As a man of success, Alfred Nobel stands on his own precious rugs, with his new secretary at his side. They are on the second floor in the house at Avenue Malakoff where the windows give a fine view of Paris. Above the roofs, row upon row of yellow chimney pots; a few blocks away, they catch sight of the arched back of the Triumphal Arch.

Alfred walks Bertha through the wing of the house which is being renovated for her use. The rooms are more elegant than any other place where she has lived. Then he shows her his book collection. After his move to the great metropolis, he has been buying books and created a wide-ranging library. It contains more than 2000 volumes and consists not only of French literature, but also English, German and Scandinavian. Alfred is well versed in the latest publications. The 6th edition of the most influential work of the 19th century, Darwin's *The Origin of Species*, is part of his collection, as well as major works dealing with subjects in physics, chemistry and many other scientific areas. However, the 500 literary fiction titles make up the largest part of his book collection: Large, bound editions of classical works by authors such as Shakespeare, Goethe, Schiller, de Musset and Tegnér, who he often referred to or cited.

As a boy of maybe thirteen or fourteen, Alfred had started reading the authors of the Romantic period and this became a passion that was to last all his life. His shelves held, among others, Lord Byron's *Poetical Works* in an edition from 1826: 11 small, red volumes with gilt lettering. [28] He shows Bertha the long 1812 poem *Childe Harold's Pilgrimage*, a melancholic travelogue he likes to quote, as well as fifteen books by Victor Hugo, the great author of the French Romantic period, who also was an acquaintance of his, living only a few blocks away, in 130, Avenue d'Eylau. [29]

Does he tell Bertha of the many occasions when he has dined *chez* Hugo? [30] She admires the socially engaged author just as much as he does. The list of her favorite writers otherwise includes de Musset, Zola, Flaubert, Tennyson and Dickens. [31] As the two of them discuss similarities and differences between their preferred writers, Alfred realizes that his new secretary is a fellow literary enthusiast.

But, unlike Alfred, Bertha had never written anything else than letters and pages in her diaries.

Literary ambitions

How many people in his surroundings knew that Nobel, the inventor and businessman, also wrote poetry? There are no indications that he shared this information with his friends and colleagues. But Alfred had been writing since he was a young man, often aspiring to resemble his favorite poets Lord Byron and Percy Bysshe Shelley. Loneliness, the yearning for love, and reflections about the meaning of life and the origins of the universe were recurring themes. As a teenager, he often picked up a pen to put words down on paper. During periods when he was ill, he would read. Or write. Alfred spent hour after hour indoors writing in blank verse, while his peers were outdoors playing.

Did he dream of becoming a writer? [32] There are those who think so, and hold that it was his father who convinced him to abandon this idea. Others, like his brother Robert, believed Alfred wrote first and foremost "to impress the ladies." [33]

There is little reason to doubt that Alfred took literature seriously. In his 51-page, hand-written poem entitled *Canto I*, full of deletions and amendments, he expresses the conviction that poetry is the highest form of language. Poetry is a treasure that can charge life with meaning. It can free us from everything that binds us to trivial and ephemeral things. Without "hopes and dreams and poetry", life becomes impoverished. "Let us pay homage to poetry" says the poem's narrator. *Canto I* is structured in different thematic categories: The poetry of daytime, night, love, life, benevolence and dreams. It seems that Alfred had ambitions of continuing with *Canto II, III*, but these ambitions were curtailed. [34]

Also in the dramatic sketch *Ett fantasiens offer* ("A Victim of the Imagination"; date unknown), Alfred's enthusiasm for the written word shines through. The drama's main character, the poet Robert, is characterized as having the dreamy nature of one who has turned away from worldly things. He is an incurable idealist, in short, a "victim of the imagination," who at one point declares: "What I call poetry is the soul's enthusiasm for what is noble and true." [35]

There are many indications that he had a strong urge to write. Small, crumpled pieces of paper bearing words of wisdom had crept in between the jars and test tubes in the laboratory and were discovered long after his death. As recently as in 1956, scraps of paper scribbled with his handwritten poems were found in a stack of miscellaneous clippings. Most of what Alfred wrote consisted of rough drafts. At a time when he encountered setbacks in the form of accidental explosions that led to adverse newspaper articles and the threat of bankruptcy, the 35-year old wrote to his brother Robert that he was considering abandoning his work as an inventor, and starting with something "completely different". Weary and distressed during this period of hardship, he wanted to give up on everything that goes under the name of "business life" and earn his living by his pen. [36] Alfred dared to believe that he was not wholly lacking in the ability to express himself after an English scholar commented on a poem he had written in blank verse. The Englishman was the clergyman C. Lesingham Smith, an amateur poet in his own right. After having read one of Alfred's poems, Smith sent him a letter full of words of praise, underlining that "there are no more than a half dozen mediocre lines among all 425." [37] He compared the poem to John Milton's superb epic poem *Paradise Lost* (1667), which was also written in blank verse, and encouraged him to continue writing. [38]

Despite these words of praise, it was not long before Alfred put his pen aside to pursue a vocation in engineering. Only in the late hours of the evening, he sometimes took out a pen and paper to write down a verse or two.

"Spinster"

Alfred and Bertha leave the library and go down to the conservatory, which is one of his favorite rooms. He likes being alone with his "silent friends", as he calls the flowers. [39] They are served a pot of tea and chat about all manner of things. Before the day is over, and the street lights come on, Alfred drives his new secretary back to Le Grand Hotel.

In her hotel room, Bertha takes out a pen and paper. She is satisfied with her first day with Mr. Nobel: "The conversations with him had my undivided attention. Talking with him about the world and people, about art and life, about our times and eternity was a huge intellectual pleasure." [40]

But he was not cheerful, her new employer: "He is sad and a little cynical. Perhaps that is the reason why Lord Byron is his favorite poet?" [41]

Miss Kinsky goes to bed, but is unable to fall asleep. The moon sails up over the rooftops, shining and serene. When daylight filters through the blinds, she is still awake. She gets dressed and goes down to breakfast. Then she goes out into the streets, wandering up and down along the avenues and boulevards. She walks past St. Germaine-des-Prés, across the Place St. Michel, continues past the exclusive jewelers on Rue de la Paix, where a young, wealthy Australian suitor had once purchased a piece of diamond jewelry for her. But her dream of a marriage with a rich man was shattered when the Australian suddenly returned home after Bertha had made their engagement known. Does she also walk past the famous singing school of Gilbert Duprez, where she a few years back had studied? At that time, her goal had been to become a famous opera singer, but her nerves failed her when she stood before an audience.

Bertha continues past La Cité and Porte St. Martin. She walks along the Seine. Dark leaves and branches create a lush pattern against the greenish-grey water of the river. She walks up and down along the streets. Broad and straight streets, narrow and winding streets. [42] For the first time in many years she is alone. She has time to think.

Does she sit down under the awning of a sidewalk café and order a cup of coffee and a croissant? Maybe she throws glances at the Parisian women's outfits as they stroll down the street. Bertha has always loved beauty. Beautiful people. Faces. Clothing. In the French capital, women's fashion has changed since she was here last. The wide crinoline (the bell-shaped petticoat) skirt was now pulled back and replaced by the bustle, playing out from the small of the back. [43]

Does the passing waiter react to the fact that she has no wedding ring, despite her mature age? To be past the age of 30 without having tied the knot was viewed as catastrophic in her circles. When she was younger, Bertha had had high hopes for her future marriage, but even at the time of her debutante ball, she had understood the impact of not having the prescribed number of noble ancestors. This was something that had hung over her throughout her childhood and both her mother and guardian had attempted to shield her from. The debutante ball was an extremely important event for any girl from the upper class of Vienna. Bertha had spent a long time planning her wardrobe and hairstyle. Her mother Sophie sewed her daughter's outfit herself. When the evening came, the girl was breathtakingly beautiful in a tailored ball gown covered with rosebuds. Her hair had been styled in long corkscrew curls.

Full of expectations, the 18-year old found a chair against the wall of the ballroom adorned with flowers. On each side of the ballroom, girls from the nobility sat dressed up in light-colored dresses or skirts and silk blouses with piping. Bertha craned her neck and allowed a smile to play upon her lips. A young, attractive nobleman would certainly notice her soon. But one man after the next strolled past without giving her a glance. When the evening came to an end, Miss Kinsky had not danced a single dance. Her disappointment was enormous. She realized that in this milieu neither charm, nor wit, nor intelligence mattered. Here one had to have 16 ancestors from the nobility to be considered attractive, or come from an extremely well-off branch of the family. Bertha came up short on both counts.

On the way home, she was inconsolable. Weeping, she declared to her mother that she would marry the 52-year old Baron Gustav von Heine-Gelder. [44] The baron was one of the wealthiest men in Vienna and had proposed to her just before the ball. Sophie protested, but Bertha insisted. Finally, her mother gave in and the engagement was announced. However, when the prospective bride and groom were alone together for the first time, it did not go well. The 52-year old pressed his lips against her own. Ugh! Bertha had not been prepared for this. Her first kiss – from an older man. A man for whom she felt nothing whatsoever. The next day she broke the engagement. The gifts were sent back to the baron. The episode was a source of embarrassment for all of them.

Bertha still hoped to find a good match. She was engaged to be married altogether three times, but each time something went wrong. The rich Australian suitor had returned to Australia. A while later, the Austrian singer Adolf Prince zu Sayn-Wittgenstein-Hohenstein impressed her when he sang an aria from Charles Gounod's opera *Faust*. It was not long before sweet music arose between them in real life, and this time Bertha was in love. But then a mishap occurred: On the way to a performance in America, the young singer suffered a cardiac arrest and died unexpectedly in his cabin. The incident came as a shock to everyone and Bertha grieved profoundly over her loss.

Her wounds were gradually healed, but given the years that had passed, the attractive, well-bred Bertha Kinsky no longer had an advantageous position in the marriage market. Young women who took part in the ball season *too* many years in a row, quickly acquired a stigma. "Miss Sophie B is a first-class beauty but a beauty who has been out for three years, in other words, a third-class beauty," was a nobleman's comment on an unmarried girl's appearance in the season for the third year in a row. [45] Bertha had reached the age when a single woman came under the uncomplimentary definition of "spinster".

Nevertheless, she did not lose hope. Bertha was always an optimist, who retained her faith that happiness and adventure were waiting for her just around the next corner.

Dynamite

Bertha finishes her morning coffee and leaves the sidewalk café well before she will meet with her employer.

Perhaps she hails a hansom cab, which takes her directly to her employer. Or it could be that she sets out on foot and walks past the innumerable small shops, vegetable stores, and booths lining the streets. Despite Haussmann's modernization, the French capital had preserved its agrarian roots.

On Avenue Malakoff, Alfred has been up since dawn and is already hard at work. He lets his new secretary inside and shows her the laboratory in the backyard. Here he sometimes spends 14–16 hours at a stretch, alone or with his assistant Georges D. Fehrenbach. When he walks into the laboratory, he switches to another frequency. When he bends over test tubes and tins of powder, he loses touch with the outside world.

Does he tell Bertha about the process leading up to the invention of dynamite, which created his fortune? A few years after going bankrupt, his father Immanuel had emigrated east to avoid debtors' prison. In St. Petersburg, he established a machine shop that supplied mines and steam engines to the Russian government. The Russian Tsar Nicholas I wanted to strengthen his kingdom both militarily and culturally. Both war and the fear of war meant good business for Immanuel, who could finally send for his family. For four years, Andriette and the children in Stockholm had supported themselves by running a small milk and vegetable shop, often living on the verge of poverty. In 1838 Henrietta, the family's only daughter, died. Alfred was nine years old when he in 1842 stepped on board the vessel that took him and the family east. At that time, he had not seen his father since the age of four.

In St. Petersburg, life improved for the Nobel family. In 1843 Emil, an afterthought child, was born. For a few years, Immanuel's manufactory went well, especially during the Crimean War (1853-56), when the demand for mines was great. The revenues from the machine shop made it possible for him to give his sons private tutors in languages. In addition to Swedish, the Nobel brothers learned Russian, French, English and German. They were also given lessons in physics and chemistry. Alfred excelled in all subjects.

At the age of 17, his Immanuel had sent him on a two-year study trip to North America, Germany, Italy and France. Was this a strategy to convince him to give up on his literary ambitions and become an engineer? In Paris, Alfred studied under the chemist Théophile-Jules Pelouze and learned about the liquid explosive oil nitroglycerine, produced by processing sulphuric acid and salt-peter acid. He witnessed the famous chemist demonstrate the fatal liquid by pouring a few drops out onto a table top. Then he struck the drops with a hammer. The sound that ensued was like the explosion of a powerful gunshot.

Alfred was impressed. It was the Italian chemist Ascanio Sobrero, one of Pelouze's students, who first discovered nitroglycerine. His face was seriously injured when a bottle containing the liquid exploded right in front of him. Sobrero did not think it was possible to find a solution enabling a safe, practical application of the substance.

The young student saw the potential of the substance. Nitroglycerine was approximately 50 times stronger than ordinary black gunpowder. Was this something that could become the first safely manageable explosive stronger than black powder? Alfred returned home with new knowledge and started working at his father's company Nobel & Sons. In 1859, Immanuel Nobel shut down the mine manufactory in St. Petersburg and moved back to Stockholm, accompanied by his wife and two of his sons - Alfred and Emil. As the Crimean War came to an end, he had gone bankrupt for the second time, and decided to head back home.

Alfred continued his experiments with nitroglycerine in Sweden. Could he manage to liberate the substance's powerful force in a safe manner? He became obsessed with finding a solution.

Did he tell Bertha about the accident that would change his life forever? One beautiful September morning in 1864, the Nobel brothers were working in their father's workshop in Heleneborg just outside of Stockholm. They experimented with the safe handling of nitroglycerine. Approximately 250 pounds of explosive oil were stored in various places on the premises. Alfred's light-hearted, youngest brother Emil was in the process of purifying the oil when a flame suddenly shot into the air. In a matter of seconds, it was transformed into an enormous pillar of smoke. The gigantic blast that followed was like a violent crack of thunder, and the whole laboratory was blown up. Only a few charred ruins of the factory remained.

Seven people died in the accident. Emil was one of them. The 20-year old's death came as a shock for the family. For Alfred, who was mainly responsible of the experiments, the experience was traumatic. Shortly after, his father suffered a stroke. He never fully recovered.

"The Merchant of Death" people now whispered behind his back when Alfred walked by. However, he did not give up. After the accident, the police issued a ban on the production of dynamite in the country. Instead, he relocated the enterprise to a barge that was anchored up by Lake Mälaren, just west of Stockholm.

Despite the accident, Alfred continued to devote himself entirely to the study of explosives, and to the safe manufacture and use of nitroglycerine. With a combination of crystal clear logic and a unique creativity, he continued his experiments. He soon discovered that *methanol* (or wood spirits) had a moderating impact on nitroglycerine. In 1867, he found an even better solution: He used diatomaceous earth, a soft, chalky stone that resembles clay, to absorb the dangerous substance and thereby produced the dough for the sticks. At last the nitroglycerine compound could be handled and transported in a safe manner.

The same year, he patented this material under the name of dynamite, after the Greek word *dynamis* (power). He also invented the blasting cap and fuse. Using these elements, the sticks of dynamite could be ignited.

Then Alfred started to work on developing a commercial enterprise based on his invention. The young man who had grown up in the poor district of northern Stockholm had by now succeeded in making one of the most sought-after inventions in Europe, and became a member of the rising bourgeoisie. Alfred's success was well-deserved: He had experimented with the substance for almost half of his life, from when he was in his late teens, until he was in his mid-thirties.

At last he could lay his head on his pillow at night without worrying about going bankrupt, as his father had done. Or that he would ever again need to sleep in a draughty house, with rats running around in the backyard.

A loner

It is almost time for lunch. Alfred puts the beakers and jars back on the shelves and invites Bertha to accompany him on a drive in the Bois de Boulogne, which had been converted into a park under the direction of the Baron Haussmann. Open lawns and woods with beech, lime, chestnut, cedar and elm trees had been planted. Walking trails, bike paths, riding trails and small paths crisscrossed the grounds. The park was located only a few kilometers away.

What would they talk about, when they were not discussing Bertha's work duties? According to her, the conversations were carried out "in an animated and stimulating manner." Bertha was far more open and outgoing than her employer. She received a lot of attention – from a gentleman wearing a top hat driving past in a horse and carriage, from a guest at a neighboring table at Café de la Paix. There was something about her that people noticed – was it the way she dressed, or the way she held her head? Was it the proud Kinsky- blood running through her veins?

The coachman swings the whip over the backs of the horses, the wheels of the carriage crunch against the gravel. Seated next to Bertha, is man full of contradictions. As an inventor and businessman: Focused and tough. On a personal level: Modest, almost shy. Alfred handled chemicals and explosives with great self-assurance and explained the contents of the different glass containers with elegant precision. However, he spoke little about his success. He did not like being the center of attention. Neither did he put much stock in his impact on others: "He saw himself as repulsive, incapable of contacting the opposite sex. That was without a doubt why he hadn't married," was Bertha's observation. [46]

There was nothing wrong with his outward appearance. Alfred was always elegantly dressed and as he grew older, he acquired a chestnut brown, full beard that covered half of his face. The passport described him as "of average height, with brown hair, an oval face, healthy skin and blue eyes." [47] His eyes were deep-set and the expression in them was described by a friend as "piercingly intelligent." An acquaintance characterized him as a man who "always seems extremely nervous." [48]

In his forties, Alfred began to walk leaning slightly forward and with quick, short steps and a slight spring in his stride. His health had never been robust. Despite this, he lived a hectic life. Alfred spent hours travelling in crowded train compartments – "my prisons on wheels" as he called them, zigzagging across all of Europe while he was developing his business enterprise. "My home is where I am working and I work everywhere," he wrote in a letter to a friend. [49] Fellow passengers could observe a pale, middle-aged man, impeccably dressed and with a brown leather suitcase as luggage. Its contents were items for personal hygiene, a writing set, cutlery and a lighter, all shiny silver. Alfred preferred to travel light. From 1865 to 1875, he was on the road constantly. In dusty, shuddering train compartments, in horse-drawn carriages over cobblestone streets, in hotel rooms in unknown cities – often with a book to keep him company.

Alfred was not alone in travelling a great deal. After 1879, the railway traffic had exploded in Europe. Some people were skeptical about the impact of railway travel on health. "According to physicians, the speed of a railway can create a kind of chronic disturbance in the nervous system of those who travel frequently," the English author William R. Greg wrote in 1875. [50]

Was it to soothe his nerves that the nervous man visited the Bois de Boulogne almost daily when he was in Paris?

Singing ambitions

Alfred drives slowly out of the park with Bertha at his side. Small carts of violets fill the air with a lovely scent. It is the hour of the daily promenade. People are strolling down the sidewalks. They are on their way back to Avenue Malakoff, where the servants are waiting with a meal. Does Alfred greet acquaintances as they drive past, or does he prefer to hide beneath his hat?

His professional success had not made him more secure as a human being. For Bertha, it was in many ways just the opposite. She had virtually no possessions nor "accomplishments", but was not lacking in self-confidence. There was just one thing that she was very nervous about: Singing in front of many people. This was a bit unfortunate – when as a young girl, she had decided to become a famous opera singer! Bertha had not married a rich man as she was expected to, but instead of moving in with a wealthy relative or tie the knot with an old bachelor, as many women in her situation would have done, she had dared to pursue a dream. And perhaps it was her mother's dream, too? When she was young, Sophie von Körner had wanted to become an opera singer, but her parents had insisted that she marry for wealth instead.

Bertha's singing ambitions were seriously awakened in the summer of 1864, when she heard the famous soprano Adelina Patti sing at the Baden-Baden spa. "How divine," the romantic, young girl thought. "Imagine standing up there on stage and taking so many hearts by storm with the help of art's magic!" Encouraged by her mother, she started taking singing lessons. Hour after hour were spent practicing scales. Do-re-mi... Now her life was all about art with a capital A: "And - nothing could and would cause me to turn away from my art, no temptations to leave the stage and get married would touch this proud artist. The one who is found in art's high tower, belongs forever and eternally in its service," she declared with pathos. [51]

Bertha was not the only young Viennese with an ambition to be a singer. Austria's capital was Europe's music metropolis more than any other city. According to the Austrian author Stefan Zweig, the city's atmosphere during the second half of the 19th century created a veritably "contagious" compulsion for artistic production. "Everyone" wanted to be a singer, actor or writer. [52] Miss Kinsky dreamt of seeing her name on the billboards.

Encouraged by her mother, she travelled to Paris in 1867 to study at the school of the famous tenor and voice teacher Gilbert Duprez. But during the open student recitals, something unexpected happened: Scarcely a sound was emitted from her lips. Bertha, who ordinarily was so uninhibited and extroverted, could not handle the pressure when she was about to perform. Unfortunately, this did not get better with time, and eventually she realized that she was not meant to be someone who stood on stage and took "many hearts by storm with the help of art's magic"! [53]

Now there was little left of her mother's widow's pension, which had financed her expensive singing lessons. The path from being a young, promising prima donna to becoming a social disaster was not a long one. There was a silver lining, one could perhaps say - because this led to an important turning point in Countess Kinsky's life.

Bittersweet success

Back on Avenue Malakoff, the servants are waiting with the meal.

Alfred Nobel lives a frugal daily life, but when he has guests he serves several succulent dishes. The food is as a rule French or Italian, as he is not fond of Swedish cuisine.

Alfred had visited the metropolis many times before he decided to invest in a home here. It was in Paris that he as a 17-year old first learned about nitroglycerine. It was also here that he some years later managed to get financial backing to develop his invention. His father did not have the means to offer him support. In 1864, the 31-year-old Alfred applied for a loan from the bank Société de Crédit Mobilier, which specialized in financing railway construction and public works – clearly a market for an explosive. He must have made an impression in the bank, presenting his plans in flawless French. The result was that he could return home with a loan of 100,000 francs, a considerable sum of money at the time.

It soon became apparent that Alfred had just as much talent as a businessman as an inventor. Determined to succeed, he started to build up an industry based on his invention. Alfred never considered export from Sweden to be a possibility, in part due to the dangers associated with the transport of explosives. At an early stage, he understood the importance of having good allies. He contacted one of Sweden's richest men, the Stockholm merchant Johan Wilhelm Smitt, and together they started the first company for manual production and sale of nitroglycerine: Nitroglycerin Aktiebolaget. The following year, a dynamite company was founded in Norway (Nitroglycerin Compagniet, Lysaker, for a period as Dyno Industrier). In 1865, Alfred acquired two new associates – the German brothers and business partners Winckeln, who invited him to Germany. The Winckeln brothers financed the production of the dynamite in Krümmel outside of Hamburg, while Alfred oversaw the work. Between 1865 and 1873, he lived in a modest home, close to his laboratory and the center of his business by the factory in Krümmel. After a while, the company was converted into a limited company – Dynamitaktiengesellschaft or DAG (1876).

In 1866, Alfred began looking to the west, towards the United States of America. His goal was for dynamite to be used in New York's large, new construction projects. Alfred travelled to the city to try to promote his invention. But the timing was unfortunate – there had been several large accidents and explosions of late. Alfred sought out the mayor of New York City and asked for permission to give a demonstration in a stone quarry located in upper Manhattan. According to *The New York Times*, the Swedish inventor was successful in his efforts to convince the huge crowd in attendance of the substance's merits and safe usage. [54] In the following days, American newspapers were full of articles about the experiment. Soon after, Alfred formed the United States Blasting Oil Company.

However, the American venture never became a success. Like many Europeans, Nobel was surprised to discover that the economic and social conditions for the labor market were much tougher in the USA than in Europe. As a businessman, he was known for his honesty and high ethical standards. In the USA, he experienced for the first time that someone attempted to swindle him. Was that one of the reasons why he would never again return to the continent after his first visit?

Instead he began considering the English market. Great Britain had achieved the greatest advancements in industrialization, and opened new markets in the colonies of the British Empire. He contacted the Scottish engineer John Downe, who became a partner when he started the British Dynamite Company in 1871. But the English were skeptical about the dynamite. Acting against all statutory provisions, Alfred travelled around in Aberdeen, Glasgow and Bristol with a suitcase containing more than 20 pounds of dynamite to give practical demonstrations. The otherwise extremely law-abiding businessman broke British law and risked two years in prison if somebody should discover what was in the suitcase!

After having penetrated the English market, France was next. Through the Winckeln brothers, Nobel met the French industrial magnate and politician Paul François Barbe. He had a large network of contacts, both in business and among politicians. In 1875, Barbe and Nobel started the joint-stock company Société Générale pour la Fabrication de la Dynamite. Nobel was the strategist, while Barbe was the one to play the cards. Soon large-scale buyers of the explosive from various industries were making inquiries - mining, railroad construction, and roads and tunnel works.

Between 1867 and 1876, Nobel's total dynamite production had expanded from 11 to 5000 tons. He founded dynamite companies in Sweden (1864), Norway (1865), Germany (1865), the USA (1866), France (1870), and Great Britain (1871), amongst others. While approximately 16 years had passed from the time he first learned about nitroglycerine until he obtained the patent for dynamite, it took him only about half that time to build up a successful business enterprise based on the invention.

The German - French War

Alfred and Bertha finish their meal in the dining room in Avenue Malakoff. The servants clear off the table. Soon they resume their various work tasks. When the work day has come to an end, Alfred once again drives his secretary back to the Grand Hôtel.

They have told each other about their respective backgrounds and shared some experiences. At some point, they start discussing peace. Was it in context of discussing the German-French war (1870-1871), which had ravaged the city a few years before? The war had claimed a total of 140,000 French and 47,500 German soldiers' lives. France had lost the abundant French landscapes of Alsace-Lorraine to the Germans and were obliged to pay five billion francs in war damages. In addition, the war had wreaked enormous destruction in Paris. Louvre, the valuable art museum, had been set on fire and several of the wings were destroyed. Thousands of people were killed when the city of Paris fell in 1871.

Perhaps it was the still visible traces of the war that led to Alfred telling Bertha of his opinion on the armament issue? He had been confronted with this since he was young. As a child, he had seen his father produce and sell naval mines. As a teenager, he had begun experimenting with explosives. Alfred viewed a balance of terror as the best temporary solution for keeping the peace: "The day that two armies are able to destroy each other in one second, all civilized nations will retreat from war in fear and disband their armed forces." [55] He told her that he would like to invent a weapon or machine with "such a powerfully terrifying impact that war would become impossible." [56]

How did Bertha react to this? At the time, she was completely indifferent to these questions. Hearing about the outbreak of war in Europe was just as insignificant to her as hearing "about a volcano erupting on an island in the West Indies." Her upbringing in Austria had taught her to have respect for the military. War was viewed as something given, as part of history's brutal logic. The Austrian-Hungarian Empire was full of symbols and long-standing, proud military traditions. The officers wore elegant buff coats and green plumes waved from the hats of the highest-ranking officers, something the young Bertha had found attractive. She could not imagine a world without war. This was just as unnatural for her as "a world without trees or an ocean without waves." [57]

Despite the destructions, Paris had quickly gotten back on its feet after the war. In just a brief period, the Louvre was restored under the direction of the architect Hector Martin Leufel. Haussmann's restoration was carried out with smooth efficiency.

The French on the other hand, did not take their defeat lightly. As the saying went: "Always think of it, never speak of it."

Alfred stops in front of Le Grand Hotel. They agree to meet the following day. Bertha goes to the reception and makes a request to send a telegram to Vienna.

"The riddle"

Almost a week has passed since Bertha arrived in Paris. Her employer has revealed a great deal about himself and his view of the world to his secretary during the few days that they have known each other. And he is going to reveal even more. To her surprise, Alfred asks if she would like to read a poem he had written when he was young. Unlike most of what he wrote as a young man, he had saved this poem, which he called "The Riddle". It was long - all of 425 lines. In the poem, written in blank verse, the 18-year old Alfred had employed many of the same turns of phrase and metaphors as those of his role models Byron and Shelley. The poem addresses a "you" and the tone is confessional.

When Bertha starts to read, she encounters a young man with a gloomy view of both himself and human existence. A sensitive and pale brooder who has been ill a great deal, who does not play with the other children, is rejected by the girls, and has "all of his dreams crushed in meeting with reality." [58]

Had the young Alfred been writing about himself?

Bertha continues to read the stack of crumpled pages. As if by magic, the boy's life changes when a beautiful girl appears. Suddenly it acquires purpose and meaning. However, the story has a tragic ending; the young girl dies. After her death, the man lives like a hermit, determined to dedicate his life to a "more noble" pursuit.

Was there one particular girl Alfred had in mind?

When he was a 17-year old chemistry student, he had apparently met a Swedish "sweetheart" in Paris. Nobody knows what her name was or where she came from. The sources say little about her. According to some biographers, she worked as an apothecary's apprentice. In that case, perhaps she was standing behind the counter one day when Alfred dropped in to buy pills for the headaches which so frequently plagued him? The relationship had been short-term as the girl fell ill and died. According to a source, she died from tuberculosis. [59]

Alfred never spoke about the incident.

Was it this girl's story he told in the poem "The Riddle"? Was this why he went back to the poem repeatedly, and would come to rewrite it in four versions? Does it also give us an indication of why the now 43-year-old Alfred had never become attached to a woman?

Bertha puts down the stack of fading pages and looks at him. She lets him know that she thinks the poem is "splendid". [60]Alfred puts the crumpled manuscript back in the drawer. Then he takes her back to the hotel.

Back in her hotel room, no sooner has Bertha laid down her head than her pillowcase becomes damp with tears. Her new employer's unexpected openness has taken her by surprise, however, she is far from content. Although known for her unwavering optimism, Miss Kinsky is now inconsolable.

Yet another night passes into morning without her having dozed off.

"Are you fancy-free?"

On Avenue Malakoff, it is quiet. When daylight filters in through the window, Alfred is already seated bent over papers, pen and ink and preparing for the day's meetings. Occasionally, he leans his head on his hand and looks out the window.

Despite his success, he is not happy. To his friends and close acquaintances, he often speaks of his great loneliness. In a letter to his childhood friend and colleague Alarik Liedbeck, he writes: "As others do, and perhaps more than others do, I feel the heavy burden of loneliness and for years I have sought to find somebody whose heart can find the way to my own." [61]

He has shown his new secretary a poem of a personal nature. His next step is to ask her a question that was at least equally personal. One day, he asks Bertha: "Are you fancy-free?" [62]

Was he considering a more prominent position for her, a position that would also put an end to his loneliness?

Bertha's answer was an honest "no".

Alfred continues to enquire. Eventually she opens up to him. She tells him why she is lying awake night after night at the Grand Hôtel. She lets him know about her love for the young Arthur von Suttner, whom she met while working as a governess for Baron von Suttner in Vienna. She tells him that after her guardian Fürstenberg died in 1866, her mother Sophie landed in serious financial problems, as there was little left of her widow's pension. To improve her finances, Sophie took up gambling.

It was quite common for aristocrats and wealthy people to spend time at the gambling tables during the spa seasons. But Sophie had no luck at the tables. To the contrary, she lost again and again. Soon all her money was gone, and she was no longer able to support her daughter. The still unmarried Bertha had to look for a position, something which was highly unusual for aristocratic women at the time. However, a position as a governess was considered "respectable work" for girls from good families. At the age of 29, Bertha moved away from her mother for the first time to become a governess in the house of Baron Karl von Suttner, who lived near St. Charles Church in the center of Vienna.

As it turned out, this proved to be a stroke of good fortune. The friendly noble family accepted Bertha with open arms. She got along well with the family's teenage daughters, whom she taught languages and music. At last, she could put her knowledge of languages and musical skills to use. Finally, her days acquired a rhythm, a structure. Forgotten were the failed engagements and the shattered dreams of an opera career. Forgotten were her mother's losses at the gambling tables. Her life acquired a new direction: "It was here that my real life began and I became the one I am ...The former Bertha Kinsky seems to me to be a character from a superficial picture book, incapable of touching anyone," she later wrote. [63]

Then *he* suddenly appeared. Photographs of the family's youngest son, Arthur, show a handsome young man with a high, wise forehead, blonde hair and gentle, kind eyes. His facial features were soft, and his handle-bar moustache was curling upwards. "The sunshine man," Bertha called him: "The room grows twice as bright and warm when he walks in." [64] His full name was Arthur Gundaccar von Suttner and Bertha was charmed by him while he was home on holiday from his law studies at the University of Graz. It must have been a good holiday – the 23-year old Arthur would never again return to Graz. Instead he arranged to be transferred to the University of Vienna.

Bertha's heart started beating again. Not for an officer, as she had previously dreamt of. Neither for a particularly rich man, nor a talented artist, but for a student, seven years her junior. But this made no difference whatsoever. Cupid's arrows had hit their mark. And this time, the feelings were mutual and had the time to develop. During the long summer seasons, when the von Suttners stayed at the family's estate Harmannsdorf close to the village of Eggenburg, around 80 kilometers north of Vienna, the couple learned to know each other.

The idyll lasted for three years. But one day Mrs. von Suttner found out about the relationship, which they had managed to keep a secret. Naturally, she was furious. Her favorite son was certainly not going to marry his governess, a woman who was 32 years of age and on top of everything, did not have a shilling to her name! In an icy tone of voice, she asked Bertha to pack her suitcase and leave the house. Mrs. von Suttner's demands were non-negotiable.

She was, however, helpful in finding a new position for Bertha, far away from Vienna and the family home. A few days later, she came back with an advertisement that she had clipped out of the newspaper: "A rich and highly cultivated older gentleman, living in Paris, seeks a woman of mature age with excellent language skills to perform secretarial duties and manage his household." [65]

Nobel's advertisement. And after some correspondence, Bertha got the job, packed her suitcase, and said good-bye to Arthur. It goes without saying that it was only with significant effort that she managed to board the train to Paris. And now, one week after her arrival, she sits and tells her new employer the entire story. About how much she misses Arthur. About the letters they write to each other, letters in which they express their love.

Alfred listens thoughtfully. Finally, he speaks. He praises Bertha for her bravery. However, he encourages her to break off all contact with Arthur: "Soon new impressions will fill your mind," he says. [66] Coming from a man of great reserve, these were strong words.

Back in her hotel room that evening, Bertha paces back and forth between the huge porcelain vases and the heavy, embroidered draperies. She stops in front of the window and looks out. Above the buildings on the other side of the street, rows upon rows of roof-tops are visible. On the horizon, the cupola of Sacré-Coeur emerges from between church steeples and towers, rising towards the heavens. She sits down on her bed. All the beauty and luxury surrounding her seems to make no impression on her. Was it possible for her to do anything else when she was alone but think of Arthur, write to him and read his letters?

Bertha lies down on her bed and stares at the ceiling. The clock strikes twelve, one and two, and there is not much sleep to speak of on this night either.

Two telegrams

The next day Alfred is again up at the crack of dawn. He packs his brown leather suitcase. He is going to Glasgow, on a business trip. Outside, a hansom cab is waiting. They drive off to the station and he boards the train.

The same morning, Bertha receives a message from the reception about a telegram waiting for her. The words are few, but sufficient: "I cannot live without you," it reads, signed Arthur von Suttner.

"My soul cried out: 'And neither I without you,'" she later recalls.

The very same day, another telegram arrives in her name from Glasgow. "Arrived safely. Back in seven days." The signature is Alfred Nobel's.

Bertha makes up her mind without a moment's hesitation. That afternoon, she sells the expensive piece of diamond jewelry she inherited from her guardian Fürstenberg. For the money, she pays her bill at the Grand Hôtel. Then she packs her suitcase and buys a ticket for the next train to Vienna:

I behaved as if I were in a dream, under the spell of an irrepressible *idée fixe*. Thoughts flashed through my mind about this being madness, that perhaps I was running away from a potentially happy destiny and into the hands of misfortune, but I could not act otherwise, and the bliss I envisioned in the moment of being reunited was of greater import than what might per chance come to pass - even if it should be death. [67]

Bertha had remained in the position of Nobel's secretary for only eight days. When he returned from his business trip to Glasgow, the beautiful bird had flown.

Before her arrival, he had wondered whether his new secretary would meet all his difficult requirements and expectations. Now she had departed and all she had left behind was a short message, where she thanked him for all the trust he had placed in her, but explained that under the "current circumstances" it was impossible for her to remain in the position as his secretary.

The sources tell us little about how Alfred responded. We only know that he would not advertise for a private secretary for another ten years. The wing he had renovated for Bertha would remain unoccupied.

Instead he bought himself a new and more manageable copy machine. [68]

Chapter 2

Years in the Caucasus – An author is born

The honeymoon

Back in Vienna, Bertha took a room at the Hotel Metropole. From there, she sent for Arthur by messenger and asked him to come to room 20 where "a lady from Paris was waiting to give him a message from Countess Kinsky." [69] With a pounding heart, she listened to every footstep passing by in the hallway until she recognized the steps of her beloved. The door opened - and there he was!

The couple were overjoyed to see each other again. Forgotten was Alfred Nobel, forgotten were Mr. and Mrs. von Suttner. Forgotten was just about everything outside the doors of the Hotel Metropole, at least for a few days. When they finally stepped out onto the streets of Vienna, they were determined never to separate again. Over the next few months, they made plans, and on June 12, 1876, Arthur and Bertha married in secret in a small, suburban church outside of Vienna, with only a best man and maid of honor in attendance. [70] Miss Kinsky became Mrs. von Suttner and the countess title was replaced by the title of baroness.

Bertha had no doubts about having made the right choice. Whereas Alfred Nobel was melancholy and a brooder, Arthur was playful and happy. He made her laugh and brought out the lighter side of her personality. But they both knew that his parents would never recognize their marriage. Arthur would have great difficulties in finding a job and a place to live. What were they to do with themselves?

The couple decided to leave Vienna. Bertha wrote to a friend who lived in Caucasia, or more specifically, in Georgia. This friend was not just anybody. In the summer of 1864, when the young Miss Kinsky had been on the look-out for a dream prince, she had instead met an actual princess. At the Homburg Spa, Bertha encountered princess Ekaterina Dadiani from the powerful Dadiani dynasty of northwest Georgia. The Dadiani family had ruled the Principality of Mingrelia since the 12th century. Bertha was immediately fascinated by the princess, who had a strong spirit of adventure. She told Miss Kinsky about how she had ruled in Mingrelia for four years after the death of her husband David. And about the time when she had defended the region against Turkish invaders and performed bold feats on horseback, feats never before done by a woman. She shared stories about the suitors she had had – and who continued to appear - Spanish noblemen, Russian adventurers and English landowners... [71]

Ekaterina and Bertha became close friends, despite the 25-year difference in their ages. Soon the young countess became a regular guest at the princess's oriental-inspired apartment at the Homburg Spa. The exotic scents of orange blossom perfume, Russian cigarettes and leather tickled her nostrils when she walked in. [72] She was introduced to her daughter Salomé, who her mother hoped would meet a bachelor with blue blood in his veins. For this reason, Ekaterina and her daughter spent the winter season in Paris. Salomé taught Bertha beauty rituals designed to make girls attractive to admirers – such as powdering oneself with rice flour using a rabbit's foot, or mastering the right technique for emanating a fan of sandalwood. She even gave Bertha a sandalwood fan.

Salomé lived up to her mother's expectations when she married the French Prince Achille Murat, who was one of the most attractive bachelors in Paris society. In May 1868, the wedding took place - a big event in Paris high society. An enthusiastic Bertha attended the wedding as maid of honor during the orthodox part of the ceremony.

Eight years later she was now married herself, and wrote a long letter to the princess in which she informed her of the happy tidings. She also explained the situation in which the couple found themselves. Might they perhaps come and visit the princess in Caucasia? Bertha was feeling optimistic about the princess's position and influence in the court circles. She was hoping that her son Niko could help Arthur to find a position there. A brief time later, the overjoyed telegram from Mingrelia came in response: "Welcome!" [73]

The couple spent a few months looking for the necessary funds for the journey - predominantly loans that Arthur took out, before they set out on the long trip to Georgia. First by horse and carriage, because the railway covering the distance to this region had not yet been built. From Odessa in Romania the trip continued across the Black Sea by ship.

They were both excited. Just like the legend of Romeo and Juliet, they had defied their parents' wishes and chosen love, but unlike Shakespeare's famous lovers, they had managed to escape together. Now they were on their way to a country they knew little about - other than the titillating adventures of Ekaterina - stories that Bertha always associated with the scent of incense and orange blossom perfume. Would Georgia live up to their expectations? [74]

"In Wonderland"

Bertha and Arthur were not the only ones travelling eastwards full of expectations. The 19th century was above all the century of travel and emigration. Thousands of people left their villages to find means for earning their daily bread in more urban areas; others had more remote destinations. The railroad and steamship facilitated travel. New parts of the world were discovered, colonies established.

Many of the travelers were people upon whom fortune had not smiled kindly in Europe and who hoped to build a better future. One of these was Immanuel Nobel, who had travelled eastward 44 years earlier. Others were adventurers who wanted to explore a new country. An example of the latter was the famous Norwegian author Knut Hamsun, who visited the country in 1899. He gave a vivid description of the Georgian way of life in his travelogue "In Wonderland", expressing that he was particularly enchanted by the country's nature and the majestic Caucasus Mountains in the north. They were forming a precipitous border between Europe, Asia and the Middle East. [75]

Bertha and Arthur were also exuberant about the beautiful sights that met their eyes as their ship glided in towards land. "We are in Asia!" Arthur cried. "Asia, or Australia, the Earth or Mars," Bertha silently rejoiced, "we are together!" [76] In the harbor, they were welcomed by one of the princess's emissaries, a smiling Cossack who was wearing the local costume of a caftan with a bandoleer across his chest, a *bashilk* on his head and a dagger in his belt. Accompanied by the Cossack guide, they set out on another boat trip - up along the coast of the Black Sea and to the marshy sea port of the city Poti. From there they continued their journey on foot, now with a new emissary: The Count Rosmorduc from Brittany, who was married to a local woman.

The journey to the north was full of surprises, at least if we are to believe Bertha's descriptions. Wherever the newlywed couple went, banquets were held, and concerts and dance performances were put on in their honor. Singing and dancing were important for the Georgians as a means of preserving their culture after Russia's having incorporated the country under its rule in 1801.

Georgia is particularly known for its abundant flora and fauna, and an enthusiastic Bertha observed "roads filled with blossoming mimosa" and "hedges bursting with roses". The sensual impressions were powerful: Exotic aromas, fruit trees laden with produce and foreign plants. Bertha's depictions of the journey are representative of the state of mind of the newlyweds - *everything* was marvelous - the architecture, the Georgians who welcomed them in the villages, the unfamiliar language, the unfamiliar scents - yes, even the smell of buffalo dung was "enchanting"! [77]

On the final leg of the journey towards Gordi, where the princess lived, they rode in the intense heat in a troika. Eventually they reached "Pompey's Bridge" in the Mingrelia region. At this point they were obliged to leave the carriage and travel the rest of the way on horseback. Prince Niko accompanied them on the final stretch, riding beside them for seven kilometers on narrow, steep trails. Finally, they ascended the mountain plateau where they looked out across cold, windy plains. In the distance, they could see mountain peaks and on the horizon, glimpse the Dadiani's residence in the village of Gordi. The castle was situated against the side of a mountain, and was broad and ornamented with towers, countless balconies and terraces. In front on either side were small, attractive wooden houses in a typical Caucasian style, each with a wrap-around porch. The princess was standing on one of the latter, waving to the couple.

It was a heartfelt reunion. With her raven-black hair, walnut-colored eyes and pale skin Ekaterina was still "radiantly beautiful", according to Bertha. [78] Impeccably dressed in a full-length dress from Worth, adorned with white pearls, she welcomed the couple and led them to an open terrace where the servants were setting the table for dinner for more than 30 guests. A magnificent reception had been organized, with singing, dancing and fireworks on a plateau bathed in moonlight. It was midnight before Bertha and Arthur tumbled into bed in the small wooden house the princess had fixed up for them for the summer season.

Their stay in Caucasia had had an impeccable start.

Daily life

In the days that followed, Bertha and Arthur explored their new surroundings. Ekaterina showed them around the family estate, which was valuable with forests and mines that were many centuries old. She also introduced them to Georgia's history.

The country was originally an old Christian kingdom that had its heyday under the rule of the powerful Queen Tamara in the 12th century. Under Tamara's rule, trade expanded, and painting, handicrafts, and architecture flourished. The queen was a skillful leader who, according to history, motivated the troops to win all battles, warding off would-be conquerors. In countless national legends and poems, homage was paid to the queen befitting a goddess. Tamara was viewed as "the true and perfect ideal of femininity – a radiant beauty like the sun itself." [79] The queen was a source of inspiration for many visitors and authors, such as Knut Hamsun, who wrote a play with her name as the title. [80]

Could Ekaterina Dadiani's position be compared in any sense with that of Queen Tamara?

To her chagrin, Bertha soon discovered that the princess was far from being as powerful as she had expected. In 1857, Russia had usurped the Dadiani family's power. Although the Tsar had given the princess and the Mingrelians a large degree of self-rule, Ekaterina and Niko had very little political influence. Bertha's hope that Arthur should get a position in the court was shattered. And now the rest of their money had almost run out. What were they to live on? Arthur's parents had severed contact with them. [81] Sophie Kinsky had given their union her blessing, but she had no means of supporting the couple financially.

Luckily, the princess found a solution. Through some families she knew in the city of Kutaisi, Bertha and Arthur were offered positions as tutors for the children of Russian nobility. These were familiar with the romantic story of the couple and their close ties with the Dadiani family, something which possibly made them attractive additions to the household. Bertha began tutoring in French and music, and Arthur in German.

War breaks out

Georgia was far from a suitable destination for an idyllic honeymoon, if that's what they had imagined. For centuries, the country had experienced a great deal of unrest and several regime changes. It had been a bone of contention between Russia, Persia and Turkey. The Russians wanted to expand their empire to the west, so they would gain access to the Mediterranean and thereby crush the Turkish hegemony in the Balkans. On April 24, 1877, the Russians declared war. A period of great unrest and instability followed.

Bertha, who only a couple of years before had been ignorant and indifferent when Alfred Nobel had told her about the French-German war, was still ignorant but no longer indifferent as the Russian and Turkish troops were battling it out in the country they were living. [82] She was still easily influenced by her surroundings, the Dadiani family and their close affiliations with the Tsar. Like the princess, she sided *with* the Russians and uncritically accepted their arguments about "their benevolent objective of freeing their Slavic brothers from Muslim oppression." [83] But she no longer shrugged her shoulders and sighed "C'est la guerre" with indifference, as she had done before. [84]

Living in a country where acts of war were taking place had an impact on her. Although she did not personally know anyone who had been killed or seriously wounded, the losses she read about in the papers and heard about through the local population made a strong impression.

A thrifty life

Like many others, Bertha and Arthur volunteered for service at the military hospital. But the couple made one requirement - that they be allowed to work at the same hospital. After the week that Bertha had spent in Paris, they had vowed never to be separated again.

However, their request was turned down because the rules stipulated that men and women had to work separately. Instead, the couple helped out at charity events to raise money for poor and needy soldiers. Bandages were made and money, tea and tobacco were collected and sent to the soldiers out in the field.

The war lasted for one year. The Turks were pertinacious, but the Russians won. On March 3, 1878, a peace agreement was signed between Turkey and Russia. The Russians had increased their power in both Caucasia and the Balkans. That summer, the Russian victory was celebrated in the home of the Dadiani family. Bertha and Arthur were naturally among the guests.

However, the war had taken its toll on the couple's opportunities to provide for themselves. Few families could afford tutors any longer. "Some days we even made the acquaintance of hunger," Bertha later recalled. [85] For a period, they moved around. Eventually they settled down in the region's capital Zugdidi, approximately 100 kilometers east of Gordi.

Once again it was the princess's contacts who came to their rescue: Her son-in-law Achille Murat was to build a new palace for the royal family, and Arthur was taken on as a supervisor for the construction work. Bertha was going to tutor the princess's grandson Lucien Murat in German.

By the standards of our times, Zugdidi was virtually a large village: It was built around a single, long, main street called "the bazaar", where there were rows of Oriental buildings with open booths. The couple rented a cottage on an out-of-the way farm. A huge wooden table served as a desk for them both. The sitting room's most prized furnishing was a *takhta*, an enormous sofa covered with a colorful tapestry and filled with large, patterned pillows – a typical piece of furniture in every Caucasus home. Otherwise the place was simply furnished.

Bertha's life had always been full of contrasts – from a relatively carefree existence as a young countess to earning her own living as a governess and language tutor. Now she would reap the fruits of yet another experience: A frugal life in a foreign country. The contrast between the primitive farmer's cottage, with jackals barking at the edge of the forest and von Suttner's elegant *Schloss Harmannsdorf*, with its English parks and marble statues, was large. Far away from Vienna and its animated coffee houses and various attractions, the couple now lived a quiet life, close to nature.

It was a thrifty life: Sometimes they only just managed to pay for the rent and their spartan diet.

It was a simple life: They got up in the morning when the cock crowed, had breakfast, went their separate ways to work, had lunch together and then went out to work again in the afternoon. When evening came, they sat side by side, reading and writing.

It was a solitary life: Sometimes weeks would pass before they saw another soul. Because of the language barrier, making friends with the neighbors was a challenge.

Nonetheless: It was a rich life, at least if we are to believe Bertha's descriptions: "There were some days when we barely had anything to eat, but there were no days when we did not joke, touch each other lovingly or laugh! ... Nothing bad could happen to us, because we had each other." Life was short on money, but it was "abundant with adventure and events, although the source of these was our books and our hearts." [86]

Bertha's own accounts are the primary source of information about their stay in Caucasia; many of the letters the couple wrote home have been lost.

A new passion

Bertha did not make many close friends among the women in her surroundings. She didn't master the local language and besides, most of the women her age were predominantly busy raising their children. How should she spend her free time? It had been a while since it had seemed important to spend time coaxing her hair into the requisite corkscrew curls. Or learning to master the right technique for emanating the sandalwood fan that was a gift from Salomé.

A former passion was reawakened: Reading. Square, hard packages from Europe, wrapped in thick paper with her name written on them, began appearing in the mail. With her fondness for powerful metaphors, Bertha described the sensation of tearing the wrapping off the books as a "delight she would not trade for any of her former pleasures!" [87] Soon books filled the wooden table in the sitting room and found their way onto the *takhta*, where she read by the light of a paraffin lamp. Night after night, Bertha stayed up reading. The books "illuminated a new horizon" for her. The lively and sociable Miss Kinsky was now loath to allow anything to distract her from whatever book she had in her hands. She had thirst for knowledge, a more pressing need to understand the world.

Here, in the quiet surroundings, she found the time to reflect upon what she was reading. To let the words sink in. To think beneath the surface.

A critical perspective

Was it all the reading and reflection that led her to renounce her previous way of life and acquire a new perspective on her own country? In Caucasia, Bertha began to regard with a critical eye the way the women of the aristocracy were raised to believe that the most important thing in life was to marry a man from the elite. That the education they received was for the sole purpose of learning to please others - and their husbands in particular.

She began to distance herself from her earlier life and from Vienna and its various diversions, the theatre and concerts. According to her, the frugal life in Zugdidi had far greater benefits than her former life's wearying attempts at pleasure: "I wouldn't exchange any of my pleasures now with the pleasures of my youth." [88]

Here it is tempting to draw a parallel to Leo Tolstoy and his critique of the nobility's "superficial life". Like Bertha, he came from the aristocracy and like her he would denounce this class's way of life in biting terms until he in the end gave up all his earthly possessions to live an ascetic life in the countryside. Tolstoy's criticism of the West's frenzied culture and urban society was crass, he saw life there as "exceedingly pathetic." [89]

Bertha did not go that far in her criticism. And unlike her Russian colleague, there was a great deal about Western culture that she appreciated, including the advances of science, an appreciation reflected by the growing book collection in the couple's cottage outside of Zugdidi.

Optimism regarding progress

On their bookshelves, it was the prominent authors of the day who were allotted the most space. While Arthur was mostly interested in the classics, Bertha's interest was primarily in literature with a contemporary relevance. "The period we are living in is just as much our homeland as is our geographic location," she wrote. [90]

In that way, Bertha was child of her time. The end of the 19th century was first and foremost characterized by optimism about progress: A belief that new inventions would make society better and human beings happier. A faith in science had informed the intellectual life of Europe since the 1600s, but never had so many people shared this view as during this period. Scientists like Alfred Nobel were looked upon as "heroes", because of their contribution to technical advancement.

In Caucasia, Bertha read the philosopher Herbert Spencer and the biologist Ernst Haeckel, who both expanded upon Darwin's teachings about evolution, developing them into a comprehensive philosophical system. According to Spencer, the same laws that applied to the origins of biological species, applied to the development of society. Evolution was a constantly ascending progression towards higher knowledge and morality.

However, the author who would come to have the greatest importance for her was the English historian Henry Buckle and his book *History of Civilization in England* (first volume published in 1857, second in 1861). In this work Buckle argues that mankind is evolving from bestiality to humanity, from vice to virtue, from hate to love. The result of this development will be peace, according to the author.

Bertha was immensely inspired by Buckle's visions. Now she felt the urge to pick up the pen herself.

Literary debut

Why did Bertha begin to write? Unlike Alfred Nobel, she never had a dream of becoming an author when she was young. She later explained that "a competitive instinct" was awakened in her when her husband's writings were published. During the Russian-Turkish war, Arthur had begun to write articles for the Austrian newspaper *Die Neue Freie Presse* and continued doing so after the war ended. He described the Georgian daily life, the natural habitat around him and the local customs.

If her husband could earn money writing, why shouldn't she? As usual, Bertha didn't lack courage. In 1878, she wrote an essay entitled "Fans and Aprons" and sent it to *Die Neue Freie Presse*. Like many of the women authors of this time, she wrote under a pseudonym, as she feared her work would not be taken seriously should it be disclosed that the author was a woman.

However, Bertha hit the bull's eye on the first attempt. The response from *Die Neue Freie Presse* was to send her 20 *gylden*. This was the start of Bertha's writing career: "[E]ver since that moment I have written like a bloodthirsty tiger." [91] Now she threw herself passionately into her writing. And she was successful: An increasing number of checks in her name began appearing in the mail.

A new era commenced in Bertha's life. Envelopes containing short stories written in the style of weekly magazines for women were sealed and sent out on the long journey between Georgia and Austria. The subject was often "true or untrue love": Men and women with blue blood who were hunting for their heart's desire, noblemen courting in competition with the garrison boys, and fluttering hearts and shattered expectations. Or nerve-wracking proposals and blessed unions.

One serial story that became popular was "From Society. Pages from the Diary of Countess X". Through diary entries, the reader gained a glimpse of a young, unmarried countess's life. Card games, knitting, piano playing and social intrigues were the ingredients of daily life and the highlight of the year was the ball season. The fact that Bertha knew both the milieu and the characters so well was probably one reason why the short stories became a hit. In addition, she had a witty and distinctive pen.

Bertha gradually developed her short stories into a full-length series. In 1881, the story of the noblewoman "Hanna" was published as a series in the magazine *Gartenlaube* - the most popular family magazine in Germany in the 1870s. She wrote under the name "B. Oulot", short for her nickname, "Boulotte". Bertha seldom let herself be stopped by a rejection: "If an article or short story is rejected by five or six newspapers, it can still be accepted by the seventh," she wrote in a letter to a colleague who had received several rejections. [92] The distance between Georgia and Austria was great, and a long time could pass before the editors replied. Despite these difficulties, Bertha's writing ambitions continued to grow. She took on increasingly more demanding assignments. The 39-year old's goal was "despite my mature age - to learn, learn, learn." [93]

The fan of sandalwood was replaced by an increasingly harsher pen.

Inventory of a Soul

Bertha soon put aside the diary entries about the comings and goings of "Countess X" and started writing her first scholarly article. In "Truth and Lies" published in the new journal *Die Gesellschaft* in Munich, she accuses all old art of being "the art of lies". She was influenced by the French author Émile Zola, who in the 1860s had developed the principles of naturalism. According to Zola, literature's most important function was to serve the truth. The author was to be like a scientist in his laboratory.

Bertha subsequently began working on her first serious book, *Inventory of a Soul* (*Inventarium einer Seele*), written under the pseudonym B. Oulot. The inspiration from the authors and philosophers with a belief in progress is evident here: "A fundamental principle for life's development is the belief in progress," she wrote:

Whichever way I turn, I find confirmation of this wonderful principle. I see it in the garden, where the aromatic *malmaison* has been developed from the wild Scottish rose, I see it in my classics, where the first babblings of human speech have evolved into majestic poetry; I see it in outer space, where the first cosmic clouds have gathered to form suns. The eternal evolution is simultaneously an eternal purification - the striving for development, beautification and perfection is an inherent, vital force in all things.

Inventory of a Soul contains visions of a more peaceful and just society. Bertha's faith in these visions shines through. She was filled not just with a belief but with a "jubilant expectation" for all that was to come. In the book, she touches upon the topic of war for the first time. War will soon belong to an earlier stage in the development of culture, she wrote. War is not something naturally given, as the prevailing view in Austria held:

One need not participate in a war to become a hero. Objectives more noble than that of the battlefield can entice men with ambitions. The fight against poverty and suffering also requires heroes. To demolish mountains, build dams, create art, put out fires, visit hospitals, and alleviate famine - these are not cowardly acts. [94]

Bertha's joy was probably further augmented when in 1883, after a three-year writing process, she succeeded in having the book accepted for publication at a small publishing house in Leipzig.

"An indelible impression"

In Paris, Alfred Nobel read Bertha's debut book and was moved by it. On a spring day in 1883 when he went to pick up the mail on Avenue Malakoff, he found a thick envelope from his former secretary. Inside it was a copy of the book, which he read and immediately wrote the author an enthusiastic response: "I am still under the spell of your wonderful book. Such style and such philosophical thoughts founded on the profoundest of sentiments! Thank you for giving me the pleasure of reading your work and kindly accept my most reverent tribute and the deepest affection, inspired by a memory and admiration that is unforgettable and indelible." [95]

Seven and a half years had passed since Alfred and Bertha had spent a week together in Paris. At the last juncture, Bertha had not behaved like an adult woman of good breeding should. To the contrary: She had abandoned her employer while he was away on business, virtually racing out of the hotel upon receiving the telegram from her lover. The idea that she could have just waited just a couple of days until Alfred came back from his business trip, had not even crossed her mind.

Alfred did not comment upon Bertha's abrupt disappearance in his reply. Instead he compliments her on her book; he is still "under its spell"! He makes no further reference to the book's contents, perhaps he had no time to expand upon it. Bertha's letter was certainly not the only one lying in his mailbox that day. The inventor still received a considerable number of letters a day.

How were his own literary pursuits evolving? Alfred used his pen predominantly for business correspondence, but he had not ceased writing poems entirely. Around 1880, he wrote the ten-verse long poem "Night-thoughts", also called "Wonder", in blank verse. While his previous poem "Canto 1", had paid tribute to poetry, "Night-thoughts" was a tribute to the natural sciences and the natural scientist Isaac Newton. The poem expresses a pantheism and conception of God close to the ideas of the Dutch philosopher Baruch de Spinoza, who was one of Alfred's favorite philosophers. During the quiet midnight hours, the poem's narrator lets his thoughts wander and ruminate upon how the universe is designed. He is humbled by how everything is interconnected: What is infinitely small reflects that which is infinitely great. Particularly fascinating is the "mystical force" that holds it all in place: The universal power of attraction.

The end of the poem takes a surprising turn as it pays tribute to "the heart's magnetism": The heart follows the same laws as the universal power of attraction. As the atoms and the sun obey the laws of gravity, so does all living matter, but it assumes more beautiful forms as it is drawn towards the heart. Inanimate and human ties are the same, and this is evidence of a form of ethics that should inspire us to humility.

Despite the Englishman C. Lesingham Smith's words of praise of his writing style, Alfred did not attempt to have "Night-thoughts" or any of his other works published. It appears as if he grew increasingly more critical of the literary quality of his writing with age. [96] He still read a lot. Since Bertha spent a week in Paris, he had expanded his library on Avenue Malakoff. He acquired many books from The Galignani Library on the Rue de Rivoli, or from Vieweg's well-stocked publishers' bookstore on Rue de Richelieu, across the street from the Bibliothèque Nationale. The books had a simple binding and were without superfluous ornamentation. [97]

However, most of his time was spent working. Alfred sat bent over paperwork or accounting while travelling to different dynamite factories, whether it was in train compartments zigzagging across all of Europe, or in hansom cabs passing through deserted landscapes and densely populated, urban areas. In 1882: London, Glasgow, Paris and Stockholm. 1883: Marienbad: 1884: Aix-les-Bains, Stockholm and Paris. Despite his poor health and a headache that hardly had been alleviated by the many hours he spent in the same room as the potent explosive oil, he worked just as much as before.

When he was at home on Avenue Malakoff, the days acquired another rhythm. Every morning he got up at dawn and worked for several hours in the laboratory. Upon concluding a session, he browsed through *Le Figaro, Le Matin, The Times* and, after 1877, *The Times Literary Supplement*. In the evenings, he dozed off in the armchair in the library with a book in his lap. If he managed to tear himself away, he might accept an invitation to dine. Or he visited the salon of the famous Paris-born editor Madame Juliette Adam Lambert. Here he was often observed in conversation with intelligent women, where the conversations maintained a level that he enjoyed. But one could just as frequently find him sitting at a solitary observation post in a corner.

His civil status was the same, even though he had a new female acquaintance.

The flower girl

Was it just a coincidence that a few months after Bertha left Paris, Alfred formed a relationship with another dark-haired Austrian beauty? He met Sofie Hess at the health resort Baden bei Wien near the Danube in June 1876, on his way home from a business trip.

Perhaps it was his love for flowers, his "mute friends", as he called them, which caused Alfred to enter the shop? [98] The dark-haired beauty stood among the roses, carnations and lilies, wrapping up flowers in silk paper. [99] A pair of greyish-blue eyes glittered towards his own when she handed him the bouquet. Was it the boldness of her gaze that gave the reserved man the courage to invite her on a drive through a nearby wooded area after her working day?

The last time Alfred had ridden around a park with a woman at his side had been with Bertha in the autumn of the previous year in Bois de Boulogne. Like Bertha, Sofie was from Vienna and like her she was talkative and outgoing, but there the similarities ended. Sofie was a typical *Wiener Mädel* – a popular expression for a light-hearted and simple Viennese girl, far from the refined and highly educated women he usually liked to associate with. She had no *Bildung*; to the contrary, she could barely read or write. Sofie was a woman from the lower middle class, who sold flowers for a living.

What did they talk about as they drove around in a brand-new hansom cab, drawn by a white horse outside of Baden bei Wien?

Perhaps Sofie told Alfred about her family background. The Hess family was of Jewish descent. Sofie's mother had died when she was only five years old. Her father, Heinrich Hess, had married again and ran a sweetshop on Praterstrasse in Vienna. The family income was meagre, and this was why Sofie worked in the flower shop. Another reason was that Baden bei Wien was frequented by some of Europe's wealthiest men. Young officers with gilt-edged distinctions, English lords wearing glittering silver pince-nezes and French counts who owned *chateaus* in the countryside strolled in and out of the flower shop. Sofie's stepmother Julie was hoping that her step-daughter would soon make a good match. Mrs. Hess encouraged her to take diligent care of her looks. Every morning Sofie had to wash her hair so it shined. Her skin had to be softened with scented oils and creams. Her working attire had to be laundered and neatly pressed.

If Sofie succeeded in making a good match, Mr. and Mrs. Hess might benefit as well, and could look forward to a life of comfort in their old age. No wonder Mrs. Hess clapped her hands in excitement when Sofie told her about her new gentleman friend, the wealthy inventor Alfred Nobel.

Sofie, on the other hand, did not provoke the same amount of enthusiasm when Alfred's family learned about her. His relationship with Sofie would amaze, astound and scandalize those in his most intimate circle. His brother Ludvig pointed a finger of admonishment at him. In a letter, he warned Alfred about his new lady friend, emphasizing that she did not come from a "good family", and expressed that he should not engage in a relationship with her. [100]

Professor Higgins

The brothers' warnings did not have much of an impact on Alfred. Was it "the heart's magnetism", which he had paid tribute to in the poem "Night-thought" that made him indifferent to Sofie's lack of breeding? The tone of his letters during the first year of their relationship is one of love and tenderness. He writes that Sofie has been the "victim" of unfortunate influences and that he wishes to help a "fundamentally depraved child find a better path." [101] Like Professor Henry Higgins in Bernard Shaw's drama *Pygmalion*, he sets about trying to transform his flower girl into a fine lady. One of the first things he does is to buy her a 24-volume set of a standard encyclopedia. But the gift remains untouched. Instead he encourages her to read a novel. "It would be good for you to try to learn something and it would give me immense pleasure. Buy yourself the novel by Balzac entitled *Deux Jeunes Mariées* [*Letters of Two Brides*]. It is written as an epistle and the language is very simple," he writes to her in September of 1878. [102]

Perhaps he was hoping that Sofie could acquire "breeding through reading"? The theme of *Letters of Two Brides* was friendship and love. If Sofie was to read it, she would also improve her French.

But Balzac's book of wisdom never found its way into Sofie's lap.

Alfred makes another attempt. Just after his arrival at the Aix-les-Bains spa, he writes to her: "I spent large portions of my journey reading the novel by Turgenev I had brought with me, which is extremely beautiful, natural and moving. I will send it to you and I think it can fill some idle hours for you, if you should have any." [103]

He was probably referring to Ivan Turgenev's lovely, but sad love story, the novel *A House of Gentlefolk* (1858) - a poetic and realistic depiction of the Russian landed gentry in the 1840s. Alfred had a Russian edition of the book in his library. Now he purchased an edition in German translation – *Das Adelige Nest* – with Sofie in mind.

But Turgenev did not capture Sofie's interest.

Alfred was at a loss. What could he give her to read? Lord Byron or Percy Bysshe Shelley would probably not be to her taste. There is nothing to suggest that he showed her his self-written poem "The Riddle" either.

Perhaps he had locked it away in the drawer for good.

Back to "Countess X"

In the meantime, he receives letters from Caucasia, from his former secretary, now Mrs. von Suttner. She, on the contrary, had used her time productively. She had read and cultivated her mind, even written a book full of edifying ideas and with a passionate belief in the future!

Why had Bertha sent Alfred the book? Was it meant as a promotion of her burgeoning literary career? Alfred was not the only one she sent it to. In the 1880s, Bertha had begun contacting authors and critics in Europe.

Inventory of a Soul received several brilliant reviews. However, not everyone was equally enthusiastic. The leading Danish critic Georg Brandes was skeptical about some of the ideas the book presented. Brandes' lectures had introduced the idea about progress and literary realism to the intellectual world of the Nordic region. Like Bertha, he believed that authors should be socially engaged and create a debate about the larger issues of the times. But unlike his Austrian contemporary, the Danish critic did not agree with those who sought to apply the newly discovered laws of the natural sciences to social, psychological and artistic phenomena. After having read *Inventory of a Soul*, Brandes wrote her a long, direct letter where he gave the book lavish praise, but his praise was not without qualification: "You are far too gullible, countess ... Evolution, you say? Are you certain that Spencer is not mistaken when he holds that this evolution, which Darwin attempts to prove in the animal world, also exists in the intellectual world? I would maintain that he [Spencer] is mistaken and that despite his enormous knowledge, he has a trivial mind (*ein trivialer Kopf*)." [104] Bertha's answer to the Danish critic is unknown.

Despite all the attention and reviews, *Inventory of a Soul* did not sell well. Bertha had to resume writing stories about the ups and downs of "Countess X" to make a living. From the cottage on the outskirts of Zugdidi, she threw herself into another round of stories about opera balls, intrigues and "true or false" love.

She had quite a lot of time on her hands. The couple's love-filled existence had not borne fruit during the years in Caucasia. Had they ever wanted children? Bertha never expressed such a wish to the outside world. To the contrary, she always spoke of how Arthur satisfied all her needs, as a friend, discussion partner and playmate.

Then again, Bertha was always known for her tendency to present things in a positive light.

Whether or not it was a personal choice, it is most likely that the absence of any dependents freed up time and energy for writing.

Homesickness

During the next three years, Bertha and Arthur experienced two great losses that increased their homesickness. While they were summer guests as usual at the princess's home in Gordi, Ekaterina suddenly fell ill. Her health deteriorated quickly and after being bedridden for a few months, she died in August 1882. The princess's death came as a shock to everyone. She was buried with pomp and circumstance in a monastery in Gordi.

Ekaterina Dadiani lived to the age of 66. Bertha and Arthur mourned her deeply. The princess had been like a mother to them and had helped them in so many ways during their stay. They had little contact with the princess's relatives. Therefore, they decided to move to Tbilisi, the capital of Georgia. It was a part Oriental, part West European city with a great deal of trade, and more than 100,000 residents of different nationalities. Here the community was more international than in Zugdidi. Arthur found himself a job in the construction trade, while Bertha continued tutoring children of wealthy aristocrats. In the evenings, soirées were arranged for European immigrants. Life became more social than it had been on the remote farm.

Bertha and Arthur had scarcely begun putting down roots in Tbilisi when in the summer of 1884 they received sad news from Austria: Sophie Kinsky had died. Bertha's almost 60-year old mother had written that her health was not particularly good, but she had not fully grasped the gravity of the situation. Now she deeply grieved the loss of her mother. She recalled the close ties they had had when she was younger – as two good friends, eagerly chatting and making plans, full of laughter, often in a horse and buggy on the way somewhere – to a spa, a party or a concert. She remembered how her mother had sewn rosebuds with care on the dress for her debutante ball and offered her support throughout her various adventures. The loss of Sophie was only alleviated by Arthur's compassionate care.

During this period, the couple began receiving reconciliatory letters from Arthur's parents, who wrote that they had forgiven them for marrying against their will. They realized how deep their love was, and expressed that they were impressed by the persistence which they had demonstrated in Caucasia. They invited them to come and live at the Harmannsdorf estate, where they now lived year-round, as they had sold the house in Canovagasse for financial reasons.

Bertha and Arthur eventually decided to go home. But before they bid farewell to their friends in Caucasia, they carried out an enormous project: A translation into German and French of the famous Georgian national epic *The Knight in the Panther's Skin*, written by the poet Shota Rustaveli. The idea came from Jonas Meunargia's, a Georgian friend of Arthur, who translated the epic to French for them orally, and they subsequently revised it in a language more suitable for publication.

The Knight in the Panther's Skin is a long, complex poem about friendship and love. It has been described as a "manifesto of living with joy". [105] The poem was written in the 12th century, during the Georgian Golden Age. Translating this enormous work gave them an invaluable insight into Georgian history and culture.

With the same enthusiasm that they applied to most of their endeavors, they went to work on this extensive project, which took much more time than they had anticipated and made a serious dent in their finances and energy. But they were determined to finish – and managed to do so with their honor intact. Today's experts on Rustaveli consider their translation to be extremely proficient.

Was this their farewell to the country where they had spent what Bertha would later refer to as "a nine-year honeymoon"?

While they were completing this work, chaotic news came from the Balkans: Russia had taken power in Bulgaria. The threat of war between Austria-Hungary and Russia was imminent. Suddenly they were in a hurry to return home. Voluntary exile is one thing; being stranded in a foreign country at a time of war is another.

They quickly packed up the few belongings they had – some Caucasus carpets, decorative coats of arms, and not least – all their books. After having packed up everything they owned, the couple said a tearful good-bye to their friends and boarded the Russian steamship "General Kotzebue", which would take them across Batumi and the Black Sea to Odessa.

A new perspective

During the five-day long journey home, the steamship stopped at several of the small ports along the way. When they reached Kerch, located in the eastern part of the Crimean Peninsula, Bertha observed the destruction wrought by the Regent Alexander, who had been given the nickname "The Great":

> Oh yes, 'the Great' – despite this, he conquered the Roman Asia Minor where he had all of the Romans – some 80,000 – murdered. That is the standard by which a king's 'greatness' was measured in the history of Antiquity – the murdered masses, the peoples enslaved, the ravaged land areas and all the burned down cities ... The amount of praise and honour lavished on the conquerors was just as great as the amount of fear and terror they generated. [106]

The damages caused by war and unrest were now something she noticed, but also the difference between the steamship's passengers had become apparent to her:

It's raining and it's cold outside - in the salon, the first class passengers drink tea, play cards and flirt with one another, the atmosphere is good ... The third-class passengers, on the other hand, sit on deck outside - the families of Greek emigrants, poor monks and others. The wind howls and they huddle together to stay warm ... Life is hard for many. [107]

The challenging years spent in Georgia had done something to Bertha: She had become aware of inequalities and injustices that she had not noticed previously. She recognized that many people on earth were lacking a great deal: "The minority are instead those who are able to live what we think of as being a dignified existence."

Bertha's experience of reading works of authors who shared her faith in progress, while the couple lived a frugal existence in a war-ravaged country led to a turning point in her life. She would never again shrug her shoulders and sigh indifferently "C'est la guerre", as if war and injustice were not her concern.

On the contrary, she began writing about the injustices she saw around her.

Chapter 3

Back in Austria – Alienation and social criticism

Conservative surroundings

In May 1885, Bertha and Arthur returned to Austria after nine years abroad. First, they went to the town of Gorizia (presently part of Italy) and planted a rose on Sophie Kinsky's grave. Afterwards they took the train to the village of Eggenburg, the station closest to Harmannsdorf, the family estate in Lower Austria. At the train station, they received a warm welcome from Arthur's parents and sisters.

It was a memorable moment when the family drove home together along the boulevard lined with leaf-laden trees and across the drawbridge over the moat. The trees and fields were green and lush, and rows of sunflowers stretched in all directions. Around the family estate the violets were in bloom, the larks were singing and there was bird life teeming all around. "The sound of the blackbirds and cuckoos is after all more pleasant than the sound of barking jackals!" Arthur commented, referring to the jackals at the edge of the woods outside of their home in Zugdidi. "Welcome home, my wife!" he said and kissed his wife. It was a moment Bertha would never forget. [108]

Although they were happy to be home and were given the best wing of the house to live in, not many weeks passed before Bertha began to feel like the walls were closing in. Accustomed to the silence and solitude in Georgia, she found it challenging to adapt to life in an extended family. In addition to Arthur's parents and two unmarried sisters, a handful of servants lived on the estate. His married sisters often came by to visit with their families. The sound of voices hummed continuously from the big kitchen where the family meals were consumed. The floorboards creaked when somebody walked up and down the stairs and in the salon, where the women sat up doing handiwork, one could hear whispering until late at night. Bertha was no longer interested in listening to gossip about who had danced with whom at the season's debutante ball, or who would be the heir of the duke on the neighboring estate. Many of the topics she had previously found exciting, she now found to be meaningless.

In addition, the worries hung over the estate like dark clouds. Harmannsdorf was in a state of decay: The bars on the windows were rotting, the curtains were moth-eaten, and the doors had peeling paint. All the outbuildings needed maintenance. The estate's quarry had been poorly managed. Arthur's parents suffered greater losses with each passing year.

Things she hadn't noticed when she was young became visible to her, such as how conservative her parents-in-law were, and how arrogant the landed gentry of Eggenburg could be. They had erected mental walls against the outside world; walls that were just as high as those protecting the enormous estates they inhabited.

When Bertha needed to get away for a bit, it took an hour and a half by horse and carriage to reach Eggenburg or three hours on foot. Going to the medieval village to run an errand was like coming to a place where time had come to a standstill. On either side of the cobblestone streets, the silent, ancient wooden houses seemed to sag against one another. Insipid plaster decorations and cracked statues of angels attested to former days of glory. The village's narrow streets opened onto a deserted square where a vendor's wife wrapped in a shawl announced the day's sale of eggs and poultry. She alone broke the silence. It was seldom that Bertha saw the face of an outsider, or heard anyone speak anything other than the local dialect.

Upon returning to the estate after an outing, she passed quickly through the heavily furnished sitting rooms with walls bearing paintings of Austrian emperors, such as Rudolf of Habsburg, and up the stairs to Arthur. Here, on the estate's second floor, the couple had outfitted a study where they had created a personal atmosphere. Most of the furniture consisted of mementos from the decade in Caucasia. Works by their favorite authors were lined up on the bookshelves: Darwin, Zola, Buckle, and Spencer among others. Persian and Oriental rugs decorated the walls and floor. In front of the large, bright windows they had installed two desks. A single lamp symbolically illuminated both work areas. [109]

From here Arthur and Bertha continued the custom they had acquired in Zugdidi of sitting side by side, writing and reading. Surrounded by their favorite authors and strengthened by each other's company, they looked ahead, high above the thick walls surrounding the estate. Both believed that the fresh winds of the future would soon come and blow away the dark clouds that were looming overhead.

"A shipwreck of youth"

A few months after their homecoming, Bertha wrote to her friend in Paris. In a heartfelt letter, she let Alfred Nobel know that the couple was back in their home country and living on the family estate. The estate is large and has many empty rooms (44, to be precise!), she writes - would Alfred consider coming and pay a visit?

Alfred was not the only one Bertha invited to the beautiful, dilapidated estate. Many of those with whom she corresponded received an invitation to Harmannsdorf. On one occasion, she would send an invitation as far north as Norway, when she invited the author and peace activist Bjørnstjerne Bjørnson to come and visit with his wife. Her invitations illustrate that the couple may have missed contact with the outside world.

In August 1885, Alfred answers her invitation and politely declines, even if he happens to be in Vienna at the time. He writes that he is pleased to hear that Bertha is happy and safely home "with all of your struggles behind you." However, he does not want to be the cause of any "disruption" for the couple, "on such occasions I am just as shy as the most sensitive of women," he continues.

Would the reserved Nobel have felt out of place among the many members of the von Suttner family? The letter gives the impression that the inventor's state of mind is far from untroubled: "What do you want me to say about myself – a shipwreck of youth, of joy and hope? A soul whose contents are a blank page – or grey," he concludes. [110]

Why the sad tone? Alfred's health had never been good, but in his 50s it had taken a turn for the worse. All his travelling most likely contributed to compounding the headaches, stomach problems, feelings of fatigue and the other physical ailments he struggled with. These were expressed in detail in his letters to Sofie Hess. [111]

Professionally he continued to experience success. He acquired new patents all the time – and within different fields: Art. Silk. Aluminum. Gas. He had an abundance of ideas: "If I have 300 ideas in a year and one of them is tenable, I am satisfied," he wrote to a friend. [112] One important patent he had acquired (1876) was for the invention of gelignite or *blasting gelatin,* a waterproof explosive composed of nitroglycerine mixed with nitrocellulose (gun cotton). The gelignite is stronger than dynamite and used for underwater blasting. This invention is considered by experts to be Alfred's third most important. [113]

In 1880, he merged the Italian and Swiss companies to form Dynamite Nobel. The following year, dynamite was used in a gigantic project: The blasting of the approximately 80-kilometers long Panama Canal connecting the Atlantic Ocean and the Pacific through the Isthmus of Panama. The work was not completed until 1914, after the United States in 1904 took over what originally had been a French project.

Not all his ongoing ventures were successful: In 1875, Alfred acquired a patent on a gas burner for lighting that was more efficient than former designs. The invention came about after a series of fire disasters in Europe in the 1870s. "Nobel Eclairage" was safer than ordinary gas lighting and was praised by the fire chief of Paris. He was preparing the invention for serial production when the electric incandescent lamp came onto the market in the beginning of the 1880s and "Nobel Eclairage" was made redundant.

As the managing director of a dynamite company with more than 100 factories, Alfred had a lot of responsibility. Accidental explosions occurred, causing human casualties. In 1883, an accident in his Italian factory in the town of Avigliana claimed the lives of 23. The following year there was an explosion accident in a dynamite factory in Ardeer, Scotland.

How did Alfred react to accidents and fatalities related to his invention? The reserved man seldom expressed his thoughts about this. He never wrote to Bertha about it.

Did he tell her about the Nobel brothers' oil adventure in Baku? He might have, since Bertha and Arthur had lived for several years not too far from where the brothers were living in the Azerbaijan region. In 1876, his brother Robert decided to try to drill for oil in the Baku region. Soon both Ludvig and Alfred were made partners in his oil-company Branobel. The Nobel brothers' Russian oil adventure was successful. After only one year, Branobel produced 2,500 of the 75,000 tons of paraffin oil produced by all of Russia's 200 oil companies! This was the beginning of the end of the American hegemony on the Russian oil market. At the turn of the 20th century, Branobel was producing ten percent of the world's oil in Baku and its surroundings.

Alfred was heavily involved from the start, both as an advisor and financial partner. But he seldom boasted of his accomplishments and never in his letters to Bertha.

He wore different hats: Engineer. Scientist. Salesman. Advertising Executive. Treasurer. Advisor. Secretary. With so many different responsibilities he was often under pressure. Conflicting pressures were not uncommon. But he was an orderly man who created detailed lists of his different projects, or "ongoing matters" as he called them. They were ticked off one by one as they were completed.

The education of Sofie Hess, however, was a project he was not able to tick off his list.

"The troll"

Alfred attempted to make his "flower girl" understand that it was in her own best interests to learn something. "To become truly happy, you still need an education in keeping with your position in society and you must therefore continue to work diligently," he wrote to her in 1878. [114]

But if Alfred was an eager Professor Higgins, Sofie was a reluctant Eliza. The French lessons he paid for seemed to be in vain. In her letters to him, handwritten in her chicken-scratch scrawl, Sofie spelled *monsieur* without the "n". Alfred became sarcastic when he corrected her for writing that he should go shopping for *pieds* (feet) instead of *chaussures* (shoes): "*Pieds* does not mean anything other than 'feet' and because there are no feet for sale at Louvre, it was not possible to satisfy your desire. Human feet that have been cut off are not very common commodities or fashion accessories in civilized nations," he wrote to her in September 1884. [115] With time, he also became irritated by the amount of money she spent. He gave her the nickname "The Troll" in his accounts of her increasing expenses. [116] Alfred issued admonishments. Gave advice. But to no avail. Sofie turned a deaf ear to his words.

At the beginning of the relationship he took immense pleasure in her spontaneous joy over the comforts he personally had such easy access to. The gifts that nobody in her family at Praterstrasse could afford – sweets, jewelry and stylish dresses. During his bustling workday, he rushed around in French fashion boutiques and ordered clothing for Miss Hess. [117] Letters show how he slaved to her whims: He even bought her a flat so she wouldn't have to live with her parents at Praterstrasse. He gave her a living allowance, so she could cease being dependent upon her family.

But Sofie's health was not so good – at least that was the reason she gave when she suggested that Alfred rent them a house, located by Ischgl – a small, attractive spa known for its healing waters. And Alfred complied with her request – he rented a *15-room* house for them.

The house was never used.

Then Sofie suggested that Alfred find her a flat in the French capital, close to his home. In July 1880, he found her a flat in Paris. Miss Hess packed her suitcase and boarded the train. Just like Alfred had met Bertha at the railway station five years earlier, he now welcomed Sofie in the metropolis. He drove her in a horse and carriage to the flat on Rue Newton. A brief time later she moved to N 10, Avenue d'Eylau in Paris (later Avenue Victor Hugo), located within walking distance from his home. The interior was stylish, with damask furniture, ottomans upholstered in silk, and velvet drapes. [118] Alfred hired a cook, a companion who was to teach her French, and a lady's maid who was to take care of practical affairs and keep her company. In addition, he gave her a dog, Bella. Everything was arranged to ensure that she would have a life of comfort.

But Sofie did not sit still on an ottoman upholstered in silk and read. Nor embroider slippers in petit-point, for that matter. She went into the city center. In and out of department stores with her lady's maid in tow. In the world's fashion mecca, there was a great deal to see: Silk, feathers and hats. Eccentric garments: What about a dress with a huge peacock embroidered on the back? Feminine clothing: What about a cascading skirt of sheer fabric? Or an irresistible dress of tartan taffeta with long, bell-shaped arms? A hat decorated with scarlet piping?

When Alfred came to call at Avenue d'Eylan, dresses, jewels, and pearls lay scattered around the flat. He could barely hide his disappointment. Why couldn't Sofie spend her time sensibly?

The letters he wrote to her in the beginning of the relationship, indicate that he had envisioned a relationship of a more conventional and long-lasting nature. However, as time passed he continued to keep the doors to Avenue Malakoff closed to her. The wing he had renovated for Bertha remained unoccupied.

Sofie, for her own part, did not settle down in Paris. Soon she was out travelling almost as much as her benefactor. The summer seasons were spent at different spas. First, she travelled to Trouville near the French coast, subsequently to Ishgl, Salzkammergut, Karlsbad, Wiesbaden, Franzensbad, Meran and Bozen, respectively. [119] To the snobbish and class-conscious Parisians, it was clear that she belonged to the lower middle class. At the spas, there was less of a class consciousness. There was a tantalizing social life, horn music and laughter. In the evenings, while the guests played cards on the terraces and the crickets sang in the bushes, the Austrian beauty with the long, dark curls received a lot of attention.

Perhaps it did not come as a surprise to Alfred when Sofie decided not to return to the flat in Paris after the spa season in 1883. Instead, she bid him farewell and boarded the train back to Vienna. Once again, the inventor was alone. In his letters to her, he expressed his great loneliness. [120]

Did Sofie's departure contribute to the sad tone when Alfred wrote to Bertha, expressing that he felt like "a shipwreck of youth, of joy and hope"? Bertha's invitation had emanated energy, optimism and an intellectual passion. Perhaps he compared her soul's "inventory", which was bright, with his own soul's contents, which were "a blank – or a grey page"? [121]

Back home on Avenue Malakoff, Alfred sought consolation in his library. It seems he found relief in communion with other scorned souls in the world of books. "*Bien!*" he wrote in pencil in the margin next to gripping lines that were permeated with the feeling of loneliness in Maupassant's short story "Happiness", published in 1885.

At least his work gave him satisfaction: It chased away "the doldrums" or "the spirits from Nifelhem", as he called them. [122]

Critique of "the artificial life"

Bertha was not only "happy and contented" to be back in her native country, as Alfred had put it. She was frustrated about finding herself in a "terribly backward setting", as she called her home surroundings. [123] Except for "My own" (Bertha's pet name for Arthur), everyone around her was "as medieval as could be. If the two of us did not have each other, we would *suffocate*," she wrote in a letter to a friend. [124]

Not only were the people in their close surroundings conservative, but it was the prevailing mentality in the dual monarchy of Austria-Hungary. The Austrian author Stefan Zweig offered a similar critique when he wrote that in the monarchy "everything was apparently unwavering and unchanging, and the state itself was the primary guarantor for ensuring that everything remained as it was." [125] Emperor Franz Joseph was the very incarnation of this immutability. He ruled for a total of 68 years, from 1848 till 1916 – the third longest period of rule for a monarch in Europe. His strict, Catholic upbringing made him conservative in both his life conduct and politics. The regulations were followed to the letter. He showed profound respect for the military by always appearing in uniform. In Vienna, everyone was dependent upon the emperor and the aristocracy's power. [126]

Vienna Gloriosa, as it was called, was a city full of aristocratic ornaments and memorials. It was surrounded by the magnificent, broad chestnut avenue - *Kastanienallee* – where the aristocracy and the wealthy bourgeoisie's buggies and carriages paraded. However, beneath the cheerful surface lay another, bleaker Vienna. When the coffee houses, or "salons" as they were also called, became so popular in the Austrian capital, it was also because the housing conditions were so horrendous that thousands of people were obliged to pass the time with a newspaper and a cup of coffee in their local café. Vienna was also the city of suicide, regardless of how Catholic Austria was.

When Bertha occasionally visited the capital, she was struck by its contrasts. Unlike before, she now noticed Vienna's unfortunate souls: The homeless huddled together in a corner for the night. The beggars who held out a cap to passersby. The streetwalkers with soot-blackened eyes who leaned against door openings while scouting for clients. On the same streets, aristocratic girls strolled merrily past on their way home from a visit to Schönbrunn or The Burgtheater, as she herself previously had done.

People she had overlooked, became visible for her. People whose existence she had not cared about, now touched something within her. The injustices she saw around her were something she began to write about. From the writing desk on the second floor of Harmannsdorf, she continued her diligent, hardworking life. She resumed her study of the new authors and the progressive ideas of the time. Her main interest was literature that could move the world *forward*.

Bertha continued writing easy-to-read novels that would earn them money, but nevertheless had some social significance. In her next novel, *High Life* (1886), she took the Austrian nobility's lifestyle to task. She attacked the aristocrats' focus on facades and form: What was important was to dress in the right clothes, assume the right attitudes and associate with the right people. "Form is everything," she wrote ironically, "for how can one [the aristocracy] distinguish oneself from the ordinary masses if it is not through *form*?" [127]

The significance of form found expression in the clothing, particularly women's clothing. Women wore cumbersome garments that in fact inflicted violence upon the body. Zweig illustrates this when he paints a portrait of a young, Austrian noblewoman wearing a suffocating corset:

Her waist was laced up like a wasp, within a corset of hard fishbone, while the lower body swelled outward like a giant bell; the neckline went up to her chin, the feet were covered to the toes, the hair piled up with countless small clasps and combs beneath a majestically waving monstrosity of a hat, and the hands squeezed into gloves even though it was midsummer. [128]

However, it was all form without content. As an example of this, Bertha refers to the Catholic congregation's words, singing and gestures, which according to her, consisted of "nothing but an empty ritual". The sign of the cross, performed by church goers with a stately and serious facial expression, was an act without meaning. The proper courtesy to be dropped before royalty and the nobility was supposingly a demonstration of piety, but behind the pious faces untruths and lies prevailed.

In *High Life*, Bertha ridicules the superficial life of the aristocracy in Vienna: "Irritating noise and annoying surfaces. Tinkling gold jewelry and over-excited laughter. Swaggering fools with handlebar moustaches on the way to the opera." The author warns against this lifestyle: "From this overstimulation of pleasure arises our century's ailments: indifference, neuroses, and anemia – this condition is called *modernity*." [129]

The novel's main character is an Austrian woman from the nobility whose daily life consists of a "hectic rush" between riding classes, shopping expeditions, five o'clock teas, various diversions etc. According to the author, this existence allows "no time for reflection, for the interests of the mind, for asking questions about the period in which she is living." [130]

Bertha writes ironically about the nobility's need to cling to the *status quo* when she puts this line in the mouth of a landed count:

A desire to change the world – what blasphemy! A world that is so beautiful, so proper, so harmonious, so blessed by tradition and led by providence! And virtuous! Are we not – those of us who represent the status quo – are we not filled to the brim with virtues? Loyalty, compassion, courage, self-sacrifice, patriotism: We know everything about it ... so spare us the eternal calls for change and your accusations. [131]

During the writing process, the author was confronted with her own past. Had she really indulged in this superficial way of life? When she was young, she had allowed herself to be caught up in the frenzy of pleasure-seeking women and men with blue blood – going from frivolous parties to elegant spas in the hunt for Mr. Right. She had ignored society's injustices. Bertha's own transformation strengthened her belief that also other people could change – a belief she would hold onto for the rest of her life: "When people tell me that change is not possible, that people cannot change, I know that they are wrong. I need only refer to my own life to disprove this." [132]

High Life gives concrete, virtually photographic depictions of the daily life of the Austrian nobility towards the end of the 19th century. For sociologists of today, the novel is a useful source of information about the life conduct of this class of society.

Inspired by Zola, Bertha saw writing as a tool for the improvement of society. This process could be compared to tearing down a house built from rotten boards. When the final board went down, one could start rebuilding. Bertha was well underway with the task of demolition and she did not hold back. In *High Life*, she attacks the lifestyle of the privileged classes, not only in Austria-Hungary, but also beyond the borders of the country. Whereas the Austrian nobility was "arrogant", the English was "prideful" and the French "vain". What they had in common was that they resisted all attempts at change, terrified as they were of losing their privileges.

Was there also vulnerability behind the book's biting criticism? Bertha had not forgotten about the time when she had not been accepted into the nobility's highest circles, because she lacked the correct number of ancestors. She would always remember the feeling of inferiority from when she was 18-years old and went to her debutante ball, only to be ignored.

Bertha was not the only author in this period who criticized the privileges of the nobility. Several of her contemporaries had enlisted in the same type of campaign. [133] For this she had to tolerate much contention from those in her close surroundings. Arthur's parents raised their eyebrows at their rebellious daughter-in-law's writing pursuits. For them, literature was a field that was "stranger than a crater on the moon". Shakespeare or Homer were acceptable reading, as were the German classics. But the authors Arthur and Bertha had as role models, they decried with a vengeance. The conflict escalated on the day Mrs. von Suttner attempted to set fire to Bertha's Zola collection! Bertha only just managed to rescue her role model from the dancing flames of the fire. The situation became so tense that the couple considered immigrating to Switzerland, but for several reasons the move never happened.

Despite this, Bertha did not lose heart. To the contrary, she continued her daily writing. In this sense, she lived according to Victor Hugo's motto: *Nulla dies sine linea:* Not a day without a line.

The Machine Age

Her energetic, daily writing eventually led to a new book, *The Machine Age (Das Maschinenzeitalter)*, completed in 1887 and published two years later. The book is considered by many to be Bertha's most ambitious work, intellectually speaking. It contained a shift away from criticizing the nobility's privileges towards a more wide-ranging social criticism. She wrote the book under the pseudonym "Jemand" ("Someone") and gave it the subtitle "Future Lectures for our Times".

The Machine Age is structured as a lecture series, with nine lectures in all. The narrator is a professor who lives in the year 3000 and looks back with a critical gaze on the situation in Austria-Hungary between 1885-88. The "unwavering and unchangeable" aspects of the dual monarchy were the focus of the critique, presented systematically. The professor condemns the Austrian educational system for being "outdated": It did not give girls the right to public schooling - something which made them unable to support themselves.

In another lecture, he takes Catholicism to task: Its oppression of life conduct, not least sexuality, produces an inhibited, puritanical attitude towards life, and a sexual double standard. Finally, the professor focuses the spotlight on the negative consequences of nationalism and patriotism, and warns against the gigantic dimensions of a European great war.

Nevertheless, the professor finds a glimpse of hope and uses the analogy "autumn leaves on the trees in April". In April, withered leaves from the year before still hang from the tree branches, but beneath these leaves, new, green buds are sprouting and growing. The month is a period of transition in nature, just as 1885−1888 is a period of transition in the history of humanity. The book's conclusion is in tune with the author's optimism: Soon the old values will be phased out and a new and better society will emerge!

Bertha was satisfied when she had written the final sentence. The publisher was also pleased with her manuscript and gave her an advance on her fee. The couple decided to spend the money on a trip to Paris. They longed to get away from Harmannsdorf's stuffy parlors and Eggenburg's narrow streets, and gain new impressions. Before they set out on their trip, Bertha wrote to Alfred and informed him of their travel plans. [134]

Chapter 4

In the salons of Paris – Intellectual awakening

La Belle Époque

Bertha was bursting with anticipation when she boarded the train that would take the couple to Paris. 11 years had passed since she had visited the French capital. On that occasion, she had left Arthur, her secret fiancé, to start working for an international businessman she had never met. Now she was on her way back with her beloved seated beside her, something which must have made the trip special. Arthur had never been to Paris, and Bertha was looking forward to showing him the city.

Bertha was not the only Austrian who longed to visit Paris at the time. Leaving Vienna for the capital of France was described by one author as moving from "the darkness into the light, and from repression to light-heartedness and frivolity, from a troubled to a superficial existence." [135] Paris was experiencing a cultural bloom, a golden age that came to be known as *La Belle Époque* and lasted until the First World War. A lengthy period of peace between France and its neighboring countries followed the German-French war of 1870-1871.

It was a time when beauty, the arts and culture blossomed, and painters, sculptors, composers, poets and authors came to Paris seeking inspiration for their work. The great painters of the period, Manet, Cézanne, Renoir, Degas, Monet, Gauguin and van Gogh all became established as artists during this time.

It was a time of *joie de vivre*. In the cabaret halls of Montmartre, champagne toasts were made, the most popular drink of the period among those of the upper class, and every night the dance halls were full. The scent of exotic dishes from the newly opened dining establishments tantalized the noses of tourists and famous restaurants such as Maxim's opened during this period.

It was also a time for optimism and grandiose projects. The Eiffel Tower was completed in 1889 and its 300-meter high structure made it the tallest building in the world. Paris was the capital of fashion and art, but other French cities also grew in diverse ways and established new public hospitals, public schools and expanded libraries.

However, most of this was enjoyed by the upper class only. The social inequalities were large. Prostitution flourished. Approximately 30,000 people woke up every morning not knowing how they were going to feed themselves that day. The nobility and rich men of industry lived in homes resembling palaces, while the poor suffered under wretched living conditions. Some found poorly paid jobs in industry, others emigrated to the USA.

It was the first time Bertha and Arthur vacationed together in Europe. They went to cafes and on outings to Versailles, Saint-Cloud and Sèvres. They visited the Louvre, the Hôtel des Invalides with the shining gold cupola, the opera, the Comédie-Française, Sacré-Coeur and Notre-Dame... During the evenings, they strolled along the Seine where the new electric street lights threw rays of light across the river flowing with slow and mighty grandeur through the city. Did Bertha's thoughts wander back to her visit 11 years ago, when she had walked the same route on her own, thinking about her fiancé?

After nine years in the barren Caucasia and two years on the remote Harmannsdorf estate, they now took immense pleasure in new cultural experiences. And in meeting new people.

Dinner on Avenue Malakoff

Shortly after their arrival, they sent word to Alfred Nobel, who contacted them immediately. What was Bertha's impression of her former employer? She did not think that the 53-year old had changed much in the 11 years that had passed, except that he was "a bit greyer" and seemed "more consumed by his work and his inventions than ever." [136] One may suspect it was somewhat worn-out man who invited Bertha and Arthur to dinner on Avenue Malakoff.

What was Alfred's impression of his former secretary? As usual, there are few source materials penned by his hand. However, we know that he later complimented Bertha in a letter, stating that she looked *radieuse* (radiant) in a photograph. [137]

On Avenue Malakoff, everything was mostly as it was 11 years ago. The green vestibule was new, as was the furniture of malachite and the music room, painted in red. In the laboratory in the backyard, Alfred gave a demonstration of how he worked, using the different instruments, test tubes, and jars. Arthur showed a great interest in the inventor's experiments. Afterwards they had dinner beneath the huge crystal chandelier in the dining room. Alfred treated his guests to "the most precious and exotic delicacies" and the finest of wines. They were served "fruit directly from Africa, with names I've never heard before and the rarest vintages of Château d'Yquem and Johannisberg to go with them," according to Bertha. Their host barely tasted the wine. Nobel continued to live an ascetic daily life, but he did not pinch pennies when he had esteemed guests.

What did they talk about over dinner? Most likely Bertha told Alfred about their years in Caucasia. Or maybe she spoke about the books she has written, as she often did. Bertha was passionate about the ideas she presented in her works, both the optimistic visions of *Inventarium einer Seele* ("Inventory of a Soul") and the social criticism of *Das Maschinenzeitalter* ("The Machine Age"). In her own words, the conversation with Nobel was "a great intellectual pleasure". [138]

Bertha's impression of Alfred was that he still lives "removed from the world". [139] He saw his neighbors and pedestrians out for a stroll only when he drove off to his new laboratory in Sévran early in the morning, wrapped up in fur pelts during the winter in his carriage drawn by elegant horses. Sometimes he worked so much that he forgot mealtimes.

His work was still causing him a large amount of distress. Factories exploded. Warehouses forbade the storage of explosives. Other inventors stole his patents. His French business partner Paul Barbe tried to swindle him, an experience which the highly ethical Nobel took badly.

It was perhaps not surprising that his hair had turned grey.

About his private life he said little. In whatever free time he had, he cultivated contact with the same friends and business associates as before. The same lady friend, too. But not a word was said about Miss Hess during the long dinner. No letters written in Sofie's chicken scrawl were lying around in the apartment, and neither were there photos of the Jewish beauty adorning his tables or chests of drawers.

Was also his last great invention; semi-smokeless gunpowder, a topic of conversation that was off-limits during the dinner with the author of peace-promoting works? Semi-smokeless gunpower, or *ballistite* as it was also called, had virtually overnight achieved a technical knock-out of the formerly used black powder. Alfred developed the invention in collaboration with his colleague Georges Fehrenbach, and received a patent for it in 1886. Ballistite was used for canons and had revolutionized the war materiel industry, particularly the artillery and the bomb industry. Some have referred to it as Nobel's most "surprising" and "problematic" invention, because it was so specifically designed for military use. [140]

Literature was probably a safer topic and an area of common interest. Perhaps they talked about Victor Hugo's death the year before? The ideals of the liberal man of enlightenment were ideals they both held dear. In his library, Alfred had all of 17 works by Victor Hugo. In the margins of many of these, he had underlined and written comments. On Hugo's 83rd birthday on February 26 of the previous year, Alfred had sent the author a long telegram in which he wished him a long and good life and success in "enchanting the world and spreading his grand ideas about universal love." [141] Three months later, Hugo passed away. More than two million people took part in the funeral procession for the national bard. Had Alfred been among them? Probably not, as he normally shunned large crowds.

As opposed to the last time Bertha was there, Alfred has no self-written poem to show her. He could only point out what he was reading now. His book collection had grown over the years. [142] Alfred had become more and more interested in "world literature", at a time when in most countries literature was considered a national affair. He would probably have agreed with the words of Goethe from 1827 to his friend Johan Peter Eckermann about how "the time of national literature had passed and the future would bring a *Weltlitteratur*." [143]

Among the new books he had acquired, were six novels by the author and editor Madame Juliette Adam-Lambert, who was an acquaintance of his. Madame Adam was a wealthy widow and republican who published the radical journal *La Nouvelle Revue*, a publication that authors fought to write for. She was also the hostess of one of Paris's most famous salons on Rue Lambert (the street was named after her maiden name, Lambert). By the end of the evening, Alfred had invited his guests to accompany him to the popular salon.

For Bertha, this invitation would prove to be a door opener.

Madame Adam's salon

Alfred Nobel set his business affairs aside when he took the couple to Madam Adam's exclusive salon. Perhaps it was Victor Hugo, who had been a frequent guest there, who had introduced Nobel to the place the first time? Crossing the threshold of Adam's famous salon was no easy matter. The France of the 19th century was an extremely elitist society. With time, however, it had become more usual for successful businessmen to be allowed to join the traditionally elite circles. [144]

Outside of Adam's salon on the Rue Lambert, people stood lined up, waiting to enter. The hostess stood at the entrance wearing a dark red velvet dress with a long veil descending the back. Diamonds were fastened to the bosom of her dress and in her greying hair. The 50-year old was a "captivating figure", according to Bertha, whose face still had a "youthful and hungry expression". [145] In the salon it was so crowded that people stood lined up all the way up the stairway. The air was thick with cigar and cigarette smoke.

The phenomenon of the *salon* was a long-standing tradition in France. Artists, scientists, writers and diplomats found their way to the salons. Discussions thrived under the best conditions. Readings by aspiring authors were also a common element. In Paris, the salons were often held in the home of a refined woman of the bourgeoisie.

The free-spoken and liberal Madame Adam made an impression on Bertha. Like many of the female authors of the day, she wrote books under a male pseudonym – the name Paul Vasili. [146] She also wrote impassioned editorials about foreign affairs for international newspapers and did not hesitate to signal her clear political involvement. "How can a woman be so involved with politics?" Bertha thought as she listened to Madame Adam speak. "How much discomfort she brings upon herself!" [147] 43-year old Bertha was by now an established author, however, unlike the hostess, she found it challenging to stand before an audience and speak freely.

War of revenge

Suddenly, Madam Adam clapped her hands: "*Messieurs! Mesdames!*" The guests fell silent. Then she delivered a thundering speech about France's defeat in the war with Germany in 1871. She made a call for revenge, praising the French Minister of War General Boulanger.

Adam was not the only one who hoped for a war of revenge. The loss of Alsace-Lorraine and the bloodbath at Sedan in 1871 were still painfully alive in the memories of the French. Although it was peacetime in France, beneath the surface, it was simmering. For 16 years, the French had been waiting for the right moment. Waiting and waiting. The thought that they would one day conquer anew the lost provinces was always at hand.

Bertha listened to the talk of revenge with growing agitation. The last time she had been to Paris, she had been indifferent to the theme when her employer discussed it. Now she decried all talk about nationalism and war: "I was no longer as indifferent about these things as when I was young ... I already hated war with a passion and the light-hearted flirtation with its possibilities seemed to me to be uncritical and without scruples." [148] While she was listening, a burning desire to do something that could help prevent another great war from breaking out arose within her.

What about Alfred, how did he react? The last time they met, he had expressed his views on the political events of the day. Then Bertha had listened with half an ear. Now she was all ears, but what about her former employer? Did he follow the conversations attentively or did he allow his gaze to slide absently away and out the window?

Perhaps being the third wheel was not equally interesting, as Bertha had brought Arthur with her. Perhaps he had already left Rue Lambert and was wandering home to Avenue Malakoff. It could be that he collapsed into an armchair with a book in his hands. And it is not inconceivable that he fell asleep before reading a single line, worn out by his stressful life.

"World citizens"

While Alfred returned home to Avenue Malakoff, Bertha and Arthur continued to frequent the lush, carpeted salons of Paris the following weeks. The salon visits seemed to have a domino effect: Once they crossed the threshold of one salon, it was likely that they would be invited to another.

That winter the couple found themselves in the midst of a colorful carousel of French free-thinkers: Agitators, radicals and rebellious intellectuals. François Buloz, Ernest Renan, and Alphonse Daudet were among those whom they met. The atmosphere in the salons was electric. The rooms were filled to the ceilings with ideas and visions for the future. Here, they met people who preferred reading Darwin rather than the Bible. People who went to the theatre instead of to church. Who were concerned about content and not simply form. People who were cosmopolitans, as was Bertha's ideal:

People who are well-travelled, have knowledge of several languages and are well-read in these languages, and who through this have absorbed the best of the spirits and characters of the different nations... Refined in every sense, they represent a type of person who belongs to a nation in the process of being created, and which one day will conquer the world: a nation of world citizens. [149]

Bertha's ideal of "a nation of world citizens" was something she would return to many times. In this, as in many other areas, she was ahead of her time.

Among the people they met during that winter, were the author and historian of religion Ernest Renan. He had received a lot of attention for his book *La vie de Jésus* (1863), where he writes about Jesus as an ordinary human being and not the son of God. At his place, they spent hours discussing the "convention-bound reality founded on lies." [150] At Renan's, they received an invitation from Victor Cherbuliez, a novelist and member of the highly prestigious French Academy. [151]After their visit at Cherbuliez's, they continued to François Buloz, who was a theatre administrator and editor of the prestigious journal *Revue des deux Mondes*. His home, a solid, old *palais* in Faubourg Saint-Germain, was the intellectual center of Paris and here the discussions were, according to Bertha, more "stiff, puritanical, learned – in short, academic." [152] The couple also received an invitation from the poet Alphonse Daudet, whose wife Julia held a weekly salon for poets and writers. Here a small group of people gathered around the hearth for a "long chat", something Bertha preferred over the discussions in large, crowded rooms.

Once again, she was reminded of the impoverished intellectual life of those in her home surroundings. How would the reflected individuals whom she met here react if they were to overhear some of the conversations amongst the landed gentry in Eggenburg?

How interesting it would be for people of an intellectual bent and with knowledge to take part in their (the nobility's) eternally identical concerns: where they danced yesterday and where they shall dance tomorrow – at Schwarzenberg's, Pallavinci's or the court - the passions in which the Baroness Pacher is currently indulging, which marriage proposals the Countess Palffy has turned down ... Such were the topics of conversation for the people around me. [153]

During that winter in Paris, Bertha had an encounter that would change the course of her life forever.

The new peace movement

In one of the salons, Bertha was introduced to the Romanian doctor Wilhelm Löwenthal, who told her that there existed something called a "peace movement" in Europe. The English pacifist Hodgson Pratt had founded the International Peace and Arbitration Association in 1880. His London-based association's purpose was to promote arbitration and peace as an alternative to armed conflicts and force.

Bertha was immediately intrigued: "What? Such a girl exists in Madrid and I don't hear about her until today? as Don Carlos shouts in the scene with the princess Eboli in Verdi's opera Don Carlos!", she exclaimed, with her sense for dramatic metaphors. Such a league existed, where the struggle to do away with war, had assumed form and life? Could this new movement help to prevent another great war from breaking out between Germany and France? The news electrified her. [154]

When she returned to Austria in the spring of 1887, her mind was buzzing with ideas. The visit to Paris had not only been a much-needed holiday, but had also provided useful information about something that would become very important to her. Back home at Harmannsdorf, she immediately sat down to write an additional chapter about the new peace movement in *The Machine Age*, just before the book went to print. She called it "Glimpses into the Future" ("Zukunftsausblicke") and strongly encouraged readers to support the new London-based movement.

During the visit to Paris, Alfred had been more of an invisible figure than last time she was there. Nevertheless, he had been a door opener: He had provided an introduction for Bertha in the Parisian salons, where she eventually learned about Europe's recently founded peace movement.

Thus, also this time, the visit to Paris represented a turning point in Bertha's life.

Chapter 5

Lay Down Your Arms! – The pacifist call

The novelistic format

When Bertha was asked how she came upon the idea of writing *Lay Down Your Arms! (Die Waffen nieder!)*, she replied: "All I can say is that I didn't come upon the idea, but rather that the idea came upon me. But why? I don't know anymore...I didn't act according to a set plan or an impulsive decision. It all happened 'by itself', gradually and altogether differently than I had thought." [155]

After returning home in the spring of 1887, she was utterly determined to do something to support the new peace movement. Bertha was tremendously driven. War was directly opposed to everything she stood for, it was contrary to the whole idea of evolution, something she emphasizes in the following passage in *The Machine Age*:

> War distorts evolution, that most distinctive of nature's mechanisms - a natural selection process that promotes the survival of the best and most adaptable - into its exact opposite: death becomes the fate of the best, that is, of the young, strong and able, while the old, weak and infirm can live and reproduce their inadequacies. In short, war is a reversal of a developmental process - an artificial degeneration. [156]

Being aware that *The Machine Age* might be received less seriously if it became known that the author was a woman, she had written it under the pseudonym "Jemand" ("someone"). When the book was published early in 1889, it received a lot of attention and praise by the critics. *The Machine Age* is considered to be among the first books to describe the results of exaggerated nationalism and armaments. However, its readership was limited. Bertha's appeal in the last chapter did not reach more than a segment of the intelligentsia. In his review in *Die Neue Zeit*, the German socialist writer August Bebel stated that it was unfortunate that the anonymous author's discourse was directed towards an intellectual minority. Whoever wants his or her message to reach the masses must write in a different mode. Was Bertha influenced by this statement in choosing the novel as the literary form for her next work? This is how she commented on her choice:

> When writing an academic thesis, you can present abstract reasoning; you can philosophize and argue your case. With this book, I wanted to do something more than that. I wanted to express not only what I thought but what I felt - felt passionately. The pain of warfare, as I imagined it, had seared my soul ... I wanted to describe real life in a historical context and that is best done in the format of a novel. [157]

Inspired by Zola's naturalist ("scientific") school of thought, she threw herself into an intensive research process. She read up on the European wars between 1859 and 1871, including the Austro-Italian wars of independence and the Prussian wars with France and Austria, respectively. She interviewed soldiers who had fought in wars, both officers and privates, and ploughed through thick history books, dusty war office documents and old archival materials. Most interesting was reports and eyewitness accounts by army surgeons who had worked in these theatres of war. Bertha aspired to write a story that was realistic. The public image of the machinery of war was of something distant and abstract - she wanted to depict it close up, and to get it under the skin of her readers.

By placing the narrative in the recent past, she gave her novel topical and current significance. The European situation was tense in 1888, something she had sensed while visiting Paris. At the time, there was a real fear of an imminent great war. From June, the war-hungry Emperor Wilhelm II ruled Germany and made threats to its arch enemy, the nation of France. The tensions were further heightened as unrest and complicated political developments in the Balkans put Russia and the Austro-Hungarian Empire on a hostile footing.

"A life story"

During the writing process, her contempt for war increased to a "painful intensity", as she "endured all the agony suffered by the heroine of my novel." [158] But Bertha was not the type to back away from difficulties, so she clenched her teeth and carried on.

In the book, the author shifts between close and distant points of view. She takes a few steps back to outline the broad historical background, only to subsequently zoom in on the experiences of individual characters. To make the narrative ring true, she created a protagonist whose life had similarities to her own. The author and her protagonist have names with a similar ring - Bertha and Martha - and their personalities and backgrounds are comparable. Martha von Althaus' father was an Austrian army general, just like Bertha's, and as a young woman, Martha loved dancing in the glittering ballrooms of Vienna, like Bertha had done. Other similarities include interest for fashion, "high society" and flirting with dashing young officers and lieutenants.

Martha soon falls for Count Arno von Dotzky, a promising young lieutenant. It doesn't take long for them to become a couple. However, the idyll is ruined when war breaks out in 1859 between Austria and France, supported in part by Italy. Arno is called to war and a few months into the war, Martha learns that her fiancé has been killed.

By now she has developed from a naïve young girl, who admires the glamor of uniforms and military virtues, into a strong woman, an ardent pacifist, just like the author herself. After four years of mourning, Martha falls in love again – with another lieutenant; Lieutenant General Fredrick von Tilling. Despite being an officer, Fredrick is weary and disenchanted with the military. In terms of both his personality and appearance, the character bore a remarkable likeness to Arthur von Suttner. The characters' partnership is very much the reflection of von Suttner's married life.

After six months, Martha and Fredrick marry, but not long after the wedding, Fredrick too, is called up. Surviving the wars of 1864 and 1866, he goes to fight in the Franco-German war (1870-71), when he suddenly disappears. Later, Martha receives distressing news from in Paris: Her husband has been mistakenly killed.

How would she react if war took Arthur from her? Throughout the writing process, this thought energized Bertha and lent passion to her writing, as well as contributing to the novel's popular appeal. Many of the readers could relate to the author's fears, especially women who had lost, or feared losing, a father, husband or son on the battlefield.

Lay Down Your Arms! is both a tribute to love and a demonstration of how war can destroy the most loving of relationships. [159] The narrator is so vividly present throughout the book, that even years later readers would confuse Bertha and Martha. The novel's subtitle – "A Life Story" – as well as the author's use of the first-person narrative, contributed to the belief that the book was autobiographical. The accounts were so detailed and apparently true to life, that when the English peace activist Felix Moscheles visited the author one year after the publication, he wanted to "present his condolences to the widow". When Arthur suddenly walked into the room and Bertha introduced him as her husband, the disoriented visitor exclaimed: "What, aren't you dead? I thought you were shot in Paris!" [160]

Many readers were astonished to learn that Bertha neither had any experiences from the wars she described in the novel. At the time of the battle of Solferino (1859), she had been staying at the spa in Wiesbaden and hardly opened a newspaper. In 1864, during the war between Denmark and the allies Austria and Prussia, she spent the summer season in Bad Homburg, listening with delight to the soprano Adelina Patti, and when Austria and Prussia clashed in 1866, the young Miss Kinsky was enjoying herself together with her friend Salomé in Paris...

Bloodbath of war

Lay Down Your Arms! provoked strong reactions: Never before had a woman written a novel containing such detailed and bloody war scenes. The narrative records the sights and smells from blood-soaked theatres of war with precision and in a way that is realistically physical. One example of this is when Martha, the heroine of the book, walks across the battlefield at Königgrätz, searching for her husband Fredrick among the wounded soldiers. In a scene, she walks past a cluster of fallen soldiers, barely alive:

> They suffered terribly. In one location, some fifty men lay close together. Their ruined limbs were rotting, the blood that covered their distorted, swollen faces was congealing ... the dead, already infested with maggots, were lying side by side with the living and had lain there, day after day. The arms and legs of the living contracted spasmodically as the poisoned blood coursed slowly through their veins. There was no hope for them.

In *Lay Down Your Arms!* there are no heroes, only victims. The author mocks the arms race between Prussia and Austria, and calls it an 'unending refrain'. In the accounts of suffering and ever-present death, the author confronts the reader with a question: Does he or she truly believe that the young men who are slowly tormented to death on the battlefield die happily with the cry "Pro Patria" on their lips? During this period, such was the normal public depiction of a soldier's death – as a fine, heroic act. The author expresses her disgust with the violence practiced in the name of "love for the mother country" and criticizes the way history is taught in the schools:

> Yes, history! It builds excitement about warfare in the young. Its study hammers into the open minds of children that the Lord of lords decides the outcomes of the battles and that wars determine how the world is ruled ...The ever-repeated observations dampen insight until war is seen only as a distant, unreal phenomenon, where the mystical scent of incense wraps itself around political history. War – the source of the highest honor and fame. [161]

Throughout the book, the author's sympathy is always with the soldiers and her anger is directed towards the men in power: The war lords, politicians and officers.

Criticism of double standards

Lay Down Your Arms! also discusses gender. Bertha confronts a society which enjoins its women to play at being patriotic wives and passive hero worshippers. Sheltered by the walls of grand houses, securely tucked away inside glazed conservatories and hidden behind large, lacy fans, young upper-class women must pretend to know nothing of blood and filth. All while they spent much of their time embroidering the banners that will flutter in the wind above the bloody battlefields... "Girls are taught that there is nothing offensive about warfare, but should they hear anyone refer to anything related to the source of life and its reproduction, they must blush and shy away. What a morality! Dreadful and cowardly!" the author exclaims. [162]

Young women were encouraged to write letters to the soldiers, tempting them with promises of love, so that they would win their battles and return home in one piece. Should a loved one return in a coffin, however, grieving mothers and girlfriends were comforted with the assurance that a soldier's death was "meaningful".

Lies, omissions and double standards were essential lubricants in the machinery of war.

Vision of eternal peace

Bertha, who never excelled at the feminine skills of Victorian women, such as prayer and embroidery, proved herself to be a talented novelist of war stories full of blood and gore.

However, *Lay Down Your Arms!* is not all death and destruction and social criticism. The novel is also entertaining. Bertha's makes the reader smile with her descriptions of young Martha and her sisters as they chase after love. Here she makes use of all the tricks she learned as a writer of serial novels. In several ways, the plot and sub-plots are reminiscent of the series of stories about "Countess X". The engaging style draws the reader into the story and towards the message of the book.

The book ends on a hopeful note: Martha, like Bertha, changes to become deeply interested in the writers and philosophers of progressive optimism. Buckle's vision of how society would move inexorably towards peace impresses her so strongly that after having studied his work, she feels "like someone who has spent all her life in a deep valley and then, suddenly, is taken to the top of a hill from the summit of which she has a view over large stretches of land and the endless waves on the ocean." [163]

To the author, "eternal peace" was not just an unattainable utopian state, but a condition which she regarded as perfectly possible if only mankind reached a higher state of consciousness. How could this state be attained? Again, the novel's political message comes to surface: Children should be brought up and schooled to prefer peace to war. Values such as love, tolerance and respect should be cultivated at an early age. The author also launches concrete proposals for the establishment of a supra-national armed forces with wide-ranging authority to intervene and argued in favor of a European peace tribunal.

Some of Bertha's arguments in favor of peace were also inserted into the conversations between Martha and her father, General Count von Althaus. The general first stands staunchly by his views on the excellence of war. A conservative man, he has neither read Darwin nor any of the authors and scientists of the new era, and rejects the latest ideas: "Change from ape into man! You don't have to be a scholar to realize that this goes against all common sense." Instead, he insists steadfastly on his arguments for war, which are also the conventions adhered to by the Austrian military establishment: 1) God - Lord of lords - sanctions war, as stated in the Holy Book; 2) war has always been and consequently, will always be; 3) without war, mankind would become too numerous; 4) lengthy periods of peace make people apathetic, degenerate and wasteful. [164]

However, the general changes his views when he loses Otto, his only son, in a cholera epidemic in the aftermath of a war. In a final moving scene, the old man on his deathbed pleads to his daughter in a whisper: "Martha, you have had your wish. I curse all wars." [165]

Perhaps this was the author's defiant salute to her own father, Field Marshal Franz Joseph Kinsky, the strapping man in uniform whom she had never met and knew only from gilt-framed paintings?

Problems with publication

Once Bertha had completed the writing process, she sent the nearly 400 pages of text to the weekly magazines that had previously published her serial novels. Every single one of the editors returned the manuscript, expressing regret: "It is expected that many readers will find the contents offensive." [166]

Then she tried various publishers, without any luck. One editor described the work as "challenging and likely to cause public outrage." In his view, it would be an incalculable risk to print a work that scorned the militarized state. [167] In another instance, the editor would consider recommending her novel for publication only if she allowed an experienced civil servant to read the text and strike out the more upsetting scenes.

Strike out passages from her book? The mere thought was revolting to Bertha. Not the tiniest fraction was to be removed: "- to get somebody to lop and trim in diplomatic-opportunist fashion such a work, which, whatever its worth or worthlessness, had at least the one merit of being hotly felt and *unreservedly sincere*, - to remodel it by the rules of that most contemptible of all arts, the art of suiting everybody, - no, sooner into the stove with it." [168]

The author was not willing to compromise. The hunt for a publisher was therefore time-consuming and draining but, as usual, Bertha stayed the course. Finally, she convinced a German friend about the worth of her book who in turn persuaded her husband, a publisher, to take it on. In the end of 1889, *Lay Down Your Arms!* was published by the small Pierson publishing house in Leipzig.

Help with promotion

Afterwards Bertha wrote to friends and acquaintances asking them to help her promote her work. One day in November 1889, Alfred found a letter from his former secretary in the letterbox. How she phrased herself is unknown, because not all her letters from before 1891 were preserved. However, its message can be gleaned from Alfred's reply:

> *Lay Down Your Arms* - so that's the title of your new book, which I am very curious to find out more about. But you ask me to promote it actively, a request that is a little merciless. If world peace ensues, how am I to sell my new powder? Unless I change the formula to make face powder [*poudre de riz*] to cover in dust those who are already about to turn to dust.

With "new powder", Alfred probably refers to his invention the smokeless gunpowder (ballistite). Could his new product instead be used as a face powder for ladies of a certain age? As it was, there would indeed be no market for it if Bertha's vision of universal peace became a reality!

The inventor is obviously in the mood for teasing irony and continues in the same vein:

> Now, apart from "Lay Down Your Arms", your benevolence will surely extend to make room for Lay Down Misery, Lay Down Old Prejudices, Lay Down Old Religions, Lay Down Old Injustice and Old Dishonour, not to speak of Old Jehovah. All of which, and whom, are truly unpleasant - as is, by the way, the Holy Spirit, who actually isn't holy at all, just like that entire lot of worm-eaten antiquities.

Alfred's letter leaves little doubt that he is a progressive man. He ends with usual politeness by saying that he would like to go and visit her, but for him, freedom was "...as unavailable as the Eiffel Tower: I can glimpse them both - but to reach them requires time and wings." [169] Busy as always, working at his desk, Alfred had a view that included the recently-constructed Eiffel Tower (1889).

Complimentary reviews

As things turned out, Bertha did not need Alfred to back her book. The support came from elsewhere. To her surprise, *Lay Down Your Arms!* was mentioned in an engaging parliamentary speech by the Austrian Minister of Finance, Julian Dunajewski: "Recently, a German woman - not a parliamentarian - wrote a story in which she included deeply moving descriptions of warfare. I implore you to set aside a few hours to study this work and should any of you retain a fondness for war afterwards, I truly pity you." [170]

A brilliant review by a friend of hers; the philosopher and politician Bartholomeus von Carneri for *Die Neue Freie Presse* also helped to create interest in the book. On March 15, 1890, Carneri wrote: "Never has militarism been described so thoroughly; how it generates suffering, how beautiful the life it despises can be." He concluded that *Lay Down Your Arms!* "ennobles in all the finest senses of the word" and that "its strength and natural quality arise from the authoress's sincere engagement and idealism." [171]

Bertha met the highly-regarded philosopher after her return from the Caucasus. Despite the difference in their ages (Bartholomeus was seventy-one years old and Bertha forty-six), they became friends. During the next decade, he became a tower of strength to Bertha – a very loyal, but also critical friend.

After Carneri's glowing review, other critics swiftly followed, and the book caused quite a stir in Austria. Some disagreed with the opinions it expressed, and a heated debate followed. It was not long before the foreign press began to take notice. Within the next few years, *Lay Down Your Arms!* swept like an epidemic across Europe, to the author's surprise. During the next decade, the novel appeared in a new language almost every year and it was reprinted in several editions. By 1905, it had been translated into 17 languages. In Germany alone, it was reprinted 31 times before 1914.

Lay Down Your Arms! became one of the greatest literary success stories of the 19th century. [172] This was partly due to a new type of readership which emerged in this period: A large segment of the middle class, among them many women, took the book to their hearts.

In an article, Leo Tolstoy compared the importance of the book for the cause of peace with what *Uncle Tom's Cabin* by Harriet Beecher Stowe had meant for the emancipation of the slaves. [173] Thanks to the novel, the international peace movement suddenly became a hot topic of debate. Bertha von Suttner had succeeded in spreading pacifist ideas more effectively than any pacifist organization could have dreamt of. Now she was celebrated by pacifists from all over Europe. Congratulatory letters and telegrams streamed to Eggenburg. Hodgson Pratt, whose International Arbitration and Peace Association had been an inspiration to her from the start, sent her a personal greeting of gratitude.

The author herself was feeling a bit overwhelmed. Even though she enjoyed the success, she took a sober view of her own role in it: "I believe that when a book does well, its success does not depend on the effect it has on the spirit of the time, but that, on the contrary, it does well because of the spirit of the time ... A flash of lightning is possible only when the air is laden with electricity." [174]

The author's aristocratic background probably contributed to somewhat to the success of her novel. In a Europe still very conscious of class distinctions, "blue blood" and "lily-white hands" were certainly useful aids for a woman author to attract this degree of attention. Felix Salten, the author of the bestseller *Bambi*, put it this way:

A woman writer from the working classes might well write a successful book. But who would listen to an ordinary middle class woman? ... However strong her presence, however articulate and politic her utterances, what would be the odds that she could impress the aristocracy, who as a class is more concerned with correct manners, forms of speech and gesture than with the meaning of what is being said? One must take care to place von Suttner on the right shelf: a baroness, born a countess and, also, an authoress. [175]

"Peace fury"

Although *Lay Down Your Arms!* was widely admired, it also received a lot of criticism. [176] Conservatives accused Bertha of being a liberal, anti-Christian supporter of Darwin's theory of evolution. "Peace Fury", "Red Bertha" and "Smug Bertha" – the author had to put up with quite a lot of abuse. People in her immediate circle of family and friends were often particularly critical. "Regrettably, aristocrats continue to be the greatest enemies of the peace movement. Thus, I have encountered the strongest resistance to my propaganda among my own cousins," she wrote about this. [177]

At the time, it was regarded as especially provocative that grim descriptions of war had been written by a woman; preferably, women should not meddle in politics. Furthermore, if they were to write books, they would do well to choose uncontroversial subjects. A little time spent at her writing desk was a respectable part of an aristocratic woman's day. She was expected to pen notes on the day's events in neat handwriting, preferably in a diary with embroidered covers. The diary, almanac and notepaper for letter writing were also seen as therapeutic means of dealing with pent-up female anger. [178] Loving letters were acceptable, perhaps with pressed flowers included as a greeting. If she were to write about love, it should be about an idealized version - naturally, without any references to physical passion. The writer Max Nordau expressed this common view: "The one subject about which you can expect women to write well is children." [179]

However, Nordau would be forced to eat his words when the author of the hitherto anonymous *The Machine Age* became known. Earlier he had praised the book to the skies in a long review, where he had also tried to guess who had written it and listed some likely candidates, all famous and all male!

Despite the success of *Lay Down Your Arms!*, Bertha earned only a modest sum through her book. At the time, this was the rule rather than the exception. There were no international agreements on the sale of translation rights and foreign publishers printed copies of the novel in translation without making any payment to the author. Even though Bertha was annoyed about this, she retained her ability to see the future in an optimistic perspective: "Our grandchildren will experience a day when intellectual property is given international protection," she wrote in a letter to her friend Carneri. [180]

"Amazon Hand"

In Paris, Alfred read the reviews of *Lay Down Your Arms!* in the French newspapers. He acquired a copy of the book which he read on a train journey from Vienna to Paris, after he had been to visit Sofie Hess. Upon his arrival home, he wrote to her about what he had read during the journey: "Fortunately I had brought along books: *Lay Down Your Arms* and *Salammbô* helped me to pass the time." [181]

While Bertha's anti-war novel had an edifying and optimistic developmental perspective, the same claim cannot be made for Gustave Flaubert's historical novel, *Salammbô* (1862), a gory and violent depiction of the Libyan war in Carthage in the year 300 B.C. Alfred did not share his thoughts about *Lay Down Your Arms!* with Sofie, but his next letter to Bertha was overflowing with praise:

Chère Baronne et amie, I have just finished reading your admirable masterpiece. It is said that there are 2000 languages – that would be 1999 too many – but there is not a single language in which your fascinating work should not be translated, read and contemplated. How long did it take you to pen this marvel? You must tell me, when I have the honor and joy of shaking your hand – this hand of an Amazon who so nimbly wages war upon war. [182]

The letter, written on April 1,1890, concludes with a flattering phrase, written in English: "Yours forever and more than ever, A. Nobel." Its tone is deferential, unlike his previous letter, which had been full of irony. [183]

In the period that followed, Alfred collected reviews of the novel with painstaking care. When he went to visit his mother in Stockholm for Christmas, he clipped out the critiques of *Lay Down Your Arms!* from the Swedish newspapers *Aftonbladet* and *Stockholms Dagblad* (dated 21 December 1890). They were found neatly folded between two pages of the novel after his death. In the latter, Alfred had underlined the following words: "This remarkable book is from start to finish written with enormous talent and warmth...One must but acknowledge the work's noble, compassionate intention." [184]

He was obviously full of admiration for his earlier secretary. In the last 14 years, Bertha had gone from being a secretary without means to a world-renowned author. When she came to Paris to work for him in 1875, *he* had been at the pinnacle of his professional career; a successful inventor. His long coming-of-age poem "The Riddle", which he had written in his spare time, had made an impression on her.

Now it was *her* turn to impress him. Bertha had experienced a breakthrough in her career and was able to earn her living by her pen, something he had personally dreamt of in his youth. She had become an author who was recognized throughout all of Europe. Not only had she made his own childhood dream of earning a living by writing come true, but she had done so with the pacifist message of his author idol Percy Bysshe Shelley.

Perhaps it wasn't so odd that Alfred's letter expressed deference. Normally he disliked the naturalistic style of writing, and what he called "propaganda literature". He had little use for Zola, whom he found "vulgar": "Zola sat in a pile of shit and spread a horrific stench," he had jeered on one occasion. [185] *Lay Down Your Arms!* was an exception. Now he set about buying Bertha's other books and placed them on the shelves of his library with care. [186]

Lay Down Your Arms! no doubt made an impression on the inventor, even if it wasn't strong enough to induce him to resolve to give up on his "armories". But perhaps it was around this time that he began toying with the idea of creating a prize in the spirit of *Lay Down Your Arms!?*

The obituary

Alfred was still not showing an interest in peace work at the time. But there is little doubt that he was longing for peace in his own life. In a letter to his business companion, James Thorne, he wrote: "I'm weary of the explosives industry, in which one only stumbles upon accidents, restrictions, bureaucracy, pedantry and other difficulties. I am longing for tranquility and want to dedicate myself fully to scientific research, which is impossible when every day brings with it further worries."

More and more frequently, Alfred expressed that what truly

interested him was science and not commerce. In a letter to another friend he wrote: "There is not a single reason why I, who have no education in running a business and hate it with all my heart, shall be plagued by such matters when I have no better grasp of it than the man on the moon." [187] The claim that he had no knowledge about how to run a business was a modest statement on the part of the successful businessman. But there is little reason to doubt that Alfred disliked this aspect of the enterprise. He shied away from conflict and preferred to visit his factories on Sundays when it was less likely that he would meet employees.

Nonetheless, he was unable to avoid unpleasantness. Claims emerged from all sides. His most recent invention, smokeless powder, was a cause of conflict with the French authorities. In 1886, Alfred had made an offer to sell the invention to France, but they had turned it down. After their rejection, he sold the patent to Italy, something which the French did not take kindly to. They accused him of espionage on the grounds of his having experimented with a military invention on French soil, and then selling the invention to a neighboring nation. The criticism from the authorities was so harsh that Alfred considered leaving the country.

This was a period of great frustration for him. When his brother Ludvig the same year (1886) attempted to persuade him to write an autobiography, he received this gloomy response:

Alfred Nobel – a pitiful creature, should have been strangled at birth by a humanitarian doctor when he made his howling entrance into this world. Greatest virtues: Keeps his nails clean and is never a burden to anyone. Greatest weaknesses: Has neither a wife nor children, capacity for joy or a healthy appetite. Greatest wish in life: Not to be buried alive. Greatest sin: Does not worship mammon. Important events in life: None. [188]

Ludvig gave up. Alfred would never write an autobiography.

Not long after this, Ludvig, who was suffering from angina pectoris, fell gravely ill. As time passed by, he did not get any better. Alfred went to visit his brother in Cannes, where he was living with his wife, Edla, and found him bedridden. He made it just in time to say farewell. Ludvig Nobel passed away on Thursday, April 12, 1888, at the age of 57.

Alfred took his older brother's death hard. A few days later, he got another shock when he read his brother's obituary in *Le Figaro*: "A man who only with great difficulty will possibly be viewed as a benefactor of the human race, passed away in Cannes yesterday. It was Nobel, the inventor of dynamite. Mr. Nobel was Swedish." The obituary went on to describe Nobel as a man "who became rich by finding ways to kill more people faster than ever before."

Through some journalistic error, *Le Figaro* had mixed up the brothers! It was not the only paper which did this, but none of them were as insulting in their comments about the deceased as this one. However, the following Monday, an apology about the mix-up was printed: "The newspaper mistakenly announced the death of Mr. Nobel, the inventor of dynamite. It was his brother who recently passed away following a long-term illness." [189]

Several people in Nobel's circles reacted to the wording of the obituary. Juliette Adam wasted no time sending a telegram: "The news of your death shocked us all. I am extremely happy to hear that you are in good health." [190] To say that Alfred was in "good health", was a bit of an exaggeration. To Sofie he wrote: "I'm so exhausted that I can scarcely manage to hold the pen." [191]

The wording of the obituary must have made him reflect on how other people regarded him. Was this what would be said about him when his time came? He had built his fortune on an invention that was predominantly used for civilian purposes: Roads, tunnels, railways and harbors. The military value of dynamite was limited. [192] Only a small part of his inventions, perhaps ten percent, had a purely military value. It was probably this part of his enterprise that *Le Figaro* had had in mind. Was the newspaper also influenced by his recent conflict with the French authorities?

Alfred had barely succeeded in regaining his balance when he experienced an even greater shock: The same year, on December 7, 1888, his mother Andriette died. Andriette Ahlsell Nobel lived to the age of 84. Alfred had been very close to her since his childhood, and always showered her with gifts along with shares, bonds and cash and spent Christmas with her in Stockholm, even though he hated the Swedish climate during the winter. Every year, on her birthday September 30, he sent valuable presents or travelled home to celebrate her day with a special dinner, often at the Hotel Rydberg or Grand Hotel. He had written long and tender letters to her throughout his whole life. In them, one finds little of the sarcastic exaggerations so typical of his other correspondence. The two brothers Robert and Ludvig had not shared his ardent love for their mother. Now she was gone as well. Yet another loss in his life.

After his mother's death, Alfred donated his portion of her estate to Karolinska Institutet in Stockholm to establish the "Caroline-Andriette Nobel's Foundation for experimental medical research" – a harbinger of greater largesse to come.

"Cupid's arrows replaced by canons"

In his private life, the relationship to Sofie did little to soothe his nerves. Miss Hess often complained to him about being lonely, lacking money or not feeling well. In her letters, she tells him about her various ailments, such as "dizziness", "nausea" or "anemia". [193] There is little to suggest that she was suffering from anything serious.

In the meanwhile, she continued the costly spa life. Mortgage deeds and debt claims appeared in Alfred's mailbox at Avenue Malakoff. In his letters to her, the ascetic inventor expressed shock and disbelief over his lover's spending habits. He was willing to put up with financing one spa visit after the next, but enormous amounts of money just seemed to evaporate. Alfred was convinced that Sofie was giving money to her family. Back home at Praterstrasse, Mr. Hess ran a sweetshop that was doing poorly and all three of her sisters were unmarried. [194]

He also disliked it when Sofie used his family name in shops and at hotels. An envelope from Karlsbad was signed "Madame S.

Nobel, Hotel Pupp in Karlsbad". "Sofie Nobel, Hotel Royal, Singerstrasse, Vienna" was her registration at a hotel in Vienna. [195] However, it was probably not so easy to be in Sofie's shoes either. At the time, marriage was the only form of cohabitation that was publicly acceptable, but there was a powerful double standard at work. For an unmarried man in Alfred's position, having a lover was accepted, in some circles almost expected. For an unmarried woman like Sofie, on the other hand, things were quite different. She had to protect her reputation.

Eventually, Vienna was not large enough to prevent Bertha from hearing about Sofie. One afternoon, the now famous author stopped by a flower shop and learned that a "Mrs. Nobel" had bought flowers there. Bertha was astonished. "Mrs. Nobel?" Immediately she sent a telegram to her friend: Was there a "Mrs. Nobel" or a *jeune femme adore* in his life? In Paris, Alfred Nobel immediately picked up his pen and wrote back. In the letter, he flatly denied that he had married or found a girlfriend:

Did you really believe that I would have married without informing you? That would be a crime, both against our friendship and against common courtesy. This old bear is not so decrepit yet. As for "Madame Nobel", it was without doubt my sister-in-law. So there you have the explanation for my secret and mysterious marriage.

Not fully honest, but at least a creative attempt at justification on Alfred's part... Was it important for him to try to ensure that Bertha did not find out about Sofie? Did he want her to preserve her image of him as the flawless, solitary Byron-reading bachelor? In the letter, it is the jilted bachelor who is holding the pen: "An explanation can be found for everything in our sullied world, sooner or later, except for the heart's magnetism...It is precisely this magnetism that I apparently lack, in that there is no Madame Alfred Nobel and since Cupid's arrows in my case have been replaced by canons." [196]

Alfred, who eight years earlier had paid homage to "the heart's magnetism" in the poem "Night-Thought" (1880), now gave the impression of being a disillusioned man when it came to love. In his letter to Bertha, bitter humor had replaced the former sensitive, lyrical tone.

How did the baroness react to this? She wrote an effusive reply where she encouraged him to look at the bright side of life. Bertha would never again mention the episode in the flower shop when she was informed of a "Mrs. Nobel".

Alfred, for his own part, wrote a letter full of reprimands to Sofie and asked her to never use his name.

Once again, he was alone in the big house on Avenue Malakoff. And Sofie was on her own as well, spending her time among strangers at the Homburg spa.

Praise from the north

Bertha's novel *Lay Down Your Arms!* continued its triumphant march through Europe. With time, it also became a success in the United States, which was rare for a book from the German speaking regions at this time. When some friends called her a "famous author", she wrote to her friend Bartholomäus Carneri: "Is that what I am? It quite simply does not sink in." She continued: "It just demonstrates how an avalanche works: as it is falling it becomes disproportionately larger – I have already wanted to stop it and I tell everyone: do not overestimate me!" [197]

Did she feel as if she was becoming an icon, the status of which she would have to live up to daily?

Focusing on her work helped to calm her nerves. Regularly Bertha was reminded of the importance of the peace cause. Letters and telegrams from all of Europe continued to find their way to Eggenburg. One day a letter of admiration from Bjørnstjerne Bjørnson, the well-known Norwegian author and peace activist, was delivered in the mail. The peace fighter of the north expressed his enthusiasm for *Lay Down Your Arms!* However, he was disappointed over his fellow men: "They say that they want justice, but they don't, that they want to abolish war, but they don't. Every now and then a beam of light like yourself appears: Energetic, prophetic, talented and beautiful – who lives for a single goal! I admire you." [198]

This was the beginning of a long friendship between the Norwegian and the Austrian peace-activist. At the time, the peace cause held a strong position in Norway, maybe due to the fact that so many Norwegians wished for a peaceful dissolution of the union with Sweden. The country was also an active member of the Inter-Parliamentary Union, which worked to find peaceful solutions to conflicts between states, including the use of arbitration. Bertha had strong faith in arbitration as a means, and her letter exchange with Bjørnson shows that he kept her informed about the development of the peace work in Norway.

Lay Down Your Arms! made an impact on other Norwegians as well. The foreign minister and historian Halvdan Koht, who later became a member of the Norwegian Nobel Committee, praised the novel in these terms: "There may be no doubt that the greatest contribution she [Bertha von Suttner] has given to the peace movement, that which has made the deepest mark, is her book *Lay Down Your Arms.*" And he added: "We can see what a strong impression this book has made on human hearts." [199]

In the other Scandinavian countries, the book continued to "make an impression on human hearts" as well. In Denmark, Georg Brandes embraced the novel. The Danish critic, who had been skeptical about some of the ideas Bertha presented in *Inventory of a Soul*, recommended the novel in print in the Danish newspaper *Politiken*. [200]

In Sweden, *Lay Down Your Arms!* was also well received, particularly in the women's movement. Its message was idealistic and edifying, as many felt that literature should be. The Swedish author and women's rights ideologist Ellen Key praised the novel in a lengthy article. The book succeeded in communicating the basic ideas of the peace message, Key wrote – ideas that had not yet achieved full acceptance with the people, but it was just a matter of time before that happened.

From near and far letters and telegrams arrived. By now Bertha had acquired global fame. However, in the village of Eggenburg, she was still able to walk undisturbed along the cobblestone streets. Here the residents indefatigably carried on with their daily chores between the lopsided medieval buildings. Nobody turned to look at her when she crossed the village square. Neither did people halt their daily routines to greet the local, world famous author. Bertha would never experience the same kind of recognition in her local environment as she did beyond the borders of her native country.

But maybe it didn't bother her that Arthur's sisters scarcely raised their eyebrows when she entered the kitchen and unperturbed continued their conversation about whom Countess Y had married, or who had danced with whom at the season's debutant ball. Instead she could focus her attention on her next step on behalf of the peace cause.

Chapter 6

"Goethe's fly" – Lobbying and networking

A vision of peace

What is the color of peace? White? What does it feel like? Like cotton? Or like a quiet wind on a summer day? What does peace look like? The Garden of Eden?

The traditional symbol of peace is a white dove with an olive branch in its beak. White symbolizes purity or innocence. The dove recalls the dove that came flying back to Noah's Ark after the flood was over. It carried a sign of land, a message of hope.

What about war? What are its symbols? The symbols for war have traditionally been large and powerful, for example a war god wearing a helmet and full armor. Or a Viking ship. Or a sword. These symbols take up space. Demand attention. Wars make noise. Wars are gunshots, fanfares, cannons. It is easy to notice war.

Peace is silent. Invisible. Like a tiny, white dove flapping silently past. It is more difficult to detect peace. Peace is "naked, poor and mangled," William Shakespeare wrote. [201]

Throughout the course of history, representations of peace have been like a tiny, pale shadow, squeezed up into a corner at the very back of the stage, while officers and generals in colorful uniforms strut around in front.

War has been associated with action and excitement, in contrast to peace which has often been related to something passive and cowardly. There are countless books about war. There are fewer about peace.

Towards the end of the 19th century, this changed somewhat. Peace started becoming visible. To acquire status. Visions, dreams and ideas about peace came to life in the form of organized societies and movements. Optimism reigned, as did the belief that progress and the new inventions would improve society and make people happier. There had not been a great European war since the Franco-German war in 1871, which was the longest period of peace in Europe for more than a century. This gave reason for more optimism. Bertha was not alone in her belief that by the beginning of the 20th century society would have "done away with war." [202]

There was a spirit of organization in the air. The 19th century saw the birth of the anti-slave movement, the women's movement, the temperance movement and the labor movement amongst others. The peace societies were part of a liberal movement for human rights and social improvements.

The humble beginnings emerged when societies were founded in England and the USA after the Napoleonic Wars of 1815. In 1849, the peace societies convened at the International Peace Congress in Paris, where intellectuals, businessmen, lawyers, church members and statesmen came together. Here, Victor Hugo held an unforgettable speech, which blew even more wind into the societies' sails. After the North American Civil War in 1861–65 and the French-German War of 1870–71, the number of peace societies increased. Towards the end of the 1880s, they were combined into the International Union of Peace Societies. [203]

Many small brooks flowed together to form a river. Swimming in the middle of that river was Bertha.

Contrary to expectations

Although she also met with resistance, she was happy. The 47-year old wrote to a friend that "she, the matron incarnate, felt like a 25-year old through and through!" [204] Bertha spoke of having found her life's calling: "There is no issue in the world that has greatness equivalent to this ...This is the conviction that lies so deeply and passionately within me (one tends to refer to such things as a calling) that I can't agree with it often or loudly enough." [205]

The upheaval in her life had been enormous. Two years earlier, she was a relatively unknown writer living on a remote estate outside of Vienna. Within a short period of time, she found herself at the center of attention for pacifist Europe and visited peace congresses and reunions in many countries. According to her colleague Alfred Hermann Fried, Bertha was not a pacifist when she wrote *Lay Down Your Arms!*, but her own book turned her into one: "The movement it triggered pulled the author into a machinery that would not let go of her again." [206]

Inspired by her conviction of being a part of something great, she threw herself into the peace movement. As the peace movement was a young movement, the first passionate souls had a profound influence. Bertha decided to do something that no woman had done before: To start her own peace society.

It was not the first time that she acted contrary to the expectations of the day for her gender. In contrast to the 19th century's criteria for the ideal woman, Bertha rarely acted according to a sense of duty or a desire to please others. She was not one to tiptoe around in Harmannsdorf's corridors speaking in hushed tones. To the contrary, she made noise wherever she burst forth, talked a lot and frequently sang. She expressed herself just as freely on paper. Bertha was not one to hold back, but stated her opinion so the newspaper columns "buzzed".

Her outspoken and rebellious commitment was something quite different than the soft-spoken and cautious contribution of most other women peace activists. More and more women became involved in the peace movement throughout the 19th century, as the women of the middle class and aristocracy acquired more free time due to economic growth. It was generally accepted that these women used their newly acquired free time on socially beneficial tasks, such as "reforming prostitutes, helping poor widows, improving prison reforms, promoting moderation in relation to alcohol, organizing bible and study groups, beautifying the city and park facilities, improving sanitation conditions and working for peace." [207]

A woman getting involved in politics, however, was not common. Women did not even have the right to vote in most countries. [208] Working for peace was on the other hand associated with women as mothers and nurturers and thus acceptable. For some women, the peace cause became a legitimate path into public service. Many of them were dedicated Christians. In *Det Norske Fredsblad*, the recently founded Norwegian peace society's own publication, the pacifist N. J. Sørensen described a group of women pacifists he observed who, "were waiting for peace to come with a religious fervor like the revelation of the thousand-year kingdom or god's kingdom on earth." [209]

Waiting was not Bertha's style. *Action*, on the other hand, was something she liked. In this way, she lived up to the original meaning of the word pacifism, which comes from the Latin *pax* (peace) and *facere* (do).

The Austrian Peace Society

All the peace societies of Europe were in this period led by men. Many of them had opinions about what the nature of women's involvement should be like. The first president of the American Peace Society, William Ladd, was one of those who had a clear view on the role of women in peace work. In a religious pamphlet with the title *On the Duty of Females to Promote the Cause of Peace* he expanded upon his view. If a woman might be in doubt about how she should proceed in her work for peace, she could simply follow Ladd's list of instructions:

- Pray
- Become informed about the peace issue by studying the Bible and peace publications
- Inspire the family by singing anti-war songs
- Read stories about peace for children
- Refuse to attend military balls

- Write children's books about peace
- Join peace societies and distribute literature about peace. [210]

Bertha would have come up short if assessed against Ladd's list! She did not pray, and she had not studied the Bible. She had not sung anti-war songs nor read stories about peace to children, neither had she written children's literature about the subject. There was only one item on Ladd's list that Bertha could cross off: She joined a peace society.

Or, more precisely – she started her own.

How did she get started? Bertha began with something she mastered: She picked up her pen. On September 3, 1891, a fervent article against war was printed in *Neue Freie Presse,* signed by Bertha von Suttner. The editor's lead-in contributed wind to the sails of her appeal: "There is nobody in Austria better suited to speak in the name of the friends of peace than the author of *Lay Down Your Arms.*" [211] The article concluded by explicitly encouraging readers to send the author their names and address to become members of the Austrian peace society.

The response was overwhelming. Hundreds of names and declarations of support poured in. Bertha knew how to strike while the iron was hot. A mere three weeks after her appeal was published, she organized a meeting in Altes Rathaus in Vienna. Here the by-laws of the Austrian peace society were passed. On October 30, 1891, *Österreichische Friedensgesellschaft* was founded and Bertha von Suttner elected as its president. Members: 2000.

Involves Nobel

Bertha's enthusiastic appeal soon found its way into the European press, where it created a stir. In Paris, Alfred Nobel read it and picked up his pen and wrote to his former secretary:

"My dear friend! I am delighted to see that your eloquent appeal against the horror of war has found its way into the French press...

And your pen - whither does it wander now? After writing with the blood of martyrs, will it show us the prospects of a future fairy-land or the less utopian picture of the Thinkers' commonwealth?"

Alfred expressed curiosity about Bertha's literary production: After having written with the "blood of martyrs" - here he was probably making reference to the realistic and grisly depictions of war in *Lay Down Your Arms!* - was she now planning to describe her visions of a more peaceful society ("a future fairy-land")? [212] Or did she want to give readers a less utopian vision of a "Thinkers' commonwealth" - here Alfred might be referring to something that resembled the writing style of *The Machine Age,* in other words, an essayistic and reasoning style?

However, Bertha had no new book project underway. She had never espoused the view of art for arts' sake – *l'art pour l'art.* [213] Her art view was rather more utilitarian. Literature was for her first and foremost a tool for improving and reforming society. Up until recently, she had been most interested in tearing things down. Now her focus was on building something up, and not only in a literary sense, but in the real world. The most important thing was to get the peace society on its feet. There was a great deal at stake: The Third International Peace Congress would take place in Rome in just a few weeks - what a perfect occasion to launch the recently founded Austrian peace society.

Bertha had indeed succeeded in starting a society- but how would she finance the journey to "the eternal city", to this important occasion? As the society's newly elected leader, it was also her responsibility to find funding for the travel costs for the other delegates and to promote the trip.

When she writes back to Alfred this time, she has a clear objective. In October 1891, she asks her friend in Paris for financial assistance: "It's now or never – you can show me if I can call you my friend. Will you give me a friend's moral and effective support for this, which is my most demanding and beloved life task?" [214] The letter she sends contains a stack of printed materials about the new Austrian peace society and the upcoming Rome conference.

Alfred did not disappoint her. To the contrary, his contribution was all of two thousand *gylden* – far more than Bertha had expected. In his lengthy response, he demonstrates an interest in her work, combined with a critical attitude. He writes that he is "skeptical" about the peace congresses, about "the kind of large tasks the movement or peace congresses can carry out." However, the letter demonstrates that he has studied the peace movement and has come up with some ideas of his own: "One must submit an acceptable plan for well-meaning governments. To demand disarmament immediately is to invite ridicule. To demand compulsory arbitration of all conflicts is unrealistic," he writes. For the peace movement to achieve success, it must be satisfied with "a modest beginning". [215] Alfred even submits a peace proposal: One way of achieving peace is through a one-year *moratorium*, in other words, an obligatory armistice. Any hostile act should be postponed until the end of this period. While the period of the moratorium is in effect, a special arbitration court may address the conflict in question. Even if no decision were to be made, both parties would be prohibited from using force while the moratorium lasts. It should be possible to extend this period of peace. [216]

Was Bertha surprised when she read Alfred's lengthy response? It was the first time he wrote about his reflections upon the issue of peace to her. Did it make her feel good that her friend in Paris now took an interest in her work?

1891 was a busy year for her. Her desk at Harmannsdorf was overflowing with letters, papers, memos and invitations. She, who neither had experience with organization work nor as a leader, now had her hands full with the responsibility for planning all the details of the trip to Rome. This included the correspondence, the press work, logistics – even purchasing the train tickets for the wives and daughters of the participants. This was before the peace societies acquired a central organization that took care of all practical matters. To the Austrian politician and peace ally, Carneri, she aired how busy she was: "Oh, what a work load I am carrying on my shoulders. But I have accepted the challenge – and I must see it through." [217]

In addition, she started an intensive lobbying activity towards

Austrian politicians. The goal was to convince them to form a group that could take part in the Inter-parliamentary Union (IPU)'s conference in Rome the same year. The IPU was established only two years before, in 1889, as the first international inter-parliamentary institution working for peace. [218]

"Come to Rome! How you can help me with your advice!" she writes in her reply to Alfred, thanking him for his contribution, which was much larger than she had hoped for: "*Merci de coeur* – my heartfelt thanks! It is a huge loan you are giving me. Now I can without difficulties make the journey." She specifies what his money will be used for: "committee work, diverse publications, correspondence, memos, and the costs of travel and lost earnings for those responsible for organization." [219]

Alfred did not heed Bertha's plea to travel to Rome. Perhaps because he had neither the "time nor the wings" to go where he wanted, as he had stated previously in a letter to her, or because he did not wish to become visible as to his support of her peace cause? [220] The businessman Nobel always had to cultivate his relations with politicians, businessmen and other people in power.

To Rome!

The pieces finally fell into place. In the middle of November 1891, an excited, newly elected leader of the Austrian peace society packed her suitcase and got on the train to Rome together with her husband and the other delegates. For the first time, Bertha would take part in an international peace congress. And what a debut! In "the eternal city", delegates and journalists from 17 countries convened in the huge council hall at the Capitol. Not a seat was vacant. After the President of the IPU, the Italian Ruggiero Bonghi, had spoken, Bertha stepped up to the podium. It was a great moment when she gave her first speech in public. She spoke in fluent Italian and "with extreme calm...without anxiety, with the certainty of one who is delivering good news," as she described it. [221] When she had finished, she received thundering applause.

The event was historical: Never had a woman stood up and spoken in this old and revered historical arena, the former political midpoint of Rome. For Bertha, this was a two-fold triumph. The paralyzing stage fright she had experienced as a young woman, had disappeared. Now she spoke freely and without trepidation before the enormous assembly of people from different countries.

In the "Eternal City", she also made the acquaintance of Fredrik Bajer, Hodgson Pratt, Frédéric Passy and other leading figures of the peace societies with whom she would develop close friendships. The experience of international solidarity made a big impression on her: "Oh, the wonderful sense of affiliation...in a community – a community for human love and human dignity," she later wrote. [222]

In Rome, she helped to establish a central office to improve organization and publicity of the peace societies, the International Peace Bureau (IPB), at first called The Bern Peace Bureau, located in Bern. The Swiss Élie Ducommun became the president, and Bertha von Suttner the vice-president. As the only woman, she was invited to participate in the Inter-parliamentary Union's conference on arbitration and disarmament, even though she was not a member of parliament. In the years to come, Bertha would attend the annual meetings in the Union, where she participated with all her force in the public debate and exchange of views where her opponents as a rule were men.

Filled with new impressions, she returned home from the Rome congress and picked up her pen to write a euphoric letter of thanks to her friend in Paris: "I have succeeded – complete success. I don't know where I have found the courage to speak in front of the full capitol, or involve myself in debates... My courage is probably due to the awareness of the great responsibility that has been given to me. If I had failed, the young Austrian peace society would have fallen apart."

Without Alfred's support, Bertha and her society would not have been able to make that first trip to Rome. His contribution to her first success was enormous, something which she acknowledged: "Without your kindly loan it would have been extremely difficult for me to carry out this journey." [223]

From now on, she viewed Nobel as her benefactor. It was a role that he in no way appeared to be uncomfortable with.

A public speaker in demand

It soon became clear that Bertha had a talent for verbal presentations. In the years to come, she became a much sought-after public speaker. "The spoken word has a greater impact than the written," was her comment to this. [224] Her lectures, which were usually given at peace congresses, brought her to many places in the world. She would travel to capitals and big cities all over the continent, as well as to the new world. [225]

The peace champion was always well prepared, soft-spoken and did not use exaggerated gestures. Bertha had the type of personal charisma and self-assurance that seemed to incite self-confidence in people. When there were arguments and disagreements, she simply stood up and the dignity of her appearance and the serious expression on her face, created the kind of calm that is a condition for consensus. According to a colleague, when she spoke, she "created an impression of royalty on the audience". [226]

Was there after all something of a performing artist's presence that came to the fore? Bertha would never "take many hearts by storm" through singing, as she had dreamt of as a young girl, but she certainly moved many hearts with her message of peace and reconciliation between different peoples. Wherever she went, she received a great deal of attention.

And about all the journeys she made, all the tasks she took on, she wrote and told her friend in Paris.

"Peer Gynt"

Alfred's next letters to Bertha showed that had begun to study the peace movement. Did this mean that the dynamite inventor might "convert" to the peace cause?

Peace and dynamite, smokeless powder and poetry - Nobel was a man of contradictions. His correspondence with Bertha and Sofie reflects his complex personality. The letters to the two Austrian women in his life are very different, in both form and content. To Bertha, he usually writes letters of admiration, in a formal tone, which are sprinkled with French oddities and polite phrases. [227] It seems as if he put a great deal of effort into the form. He addresses her as *Chère Baronne* and in respectful terms, such as "Highly honorable baroness" or "My esteemed friend". His signature bears a stamp of reverence: "Yours most truly", "Yours forever" and on one occasion "Yours forever and more than ever".

The style of his letters to Sofie, on the other hand, is more personal. There are more and longer letters, but they seem to have been worked on less. [228] In them, Alfred uses the informal "you" form. He addresses Sofie as "Dear little child", "Apple of my eye" or "My dear, sweetheart". The tone is sometimes patronizing - he writes "My poor child" or "Poor little thing". The letters are often signed as "Your Alfred" or "Your Old Alfred" or "Your Grumbling Old Bear". Despite the nature of their relationship, he never ventures any further than to write that he sends her a "sincere kiss". His most intimate statement is that he wants to "rest in her lap". [229]

His letters to Sofie are more oral in style and describe experiences from his daily life - journeys, diary notes, information about his health and meetings with different business partners. He continues to assume a role as an educator in relation to her and offers advice on what she should do or read. However, as time passes, the tone of his letters becomes less tender and more condescending. Sometimes his letters come across as a kind of "dumping ground" for his depressive state of mind. [230]

Sofie's letters to Alfred are also full of complaints. She often writes about being short of money, or she tells him about her various health problems. Health is a common theme and a subject of interest to both, as well as their loneliness. Perhaps these were the only things they had in common?

Alfred often wrote letters when he was in a foreign city, frequently late in the evening or in the middle of the night, the longest letters were written on Sundays. His letters to Sofie sometimes have marks of water stains that look like tears, yes, even blood? In a letter to her, the inventor writes that he has worked so hard that he has begun to suffer from nosebleeds. The stationary has a splotch of blood at the very bottom, just under his signature. However, when the Swedish author Per Olof Sundmann had the splotch tested by forensic technicians, their conclusion was that the splotch could not possibly have been caused by a drop of blood falling from Alfred's nose. [231] Does this imply that Alfred was lying to Sofie about his nosebleeds? Or was he just exaggerating to make a point about how bad his health was?

In his book *Vem älskar Alfred Nobel?* ("Who loves Alfred Nobel?"), the Swedish author and filmmaker Vilgot Sjöman compares Alfred Nobel to Henrik Ibsen's character "Peer Gynt", who lies and behaves contradictory. After having seen the play, Nobel wrote to a friend and he expressed his negative reaction to these aspects of the character Peer Gynt. Sjöman points out the paradox inherent to this reaction as Alfred himself contains so many contradictions. [232]

In his letters to the two Austrian women, Alfred shows his contradictory selves. The letters to Bertha usually bear the signature of the liberal humanist and man of the Enlightenment, whereas the letters to Sofie are often written by the pessimistic and scorned Alfred. They letters also reflect how his relationship to Sofie Hess becomes more and more destructive.

An ideal?

Alfred Nobel's letters to Bertha from this time are full of admiration. Had he put Bertha up on a pedestal? The memory that he came away with from their first meeting was "unforgettable and indelible". [233] Was it an idealized perspective that he would retain, a version that was intensified by what she wrote and what he read about her in the newspapers?

The poems that Alfred himself wrote often illustrate a tendency towards an infatuated idealization of women and a longing for a pure and unselfish love. [234] Had Bertha acquired the same status as the ideal woman "Alexandra", whom he had described in the poem *Canto* (1862-1864)? The long poem was not just a homage to poetry, but also a homage to the ideal woman. "Alexandra" was a truth-seeking woman with a "brilliant enthusiasm for the lofty and noble". A woman who preferred to adorn her "soul" rather than her "person". [235] Had Bertha attained a similar position, while Sofie represented nature, greed and physical needs?

Sofie was at any rate far from the ideal. A former admirer of Miss Hess also made it clear to her that "nobility of soul" was a quality she was lacking. In a letter to her, the man, whose identity is unknown, wrote that he was moved by Sofie's "helplessness", but that there could be no talk of a love affair between them, in that one "can only love people who have nobility of soul, something you are completely lacking." [236]

Poor Sofie, she had to tolerate a lot of censure from the well-educated gentlemen of means!

The Association against Anti-Semitism

For her own part, Bertha expressed that she was living in a harmonious conjugal relationship: "In spite of all the wars and conflicts that exist in the world," she was happy: "Oh, these wonderful times! Because I was happy through and through and so was 'My Own' (the pet name for her husband) ...Our kingdom lay elsewhere, it was the kingdom of our closely united, combined hearts." [237]

In their marriage, Bertha assumed the role of leader, something which was rare at the time. It was probably natural because she was the eldest of the two, as well as having had extensive experience in managing on her own before the two of them met. Arthur had, so to speak, gone straight from his mother's hands and into hers. Nevertheless, Bertha would always tone down her leader role in relation to her husband. Instead she emphasized the importance of her husband's support in enabling her to maintain a strong public face and carry out her peace work. Arthur was her "friend, lover and the bedrock of her existence." In relation to what she called her "philosophy of happiness", she wrote: "It is commendable to try and create a better existence for future generations, but one's foremost duty is first to give one's life partner as much joy as possible and always try to be happy oneself." Were they always cooing in such harmony? That was at any rate how Bertha would present their relationship to the outside world. She "always showed her nature in its Sunday-best," according to her colleague Fried. [238]

However, in her diary, she also told another story. In the 1890s, Marie Louise, Arthur's fourteen- year old niece, came to live at Harmannsdorf after the death of her father. The girl attached herself to her beloved "Onkeles" Arthur. When Marie Louise became of an age to marry, she was not interested in any of the suitors. Instead she preferred to stay at home. Together with Arthur she went for walks a couple of hours every morning, while Bertha stayed at her desk working. For the first time in her marriage she was tormented by jealousy. Quarrels broke out over trivialities. The situation worsened when Marie Louise wrote a novel, *As light dawned* (*Wie es Licht geworden*, 1898), which she dedicated to Bertha. It was published by Berthas publisher Pierson Verlag in Leipzig. It described a young woman who had a love affair with a man who was bound in a supposedly unhappy marriage. The characters had little disguise and the man was described with a portrait's likeness to Arthur. When Bertha confronted her husband with this story, he broke out in tears and insisted on his innocence. He swore that his relationship to Marie Louise was platonic. Bertha *wanted* to believe him, but doubts were nagging her. Was this just a fantasy of a teenage girl? Or was there actually something to the girl's story?

Bertha wrote a lot in her diary about this pain which she did not want to share with her family and friends. [239] As time passed by, the situation became less tense when Arthur's health began to decline. Ever since they lived in Georgia, Arthur had become increasingly more susceptible to illness. Marie Louise, who had inherited a bit of money, payed for the doctor. The two women focused on his well-being. Bertha stepped back and the situation became more relaxed.

In terms of their professional life, Arthur never experienced a success like her own. Was it sometimes a challenge for him to be married to such a successful woman? In his daily life, he mostly functioned as an overseer of the Harmannsdorf estate with responsibility for the restoration work. During their stay in Georgia, he had written short stories and articles. With time, however, his stories were no longer well received, and eventually he was unable to find a publisher for them at all. Arthur's attempts to find a job as an editor were also in vain. Even his newspaper articles were not printed any more. Resigned, he decided to give up on writing altogether.

In the early 1890s, Arthur found a meaningful task in working for the Association for the Resistance to Anti-Semitism in Vienna, which ran parallel to the peace movement. Anti-Semitism had broken out in Austria in reaction to the mass emigration of impoverished Jews from Russia to Western Europe in the 1880s. Vienna evolved into the center of anti-Semitism during the fin-de-siècle. Xenophobia was something both Arthur and Bertha vehemently opposed; it went against all their ideals for a future society where all people were integrated. Bertha described anti-Semitism as "a backslide" into the Middle Ages. When the Austrian anti-Semitic party won a great victory over the liberals in the election of 1891, Arthur was not the only one to be filled with indignation. He immediately sat down to write a draft of bylaws for an association which was going to work against anti-Semitism. Afterwards, he contacted some prominent people who could join this fight. On July 2, 1891, the association had its first meeting. Many of the people supporting the Austrian peace society were also supporting the association against anti-Semitism.

When the anti-Semitic Karl Lueger was elected the mayor of

Vienna in 1895, they were both distressed. Lueger, who was the political leader of the Christian Social Party, wanted to strengthen the German-speaking part of Austria to the detriment of all non-German speaking minorities in the empire. [240] With him, anti-Semitism became a significant factor in Austrian political life and it was to remain so in the coming decades. The new mayor knew how to use rousing speeches to win over the Viennese population to his cause, making use of anti-Semitic prejudice invoking stereotypical images of alleged enemies. In a letter to Alfred written in April 1896, Bertha aired her resentment about this:

> Lueger, the sanctimonious idol of anti-Semitism will soon be the mayor of Vienna and has in conjunction with this been received for an audience with the Emperor, in other words, this is something that is celebrated, but first and foremost – it is a victory for human stupidity. And because I know how much you despise stupidity, I thought of you immediately and I therefore am airing my resentment in a letter addressed to you. [241]

The power of words

While Arthur's pet cause was The Association against Anti-Semitism, Bertha continued her work through the Austrian peace society. In 1891, she was like a thoroughbred horse released onto the race track: The only thing that mattered was winning rounds for the peace cause. It had been a boom year for the peace movement, with many visible results: The international peace agency in Bern was established. The Rome conference had been an enormous success and the number of members in the Austrian peace society had increased from 2000 to 8000.

Bertha enjoyed a lot of respect within the peace movement. Frédéric Passy, the head of the French peace association now called her "notre général-en-chef" ("Our General-in-Chief"). [242] Earlier in the year of 1892, she travelled to Berlin and gave a lecture that contributed to the formation of the German peace association (Die Deutsche Friedensgesellschaft). The German association was based on a model from her own Austrian society. "The hall is sold out. The box office is selling to the highest bidder. Flowers from followers," she proudly wrote to her friend Carneri. [243] During the lecture she gave a reading from *Lay Down Your Arms!*

Her letters to Alfred from this period were bursting with enthusiasm: The German original version of *Lay Down Your Arms!* has sold 6,000 copies, she wrote. In Russia, the fifth edition of her novel has been published. In the United States, it has been named the book of the year! [244]

In his replies, Alfred continued to express his appreciation: "What I have in my heart is the wish to express my great admiration for your manner of presiding over an important issue. I hope that in 1892 you will see the results of your generous efforts and in that this year is close at hand, I send both yourself and Monsieur de Suttner my very best wishes." [245]

Despite his supportive attitude, however, Alfred was still skeptical of the benefits of the peace congresses. He was not alone in this - the peace movement had to tolerate a lot of criticism about its congresses: "The insecure, impractical, well-meaning and sentimental group of people that is found in all countries and nowhere as well-developed as our own - they chatter on about many things but never more in perfect harmony than when they convene to speak about peace," a critical journalist wrote. [246]

In a letter to him, Bertha addresses his critique: "My God, I know well that neither the associations nor their conferences have the power to do away with war; it's a matter of gathering and demonstrating our opinion in public so that we can influence public opinion in different countries. Have you by the way received and did you read my newsletter? I would like it if you would write an article one day." (Bertha's emphasis.) [247]

Bertha's belief in the importance of the peace congresses was unshakeable. Influencing public opinion was one of the peace movement's most efficient methods. She herself was at this point heavily involved in trying to influence politicians, the clergy and other people in positions of power.

Throughout her entire life, Bertha maintained a strong faith in the influential power of words: Words, over time, can change the world:

> Big ideas become reality slowly, these kinds of words are like seeds, or, to use a better image, the striking of a hammer. New ideas are like nails, old institutions like thick walls. It is not enough to hold up a sharp nail and hit it on the head once; the nail must be hit hundreds and hundreds of times, soundly on the head, if it is going to stay in place." [248]

Bertha would hammer on and on about the message of peace. One of those who were hit by the hammer with increasing frequency was Alfred.

Chapter 7

"Inform me, teach me" – Nobel's promise

Villa Nobel

Early in 1891, something occurred which threw Alfred off balance: He received word that Sofie Hess was pregnant. And not with him! The father-to-be was a young Hungarian officer and cavalry captain, Nicolaus Kapy von Kapivar, whom she had met at a spa.

It was Sofie's sisters, Amalie and Bertha, who communicated the news to Alfred as tactfully as they could. Most likely they were trying to avert disaster. Their letters were full of flattery and appeals to his "noble, good heart". [249]

Naturally, Alfred was shocked. His reaction was disbelief, anger. To Sofie he wrote: "When I read your last letter, a word popped up on my tongue which I out of mercy will spare you." [250] Finally, one hears Sofie's voice. From 1891, several letters from Sofie have been preserved. She writes and asks Alfred for mercy, saying she has been "unfortunate". She does not want a relationship with the captain, but would rather be with Alfred. At the moment, she is "alone and unhappy". To have a child under such circumstances is "hard and bitter" she writes. [251] But she wants to keep the baby.

Had Sofie wanted children? It was not a subject in their correspondence. However, if this was the case, she had little time to lose. The years had passed and "the child" Sofie would soon be 40 years old.

However, there is no indication that Alfred for his own part wanted to start a family with her.

The affront was great. For a few months, the letters from Alfred comes to a complete halt. Eventually he thinks pragmatically. He ends their relationship and recommends that she marry the Captain Kapy von Kapivar.

A few months later, in July 1891, Sofie Hess gives birth to a healthy girl who is named Gretchen.

At this moment, Alfred had a strong need for change. That same year, he decides to move away from France, after 18 years on Avenue Malakoff. He chooses San Remo on the Italian Riviera, a choice related to the sale of his most recent invention, ballistite, to the Italians. Because of that, he had had to endure a lot of criticism from the French authorities.

San Remo is called "The City of Flowers", because of its flowerbeds and tropical plants. The town is like a colorful garden along the shores. Here Alfred could properly revel in his "silent friends". Did he hope that the idyllic surroundings would have a calming effect on his nerves? The city's climate was likely to benefit his health.

The 58-year old invested in a villa in the charming small town. A little while later, he moved into Riviera di Pontente, a large, recently refurnished house with a view of the Mediterranean and long, white beaches. Surrounded by the sound of seagull cries and rippling waves, he prepared for a new life. He named his new home "Mio Nido" ("My nest"). But when his friend Gustav Aufschläger, director of the Hamburg Company, came to call and jokingly comments that a "nest" should have *two* birds living in it, and not just one, he changed the name to "Villa Nobel".

Bertha was quick to write and congratulate him on his new home. She and Arthur had a dream of living at the Riviera, she wrote. Would Alfred promenade along the beach of the Riviera's "paradise"? she asks. "Certainly not alone?" she fishes and continues: "If I were you, I would rest by the Mediterranean (not alone...) and in peace and quiet write a long poem in English."
[252]

But Alfred was alone. He was to remain a bachelor for the rest of his life. Instead, he buried himself in more work.

A proposal for a European Union

Bertha, on her side, continued to write to him and to try to get him more involved in the work of the peace movement. Late in the summer of 1892, she and Arthur traveled with a delegation from the Austrian peace society to Bern to participate in the Fourth International Peace Congress. The previous year's conference in Rome had been a success, and the sequel was no less triumphant. Like the year before, she had written to Alfred and invited him to take part. Like the last time, she received no reply.

Several hundred people were gathered in Bern – senators, politicians, peace workers and volunteers from more than 13 nations. [253] A resolution that recommended arbitration as the best way to solve conflicts between states was passed. This was the first step in the direction of the establishment of the International Court of Arbitration in The Hague in 1899.

Also, in Bern, Bertha put forward a motion entitled "A European Confederation of States". [254] A united, confederated Europe would be a step closer to her ideal "a nation of world citizens". Already in the novel *High Life* (1886), she had touched upon the possibility of this ideal state of affairs: "A nation is about to be created and will one day conquer all – a nation of world citizens." [255]

The idea of a European community was deeply embedded in her way of thinking. She had learned several European languages when she was young, travelled across the continent and met and discussed liberal ideas with many cosmopolitan European thinkers and authors. Bertha's focus was mainly on Western Europe, and the thinkers and authors she referred to in her works were mostly English or French. [256]

In *Lay Down Your Arms!*, she lets the protagonist Martha express her aspirations for a European league of nations that would prevent all wars: "Why don't all the European states join together in a federation? That would be the easiest." Martha believes that this state of affairs will soon become a reality. For this reason, she begins to catalogize all previous ideas about a United Europe.

For centuries, people had been tossing around with thoughts on how to secure peace by tying the nations together, with looser or tighter knots. Already in his three volumes *De Monarchia* (1315), the Italian writer Dante Alighieri (1265-1321) made a systematic attempt to analyse the concept of a world government. In this work, he describes a federal state under the Emperor of the so-called Holy Roman Empire of German Nation that could function as a secular counterweight to the Pope and his powerbase in the Roman Church: States, city states and their rulers would retain their autonomy and the Emperor would be the guarantor of world peace. [257]

Jumping a few centuries ahead, the Dutch jurist Hugo Grotius (1583-1645), best remembered as the "father of international law", called on states to create a "society" of nations, a peaceful world federation. Grotius' work *De jure belli ac pacis* (*On the Law of War and Peace*, 1625) is regarded as a foundational work in international law. [258]

As Europe began to become more secular in the 15th and 16th century, political thoughts on a united Europe became more common. A bold and widely read European confederation project called the "Grand Design" was made by the French Duke of Sully (1560-1641), supervised by King Henry IV himself. It was a draft for a Europe divided into fifteen states as equal in territory and power as possible.

A few years later, the French monk Emeric Crucé (1590-1648) proposed a federation of states consisting of a permanent Council of Ambassadors that could enforce peace by arbitration amongst themselves, or, if necessary, using force against any unruly member. His plan has been called an early precursor to the League of Nations and the United Nations Charter. [259]

Another well-known attempt belongs to the French monk, writer and politician Charles-Irénée Castel Saint-Pierre (1658-1743), who was one of the first to articulate a coherent vision of a European union in three substantial volumes plus a supplement "Project for

Perpetual Peace". [260]

The 18th century saw even more influential texts on this theme. [261] The philosopher Immanuel Kant (1724-1794) made a lasting impression with his famous essay *Zum ewigen Frieden: "Ein philosophischer Entwurf, (Perpetual Peace: A Philosophical Sketch, 1795)*. This was a more systematic and logical draft than any previous plans for securing peace. In his work, which bore connections to the work of Castel Saint-Pierre, Kant proposed a peace program to be implemented by governments where the law of nations would be based on a federation of free states, which should "eventually include all nations and thus lead to perpetual peace." [262]

Jumping into the next century and Victor Hugo's famous address to the Peace Congress in Paris in 1849, where he optimistically advocated the creation of a European Union of States with a single parliament. In poetic and elevated terms, Hugo tried to inspire the assembled intellectual elite of 670 representatives:

A day will come when you France, you Russia, you Italy, you England, you Germany, you all, nations of the continent, without losing your distinct qualities and your glorious individuality, will be merged closely within a superior unit and you will form the European brotherhood, just as Normandy, Brittany, Burgundy, Lorraine, Alsace, all our provinces are merged together in France. A day will come when the only fields of battle will be markets opening up to trade and minds opening up to ideas. A day will come when the bullets and the bombs will be replaced by votes, by the universal suffrage of the peoples, by the venerable arbitration of a great sovereign senate which will be to Europe what this parliament is to England, what this diet is to Germany, what this legislative assembly is to France. A day will come when we will display cannon in museums just as we display instruments of torture today, and are amazed that such things could ever have been possible. [263]

Hugo named his vision a "United States of Europe". But he met with resistance among those who thought the United States of America should not be a model for Europe.

So, it was on a deep historical background that Bertha von Suttner in 1892 presented her proposal for a union of European states at the Bern congress. A European confederation would, according to her, "create a lasting legal framework in Europe" without "infringing on the independence of individual countries in respect to their own internal affairs, and therefore also their forms of government." [264] The proposal would also be in the interest of business – the goal was to have a community of states without tolls and other trade restrictions.

However, Bertha's proposal met with resistance: "At that time still an idea no one understood; generally mixed up with 'United States' after the North American model, and disapproved of for Europe," was her comment to this. All in all, the 1892, congress delegates proved not ready for this proposal.

But despite the opposition, Bertha, with her usual stamina, continued to work for this idea in the years to come. "A united confederation of European nations should, for the years ahead, be the chief goal of enlightened pacifism", she said, repeatedly.

An unexpected guest

Bertha was relaxing after the day's intense meetings at the Hotel Berner Hoff when one of the employees came over with a calling card and a message that there was a gentleman waiting for her in the lounge. The calling card bore the signature of Alfred Nobel. Nobel? Bertha was surprised. His name was not on the lists of registered participants. She quickly walked towards the lounge and recognized her friend. The reunion was heartfelt. Alfred and Bertha had not seen each other for five years, since their second meeting in Paris. His journey was not a long one, as he was living in Zürich this year, where he had formed a collaboration with engineers and professors at ETH (Eidgenössische Technische Hochschule). [265]

Bertha informed him of the conference. She offered to introduce him to some of the other participants, an offer which he politely declined. Alfred had spent half the day in the gallery, listening. He was clear about his role – he was there as a private observer, not an official participant. [266] As always, the inventor was busy and soon had to leave. Before he went, he surprised Bertha by asking if he could join her Austrian peace society and said he wanted to donate 2000 franc to it. [267]And in the same breath, he asked the couple to come and visit him in Zürich after the congress.

Did this mean Alfred was in the process of changing his view on the benefits of the peace congresses?

Meeting in Zurich

Eager to continue their conversations with Alfred, the couple left the congress a day early, in order to take the train to Zürich. Here Alfred put them up at *Baur au Lac Hotel,* one of the city's most beautiful hotels. The rooms had balconies with a view of the enormous Lake Zurich. In the distance, they could see the drawing patterns of the Alps against the sky. Bertha noted with delight that they were staying in the very room that the Empress Elisabeth had just evacuated! Despite her radical views in many areas, Bertha always retained a fascination with things royal or imperial.

Soon after their arrival, Alfred invites the couple to dinner in *Baur au Lac's* exclusive dining room. During the meal, Bertha thanks him for becoming a member of the Austrian peace society, but in the same breath lets him know that she believes he supports her peace work out of "friendship" and not because he is personally convinced about the cause. She says she hopes that he will begin to *believe* in it. Alfred replies that he believes in the cause but that he is "in doubt as to whether their societies and congresses are the right means by which to handle it." Then he utters the words that have so often been cited afterwards: "Inform me, teach me, and I will do something great for the peace cause".

Bertha promises to keep him informed. She says that she will send him letters not only full of information, but of "enthusiasm". Alfred expresses his gratitude and says he likes "nothing as much as to be able to feel enthusiasm, a capacity which my experiences in life, and my fellow-men, have greatly weakened". [268]

The next day, Alfred invites the couple along on a boat outing. He surprises them with a brand-new invention - an aluminum motorboat! As a boat builder, Nobel was also ahead of his time. He understood early on that aluminum was the metal of the future, while it was only in the 1930s that it experienced a breakthrough in the shipbuilding industry. With his sense of sweet names, Alfred called the boat "Mignon" (French for "cute").

Bertha and Arthur are the two first passengers on the boat. Alfred sits at the helm, while the guests admire the panorama that glides silently past. Beautiful Swiss chalets are situated along the shore of the enormous Lake Zürich. White clouds sail across the sky. It is a perfect day to let the visions take flight: "We talked about war and peace and how wonderful the world could be if the divinity that glows and shines in the hearts of individual human beings but is still squelched beneath the brutality of ignorance, could break through," according to Bertha.

They play with the idea of writing a book together. With their diverse knowledge and experiences it could be good: "A manifesto against all of the misery and stupidity maintained by the world". [269] Alfred provokes the peace activist by saying that his dynamite factories can perhaps bring an end to war more quickly than her peace congresses - an argument he had used already when they first met in Paris. Bertha rebukes him: Does he really believe that peace can be created through *fear*? It will only take one spark to trigger an explosion that could be of catastrophic dimensions.

Again, Nobel's ambivalence comes to the surface. On the one hand, he believes that education and public enlightenment are important means of creating peace. On the other hand, he thinks that the threat factor and deterrence are critical. He expresses optimism about the future, being "full of faith in the abstract ideal about a coming proud and superior human race when people finally come to the world with minds that are better evolved," according to

Bertha. Simultaneously he is full of distrust because he meets so many "vulgar, egotistical and false people" in his daily life. [270]

Bertha airs her disagreement. Peace must be based on *trust*, not on fear. *Para pacem,* peace must be created, she argues. To work to prevent the causes of war is more important than watching over one another in fear.

That evening, Alfred has a surprise in store for them. During dinner, he mentions for the first time that he is considering leaving his fortune to some other purpose than benefiting his family and relatives. [271] He says he is thinking about giving a sum of money to peace work. In his opinion, large fortunes should go back to the public domain and be used to benefit society. Children and relatives should receive money, but only enough to get an education, so they can manage on their own.

Alfred knew what he was talking about. He had not received many handouts. Despite this, he had become one of the richest men in Europe.

The next morning the couple travels back to Vienna.

A new consultant

Did Bertha give her friend something to think about? Was Nobel beginning to discard some of his doubts about the importance of the peace congresses? An inquiry he made a few weeks after the visit in Bern, indicated a more nuanced view. In the beginning of September 1892, he wrote to the Turkish diplomat and lawyer Gregoris Aristarchi Bey: "I had an opportunity when I was in Bern to witness the work of a peace congress. On the one hand I was struck by the rapid growth in the number of qualified and serious members there, on the other hand, by the ridiculous endeavors on the part of some of those present to destroy the best of all matters." [272]

He contacted Bey through a common friend and business contact in Stockholm who asked for his help in finding a post for the retired lawyer. In the fall of 1892, Nobel made Bey an offer of 15,000 francs a year to "keep him informed on the political tendencies and the peace movement's progress in Europe and try to promote peace in the press." [273]

Was he beginning to think about what he would write in his will? In the correspondence with Bey, he discusses different proposals for conflict resolution models. As was the case in most of his undertakings, Nobel took the question of peace seriously and approached it methodologically. He first assessed the possibility for a compulsory one-year *moratorium*, in other words, a postponement of the threat of war, an idea he had mentioned to Bertha previously. [274] The idea was that as time passed, the conflict would cool down and the parties use common sense.

Then he explored the idea of a *collective security system*. This entailed that all governments in Europe should be bound to take joint action against any aggressor who threatened the peace. The system would be regulated by an international organization that could coordinate sanctions. Nobel's' thoughts about a collective security system were quite unusual at the time. It was this idea that later formed the basis of the League of Nations, established by the Paris Peace Conference after the First World War.

In a letter to Bey, he also mentioned the arbitration idea. Interestingly, he referred to the feudal tradition of a *ritualized duel*: Was it possible to develop rules for ritualized duels between states in the same way as duels between individuals? Formerly, witnesses should assess whether the parties' reasons for fighting were adequate. "The witnesses" in a modern process could be the governments of neutral states – a tribunal or a type of superior court.

However, Alfred also had the peace congresses in mind, and concluded the letter as follows: "I would be extremely happy if I, even if it were only a step, could contribute to advancing the peace congress' work, and for such an objective I would not look at the costs." [275]

Again – was it his visit to the congress in Bern that had borne fruit?

Rivalling counsellors

Alfred now has two informants or counsellors on the development of the peace movement: Gregoris Aristarchi Bey and Bertha von Suttner. He continues the dialogue with both.

At first, he does not tell Bertha about his dialogue with the Turkish lawyer. In November 1892, he writes to her and mentions Bey in what is virtually an aside: He explains that he has recently met "a former ambassador" who has "criticized the arbitration idea". He repeats his ideas for a collective security system and why he considers this the best model for conflict resolution, and expresses his belief that disarmament is "inexpedient" under "the prevailing circumstances". A collective security system would over time lead to a gradual reduction in the standing armies, he concludes. [276]

That is when the baroness reacts. On Christmas Eve itself, she writes back and addresses Bey's critique: "For those of us who are "professionals" in the peace league, your Turkish friend's doubts about the feasibility of arbitration are quite well-known," she lets him know in a tone which implies that she is not very impressed with Bey's objections, which have "already been addressed in negotiations." [277] If Alfred wishes to learn more, he can receive reading materials from *her* (the author's emphasis) in the form of a bulletin, published by the Peace Agency in Bern where she herself has written an essay.

After having dismissed Bey's objections somewhat brusquely, she returns to her usual optimistic tone: Despite all the hindrances the peace workers meet, there is also encouraging progress. *Lay Down Your Arms!* has now been published in an official English translation (a very good one, she stresses) as well as Danish, Swedish, Italian and Russian translations. Is not the success of the book a clear sign of the times' *craving* for its ideas, she asks? "If the majority of the people were of belligerent views they would certainly not welcome a work of fiction with the title "Lay Down your Arms!" [278] A tough battle against evil remains, but as long as their strength is intact, the peace movement will fight and perhaps "we will one day experience the dawning of victory!" [279]

No clear reply from Alfred to this letter is to be found. But he would never again criticize the arbitration idea in his letters to the baroness, nor mention any of Bey's different proposals and objections.

The next time he writes to her, however, he has a surprise in store.

A new ally

While Alfred continued his dialogue with the lawyer, Bertha on her side gained at new ally – with the same first name as her friend in San Remo, but more than 30 years his junior. The 28-year-old German bookseller Alfred Hermann Fried sent her a letter full of admiration after having read *Lay Down Your Arms!* Originally from Vienna, Alfred Fried resided in Berlin. His deepest wish was to dedicate himself wholly and fully to the peace movement. Was there anything he could do to help?

Was there anything! The timing could not have been better. At the time, the always busy Bertha was planning a publication that could keep the members of the new peace society up to date on the work. After a meeting with Fried, the two of them decided to collaborate on publishing a monthly peace magazine. Neither of them had funds to finance the work. All the same, it did not stop them from throwing themselves wholeheartedly into the task. Optimistically they thought that they could over time collect paying subscribers, at least five hundred. The magazine received the same name as the novel: *Lay Down Your Arms! (Die Waffen Nieder!)* It was to be more than just an organ for her society, rather "a general magazine for supporting the peace idea". [280] Bertha wrote and edited the magazine from Vienna and Alfred published it in Berlin. She commented on political events as she observed them in her daily reading of Austrian, English and French newspapers. The first issue was 48 pages long and published already in February 1892

Bertha was fortunate, she could now lean on two Alfreds as supporters!

Bertha the spider

Repeatedly, Bertha proved to be an adept networker. It came easy to her as she was sociable and passionate about her ideas. Perhaps a bit rude metaphor is to compare her to a spider queen, spinning a huge net all around her: Into it she drew different talents - famous authors, politicians and diplomats! In the one corner, she gathered some of the most politically active peace advocates, such as the French diplomat and politician Paul Henri d' Estournelles de Constant, the British politician and four times prime minister William E. Gladstone and the founder of the French peace association, the economist Frédéric Passy. In the other, she gathered authors and artists such as Max Nordeau, Émile Zola, Leo Tolstoy and the Russian painter Vasily Vereshchagin. Bertha got hold of the different talents with one objective in mind: How could they best contribute to the peace cause?

The spinning itself was done on the Harmannsdorf estate, and the threads were spread out in the form of letters. Several times a week, Bertha would seal an envelope and address it to a prominent person. Would the famous poet Peter Rosegger come to read at a public event in Vienna? Would "the waltz king" Johann Strauss write a waltz in honour of the good cause? What did Bjørnstjerne Bjørnson think about the idea of contacting the American industrial magnate and philanthropist, Andrew Carnegie, to ask for funding of the journal he wanted to start? [281]

Bertha left no stone unturned when it came to recruiting people to peace work. Almost every single prominent person in Vienna who could have the slightest interest in the cause, received an inquiry from her. When she heard that the Norwegian explorer Fridtjof Nansen would be giving a speech for 2000 people outside of the City Hall in Vienna, she immediately wrote to him and encouraged him to take advantage of the situation and to say a few words about how "after the heroic period of war comes the heroic period of knowledge and research." [282] Nansen concluded his speech accordingly: "The time of great wars of conquest has passed - the time of conquests in the land of science, of the unknown, will endure, and we hope that the future will bring further conquests and thus bring humanity forwards." [283]

Bertha also performed the feat of convincing the American author Mark Twain to give a short, improvised speech in which he declared his support for disarmament when he came to Vienna to read aloud from his latest book. Twain did it in his own unique fashion - he declared that he was ready to disarm at any time, even though a pen knife was the only thing he was carrying! [284] The newspapers highlighted precisely this statement - and there was publicity for both Twain and the peace cause.

Bertha spun and spun her web. She seldom accepted no for an answer. After receiving seven long letters, the Austrian poet Peter Rosegger finally surrendered and travelled from Graz to Vienna to give a reading in honor of the cause. She also managed to convince the intelligent and influential Joseph Lewinsky, Vienna's most famous actor, to give a performance together with his actress wife, Olga Lewinsky, in honor of the cause.

Eventually she wrote a letter to her author role model Zola and requested a declaration of his sympathy on behalf of the peace issue. The French author replied that he, too, dreamt of world peace, but believed unfortunately that it was "just a dream". Bertha wasted no time in responding that the progress of mankind was certainly no "dream", but something that would come as a natural result of the development of history. [285]

Here she was for once at cross purposes with her own role model.

She even tried to recruit Henrik Ibsen to the cause. In a letter, she asked the famous Norwegian playwright if he would write an article for her magazine *Lay Down Your Arms!* However, Ibsen briefly replied that he knew "nothing at all about the peace issue and therefore cannot write about it." [286]

Ibsen never let himself be captured by this spider queen.

Nobel, on the other hand, had received a prominent place in her web. One could almost say that the net was tightening around him.

Nobel's decision

During Christmas 1892, Alfred came to a decision. In a letter to Bertha dated January 7, 1893, he compliments her on "the great campaign against ignorance and stupidity" which she leads. Then comes the news:

> I want to donate a part of my fortune to a fund for the foundation of prizes to be awarded every fifth year (let's say six times, in all, because if within 30 years one has not succeeded in reforming the society of today, we will inevitably descend back into barbarism) to he or she who in the most effective manner has contributed to bringing about peace in Europe. [287]

The idea he had mentioned for her over dinner in Zürich, was confirmed.

In the letter, he expands upon his ideas regarding what he still views as the best conflict resolution model: A collective security system. He adds that he is still skeptical about the realism of disarmament, it can only be done "very slowly". A defense alliance of this kind will make war impossible and "oblige the most brutal aggressor to resort to arbitration or refrain from attacking." [288]

Bertha was quick to pick up her pen. She starts her reply by saying that she hopes she will live to see "this wonderful state of affairs" prevail between nations. But did Alfred really believe it would take 30 years before this came about? Bertha's beliefs were far more optimistic, she thinks it will happen within seven years: "- we will not write the 20th century and maintain this condition of anarchy and barbarism that reigns between the states today." [289]

As usual, she is clear in her opinion: Awarding *prizes* is not the best solution. Peace activists need *funding*, first and foremost, and not prizes in the manner of awards to individuals. For example, her Austrian peace society would not have existed if she had not made the journey to Rome in 1891, which in turn she could not have done without the necessary funds from Alfred.

Besides, she continues, it might be a challenge to award the prize to "he or she who in the most effective manner has contributed to bring about peace in Europe", as Alfred had written. She offers some examples of how the prize in such a case could be awarded to people who were not in material need of it, such as royals and rich bankers.

If Alfred had insisted on this formulation in his will, the prize would most likely be awarded to statesmen and political leaders. Peace activists and pacifists like Bertha would not come into consideration.

But instead, he put on his thinking cap once again.

Not only peace: Literature, hobbies and health

Alfred was not the only person with whom Bertha discussed peace in her letters. She was an avid letter writer and wrote more than 5000 letters in her lifetime, to peace activists, politicians, artists – a wide range of people. [290] She also received a lot of letters: "Signed or anonymous letters; letters from my own country; letters from other parts of Europe and from beyond the sea; letters with explosions of admiration or of coarseness; letters requesting information or making all sorts of propositions for the surest and speediest attainment of our object." [291]

Bertha's letters to other peace activists were mostly about work, such as her letters to Bjørnstjerne Bjørnson, with whom she had begun to correspond in 1892. On one occasion, she wrote and asked him enthusiastically whether he could write for her magazine *Lay Down your Arms*. [292] And unlike Nobel, Bjørnson would respond to the request and contribute to her peace magazine. [293]

Von Suttner and Bjørnson also discussed the evolution of feminism. And it is striking how, unlike her, Bjørnson connected the idea of peace to the feminist cause. On one occasion, he let her know that he had written an introduction for a new woman's magazine in Copenhagen: "This movement (the women's movement) is the dearest to my heart. Without women, the peace issue will never be victorious!!" [294] Bertha disagreed with the claim that women were greater lovers of peace and of a gentler nature than the "warrior-like" men, which was a common belief at the time. In her opinion, men and women were not so different in that regard: "enthusiasm for acts of war can be found in women and enthusiasm for the peace movement can be found in men." According to Bertha, it was not so much from nature, but from society that women had acquired the role of a nurturer.

Another well-known international figure with whom she discussed peace, was the American industrialist Andrew Carnegie. The steel magnate contributed to peace work on a large scale as his contact with the international peace movement increased. For example, he gave an annual stipend of 125,000 francs to the Bern Peace Bureau - founded after the Rome conference in 1891. A few years later, the industry baron took the initiative to build the Peace Palace in the same city. It acquired a library with the largest collections in the field of international law and a few years later became the seat of the permanent court of arbitration. [295]

Bertha did not have enough words of praise for him. After meeting Carnegie at a party, she wrote him and asked if he could donate an annual amount to her editor Alfred Fried, so that he could be able to continue his work with the magazine. Afterwards, she regretted that she had used a private event to carry out propaganda. Irritated, she wrote in her diary: "Now I have ruined this chance to become friends!" [296] But only a brief time later the joyous news came in a personal letter from Carnegie - he would support Fried with an annual donation!

Like Nobel, Carnegie held the opinion that rich people should invest their wealth in a way that benefits society. In his book *The Gospel of Wealth* (1900), he emphasized the importance of making donations to worthy causes such as education and science, so that the less privileged could acquire knowledge to move up in the world, as he himself had done. Carnegie's correspondence shows his deep social concern and desire to support the peace movement.

Bertha's letters mostly revolved around the peace cause. However, the letters between her and Alfred reflect a friendship on a deeper level. The two of them discuss not only peace, but also inform each other about their hobbies, travels and books. Bertha is very clear about her literary preferences. For example, she is critical of Nobel's compatriot August Strindberg: "Have you read the novels by your countryman Strindberg? I have just finished browsing through *The Defence of a Fool*. It is quite simply *hideous*." [297] The word "hideous" is underlined twice. Strindberg's semi-autobiographical and disillusioned novel about the institution of marriage, first published in 1893, was obviously not to the taste of the optimistic Bertha.

A couple of years later, in 1896, she wrote to Alfred with enthusiasm about the most recent technical inventions: "The X-ray is fantastic, isn't it?" The year before, Wilhelm Conrad Røntgen had discovered the rays that could penetrate materials and substances. [298] Alfred's reply to this letter is not known.

In their correspondence, they also discuss health issues. Alfred struggled with health problems throughout his whole life, and rarely wrote a letter to Bertha that did not contain a line or two about his various bodily ailments. Throughout the 1890s, it was a matter of heart problems. One letter he signs with *ami moribond* ("a dying friend"). Bertha took him seriously: "Why do you write 'dying friend', is it an expression of your foul mood or are you seriously ill ... are you suffering?" [299] Alfred tended to exaggerate in his letters, nevertheless, the truth was that he was experiencing increasing symptoms of heart failure in the early 1890s.

Bertha's letters to Alfred, on the other hand, were testimonies of a robust woman with a lot of energy. Her only physical challenge was that she easily put on weight. As the years passed, her weight gain became a problem. But in the same way that she took on most challenges, she displayed vigor: A bicycle was the answer. The bicycle was a new invention and with a long skirt it was no easy matter to master this means of transport. But soon she learned to stand up on the pedals of the bicycle and cycle around on the country roads of Eggenburg. And it helped: "The attacks of lethargy disappeared, I lost weight and sometimes I had the feeling that youth - youth bubbled through my veins again!" [300]

However, in the winter of 1893, Bertha fell ill, for the first time since the period when the couple lived in Georgia. The doctor ordered complete bed rest. In a long letter to Alfred, she describes her ailments - she cannot stand on her feet for more than five minutes without her heart pounding, and sometimes she fears that she is "about to pass out". [301] That same year, on the ninth of June, she turned 50, "horrible!", she complains. [302]

Bertha was very much aware that women who were in the public eye were scrutinized for their age and appearance. She had always been proud of her lovely hands. Now that she was aging, it showed on her hands: "You are judged by your hands. And red, fat, ordinary hands like mine can cause people to judge me erroneously," she wrote bitterly in her diary.

Her letters to Alfred from this period show another side of the self-assertive author who prides the first row in photographs from peace conferences. In them we meet a tired Bertha. A vulnerable Bertha. A Bertha who is worried about the challenges that are piling up at Harmannsdorf: The financial situation at the family estate was so bad that Arthur's parents were obliged to sell paintings and furniture to keep going. Mr. and Mrs. von Suttner had never had good business sense. Now they feared that they would be forced to auction off the estate.

The von Suttner family's situation was not unique. Their property and fortune had been passed down as an inheritance for generations, which was customary practice among aristocrats. The 19th century was a period when estates and properties managed by aristocrats heavily in debt were increasingly falling into the hands of members of the bourgeoisie and the hard-working and growing middle class. [303] In 1893, the von Suttner family was virtually drowning in debt. During this period, Bertha had begun writing novels again to make money for the household. Arthur's parents were totally dependent upon their daughter in law's ingenuity and income as an author to keep their heads above water.

Now Bertha had to put on her thinking cap. Would someone be interested in buying the estate? Could her friend in Paris be their "savior"?

"Goethe's fly"

Her correspondence with Alfred takes a new turn, when in she in a long letter tells him that her parents-in-law will soon be forced to auction off the estate, despite having done all they could to find a "suitable buyer". But perhaps might he be interested in buying a property in Austria?

In her letter, the sale of the estate is presented as a generous and almost irresistible offer to a very special and selected friend. "Who knows," Bertha writes, "perhaps you would like to have a property in Austria? It is not a plea, not a proposal, it is merely information – so that you will not by some odd coincidence say to me 'why didn't you tell me this before?'" [304]

Was it a challenge for the baroness to suggest that her friend purchase the von Suttner's family home now up for sale? If this was the case, it was not something she put into words. Quite the contrary, in the letter, written in April 1893, she demonstrates an unmistakable talent for marketing. Despite this, Alfred would not grant Bertha's wish this time around. The Harmannsdorf estate was nevertheless not sold – in one way or another the family managed to hang on to it for another few years. [305]

Books, health, the sale of the estate – the subjects of the letters between Alfred and Bertha were many. Nonetheless – *peace* was the subject they most frequently would return to. Or – to put it more precisely – Bertha was careful to pull the right strings. Sometimes she tried to engage her friend by including him in decisions she was trying to make. For example, when she wondered how she should reply to an invitation to a meeting with the English pacifist Hodgson Pratt, and asked Alfred for advice about this. The baroness was extremely popular in the Anglo-Saxon regions, but was in doubt about whether she should go. "A distinguished woman who is advocating a worthy cause will be listened to much more in England and America than in Europe," Alfred wrote back in the spring of 1893, leaving little doubt about what he thought: "How can you or will you resist Mr. Pratt's most tempting invitation? As much as I despise the word impossible, I think that for you to decline is almost an impossibility." [306]

Did Bertha ask him for his advice because she really needed it or because she wanted to make him feel like a valuable ally?

Regardless of the reason, in the end she decided not to go after all.

The same year, she wrote to Alfred and thanked for his wishes on her 50th birthday: "Happy birthday! That you will fight for a victory for the peace cause!" were his words. [307] In an informal and humorous tone, she asks if he would make her happy on her birthday by sending a "page from his cheque book" to the treasurer of the Austrian peace society. Just a symbolic amount ("a triviality"), she emphasizes, as her intention was to get his name on the list of contributors, which in turn would serve as a good example for other potential donors. [308]

Alfred did not let her down: His contribution to her society was far larger than the symbolic amount Bertha had proposed. In an effusive reply, Bertha expresses her gratitude: "My dear friend. How kind and generous you are! I had really not hoped for more than a contribution of around 20 francs...Your donation (so useful for my work) has given me great, true pleasure! It is also proof of your faithful devotion." [309] Was this the whole truth or did she know her benefactor so well that she knew he would give more than a symbolic amount once he decided to open his wallet? One thing is for sure: Bertha would thank Alfred again and again with exuberant words and turns of phrases. If enthusiasm was a "capacity that life had deprived him of", as he had put it, it is likely that she contributed to filling up his "enthusiasm tank".

Was she strategic? There is little doubt that Bertha was a woman who knew how to reconcile idealism with pragmatism. If not, she would hardly have achieved anything. She would have fallen into place in the rows of history's countless well-meaning, but invisible women. Her method was often the same: dangle the carrot, rather than to push the case. Attract attention, don't demand. Time after time, she tries to *motivate* Alfred to become involved in the peace movement: "This letter is not asking for anything, it is impossible to respond with a refusal," she writes in 1896. No, she merely opens the door for "*a wish on your part* to become active in the cause" (Bertha's emphasis). "I will keep you informed," she continues, "because 'the wonderful thing' as Ibsen calls it – may happen after all." [310]

What did she mean by "the wonderful thing"? That Alfred would begin to *believe* in pacifism? Or that he would include a peace prize in his will, as he had indicated earlier?

Throughout their correspondence, Bertha's letters illustrate a mixture of boldness and humility. She balances on a fine line between "inspiration" and "badgering". Sometimes she sends him several letters in a row with an assertiveness that was wholly at odds with the ideal for women at this time. Then she interrupts herself just as the words are flowing too freely across the paper: "Enough! You have surely received 20 new letters during one day and are a man much in demand." [311] She "fears boring him." [312]

Other times she uses self-deprecation or humor in her attempts to win the inventor over to her side. When Alfred complains that he is working all day, and that the rest of his time goes to correspondence, lawsuits and other business, Bertha replies that she will continue to disturb him, justifying it with a quote of Goethe: "He who feels that one is truly working for a worthy cause, must be a *tormentor*. One must not wait to be called, one must not pay it heed if one is sent away. One must be, as Homer sings praise of his heroes, like a *fly*, which when it is chased away, always attacks the person from another direction." In her next letters, she refers to herself in words and phrases such as: "Here is Goethe's fly again!" "Goethe's fly is keeping you informed about the peace movement and sending you some reading materials!" On one occasion, she concludes her letter by asking him not to chase the fly away, in that "the cause I serve is sacred - the most sacred of all causes." [313]

And Alfred did not chase away the fly.

On a rare occasion, she takes a step back to reflect on their friendship. 20 years since they met for the first time, she writes him a letter in an almost meditative mood. A letter that is vibrating with the feeling of autumn:

> What a strange little short story – because it was no novel... instead material for a psychological study: a thinker, a poet, a bitter and good man, happy and sad...who likes the great heights of humanity, but deeply despises reality's human beings, understands everything, but believes nothing. That's how you appeared to me. And 20 years haven't done anything to change this memory. [314]

At arm's length

Alfred's donations made it possible for Bertha to continue her work in the peace movement and to assume the position she liked best: Right in the middle of the action. She had always enjoyed being in the focus of attention. In photographs from peace conferences and gatherings from the 1890s, she is often positioned in the center, frequently beside the movement's leading male figure, Frédéric Passy. Bertha stands straight and tall, her chest held high. She is often wearing a pretty, dark, ruffled blouse with embroidery around the neckline. Her body is turned towards the photographer, and she looks proudly into the lens of the camera. She clearly enjoys her position in the front lines of the champions of peace.

Many photographs of Bertha exist, but there are fewer of Alfred. Unlike her, he disliked having his picture taken, although on most occasions he was very presentable: His beard was trimmed, his hair cut and nails manicured. In portraits and pictures, he seldom smiles. In a lovely picture of the new bridge in Dolce Aqua (Taggia),

Alfred is photographed in front of the structure. But instead of looking at the camera, he looks down towards the ground. The upper part of his face is concealed by a dark hat and the lowest part is covered by a full beard. Only his nose and two pale cheekbones stick out. [315]

Alfred did not enjoy attention nor want his name to be mentioned in the press or in reference books. He could not stand honorary titles. In addition to being modest, he feared appearing ridiculous. On one occasion, an acquaintance proposed naming a sea vessel after him. He refused with these words: "There are serious objections to this. First, it is a *she*, who would be accused of frivolous attempts to conceal her gender – and if you point out that she is comely and well-constructed, then it would seem that naming her after an old wreck is a bad omen." [316]

In San Remo, he continued to live in solitude. He had little contact with the local Italians. When his neighbor, Mr. Rossi, succeeded in persuading him to buy his property, a 20-room villa, because he felt uncomfortable living so close to Alfred's laboratory and explosives, he was for a while at a loss about what to do with the house. However, after a few days he announced to his assistant Ragnar Sohlman: "Now I have found out what we will do with the Villa Rossi. It will be good to use it as a changing room when we have been swimming in the Mediterranean. It is after all so unpleasant to be squeezed in with all the Italians in the large changing cabana and on the public beach!" [317] This is an example of how he continued to keep people at arm's length. But he willingly received visits from his brothers and their families. After work, he sometimes went out to take fresh air, seldom on foot, but usually in a horse and carriage, drawn by one of the five thoroughbred race horses in his stall.

He did not rest on his laurels nor lie on the beach and look out across the Mediterranean while he wrote "a great poem in English", as Bertha had proposed. [318] To the contrary, he was tirelessly underway with new plans and projects.

Chapter 8

"The Wonderful Thing" - Nobel's will

A draft of a will

In the fall of 1892, Alfred had informed Bertha that he considered donating part of his fortune to public purpose, and some of it to peace work. In a letter to her in January 1893, he had gone one step further and written that this would take the form of a foundation for prizes to be awarded every fifth year to "he or she who in the most effective manner has contributed to bringing about peace in Europe." [319] Bertha had immediate objections to this statement.

In March 1893, Nobel makes a new draft of his will. It is his second attempt. A first attempt from 1889 was never found. [320] In this he writes that the major part of his fortune will go to a fund, the annual interest of which should be distributed in the form of a prize for the person who had made "the most important and ground-breaking" inventions or ideological work "within the broad field of knowledge and progress" - pointing towards the science prizes. In addition, people who had been successful in "fighting against prejudices that people and governments have against the formation of a European peace tribunal" should qualify. [321]

Was he influenced by Aristarchi Bey? The lawyer had argued for a type of an international court of arbitration. The draft does not mention a collective security system - the idea that Alfred had written about earlier. Neither does it specify which areas of knowledge were to be rewarded, except for physics and medicine.

Alfred concludes the will by writing that "the remaining 20 percent" of his fortune shall go to grants for individuals and institutions such as university colleges. He also remembers Bertha – he writes that one percent shall go to the Austrian peace society.

The language of the draft is quite vague. [322] Alfred fumbles. He seems to be looking for the best wording.

Dismisses Bey

Between 1892 and 1893, Alfred had had been discussing peace with both Bertha and the lawyer. Now it is clear who has fallen short. In a letter written to Bey in the autumn of 1893, he expresses his dissatisfaction with the lawyer's efforts: "I have really tried now for one year, but I don't think that you have come one step further in your investigations of the peace issue. I do not find a single article written by you that addresses the question in print in the press." [323]

Some of Bey's comments and arguments made an impression on him. [324] For example, after the lawyer had dismissed the moratorium idea as "utopian", Nobel discarded it. He was also influenced by the lawyer's idea of a peace tribunal.

But overall, he was not satisfied with Bey's work. He had not used the press in an efficient manner for the peace cause, which had been a part of their agreement. All he had done was to write Alfred a total of some 60 letters which contained "long-winded reports and brochures." [325] In the fall of 1893, Alfred decided that he did not want to renew their contract and terminated their collaboration. Bey protested, but his employer was resolute.

Did he have Bertha's work in mind when he evaluated the lawyer's efforts? In the letter of dismissal to Bey, written on 18 August 1893, Bertha von Suttner's name is mentioned several times. Her name pops up when he criticizes Bey's lukewarm efforts, stating that he doubts whether the lawyer is committed to the peace cause at all: "I don't know whether you have converted to this issue, which Madame von Suttner is the only person of significance to promote in a serious manner." [326]

Bertha was now without any serious competitors for her position as Alfred's main informant.

The letters continue to fly between San Remo and Harmannsdorf.

"Don't complain!"

Bertha's visions were high-flying and Alfred couldn't always keep up with her. While she was full of faith without reservations, he continued to have his doubts. Or – more precisely – he alternated between belief and doubt, something which finds expression in his correspondence. In one letter to her, he writes laconically that "the only tenable peace is that which exists in the cemetery." In the next letter, he matter-of-factly expands upon his view of arbitration as a policy instrument. [327] On one occasion, he expresses his unreserved admiration for Bertha's work, another time his attitude is ironic. With one hand, he supports her peace work, with the other he dampens her motivation. Repeatedly, his ambivalence comes to surface.

Perhaps one could say that Alfred Nobel represented the duality of his day? [328] His innovations could be both useful and beneficial as well as destructive and contribute to fear. The end of the 19th century was not all about optimism and progress. It was a time with both light and dark aspects. A time characterized by inner contradictions, just like he was. One ideal was peace, while another was nationalism. The people wanted peace. So too did the governments, in principle. But instead they were arming themselves for war, and locking themselves up in military alliances. The large world expositions demonstrated the impressive technological innovations of the time, while the same technology was being used to create lethal weapons. A non-European observer, the Shah of Persia, who was travelling around Europe in the early 1870s, reflected upon this in his diary:

The Europeans have invented wonderful means of saving

people. It is strange that while they are doing so much to save people from death, they produce in Woolwich and Krupp's weapons factories all the time new machinery, canons, projectile missiles, to more quickly and on a far greater scale than previously, be able to execute a blood bath. [329]

Sometimes Alfred got on Bertha's nerves. His black humor she could take, but Alfred's gloominess put a damper on her mood: "Don't complain! I say: Life is beautiful after all. Even if there are moments of great sadness," she wrote to him on one occasion. [330]

Once she has had enough: "Don't complain. I ask you to send me some encouraging, reinforcing, gentle, happy, devoted, reassuring words - and you quote Shakespeare by saying that everyone who is over 50 years of age (you know how old I am) is in a permanently petrified state. Very, very nice!" [331]

However, she did not let it rattle her. Bertha could tolerate a great deal. If only world peace came - which it must and should!

Alternative paths to peace

Bertha's experience of solidarity in "a community for human love and human dignity", as she expressed it at the Rome conference in 1891, would endure. But with time she came to understand that disagreements and conflicts also arose *within* the peace movement. The paths to peace were many, and the champions of peace sometimes disagreed between themselves.

Some of them felt that it was more expedient to work for practical, social and political reforms. Others held that peace would only arise if everyone sought inner peace. Some again were more interested in finding global solutions. [332] Pragmatic liberals who wanted a new international legal system disagreed with Christian pacifists who felt that all war was a sin. [333]

An example of a relevant disagreement was the conflict between the uncompromising pacifists and those who accepted the need for armed forces and saw defensive war as a necessary evil. [334] Leo Tolstoy belonged to the first category. The Russian author wrote a lengthy article in defense of conscientious objection for the recently started Norwegian peace publication *Det Norske Fredsblad*. [335] In a four page-long letter to Bertha he wrote: "The longer I live, and the more I ponder over the question of war, the more I become convinced that the only solution to the question is consistent conscientious objection." [336] In *Die Neue Presse* he praised *Lay Down Your Arms* and emphasized its call for disarmament.

The baroness did not agree with him on this issue: "- I don't believe in *only ways* – there always have to be a lot of ways to be tried," she wrote to him. She had much in common with Tolstoy: Both were of aristocratic background (and would later distance themselves from their backgrounds), both opposed nationalism and both wrote realistic fiction. With the same impressive thoroughness as when she did research for *Lay Down Your Arms!*, Tolstoy had prepared himself for his masterpiece, the anti-war novel *War and Peace*, written between 1863 and 1869. He had read everything in the way of letters, war journals and biographical materials about Napoleon and the myriad characters in the book. However, in contrast to his Austrian fellow writer, Tolstoy was skeptical about the benefits of peace congresses and whether it was possible to find peaceful solutions through organized associations. Having become a wholehearted advocate for the principle of nonviolence expressed in Jesus' words about "turning the other cheek", he was uncompromising in his view that violence must under no circumstances be answered by violence. [337] In his last work, the collection of essays *The Kingdom of God Is Within You* (1894), Tolstoy wrote in beautiful and poetic terms about a society where love replaces violence, and where human beings live together in peaceful co-existence. [338] The last years of his life, Tolstoy lived withdrawn from society, in the countryside. Inspired by Rousseau, he cultivated faith in "the simple life" and "the natural human being".

While her Russian comrade advocated withdrawal from society, Bertha and her peace friends favored social engagement. The baroness belonged to the moderate wing which saw *several* paths to peace, there were "just as many paths to peace as there are paths to war." [339] Peace conferences, international agreements, the establishment of an international legal system, a European federation of states, arbitration and education were all important paths.

Another extreme view that Bertha distanced herself from, was the revolutionary ideology of the socialists. The socialist peace movement promoted the idea that workers all over the world should unite in a revolution which might involve bloodshed, *then* they would work for peace. The Polish-German Marxist politician Rosa Luxemburg was among those who held this view. [340] The guiding principle of the German Social Democrats' conferences in 1891 and 1893 was that world peace could only be brought about through the collapse of capitalism. [341]

Bertha both criticized and sympathized with the socialists. She agreed to the idea of international solidarity. But she condemned all use of violence. "Our aim is legislation, NOT rebellion," she wrote. On several occasions, she tried to establish a dialogue with the socialists, but on this point, they were unwilling to compromise. Bertha's wish for collaboration between the bourgeois and socialist peace movements proved to be impossible in the political climate of the time.

Unlike many of her contemporaries, Bertha promoted the view that the best way to bring about peace was by spreading knowledge and building awareness about war's suffering in speech and in writing. One of her favorite causes was education, which she believed was of fundamental importance for creating a peaceful society. She was progressive in her view that women's education was just as important as men's: It was the path toward a freer life that would make it possible for women to practice a profession and to think independently. Both men and woman ought to be educated towards the goal: to be a "noble human being", she wrote. [342] It wasn't until several years later that another female author was to write more in depth about this issue. In the essay *Three Guineas*, Virginia Woolf (1882-1941), a committed pacifist, discusses the importance of education in preventing war. [343]

Despite the disagreements, Bertha was an indefatigable optimist who believed that peace would soon come. In a letter to her friend in San Remo, she wrote: "We don't want to write the 20th century and maintain this condition of anarchy and barbarism between the states that reigns today." [344] And with Alfred's support, the development could be accelerated. Soon peace would no longer be "naked, poor and mangled", as Shakespeare put it, or a small, pale shadow at the back of the stage, but instead take its place in the spotlight front and center stage.

With Bertha at its side, of course.

The joy of invention

Bertha's letters to Alfred increased in number in beginning of the 1890s. In some periods, she wrote almost three times as many letters as he does. [345] Was she worried that he might forget the promise he made when they last met?

What about him, did he ever feel overwhelmed by the intensity of her correspondence? If that was the case, it was not something he expressed. To the contrary, in his letters he was usually exceedingly polite: He apologizes that he doesn't have time to write more often or can come and visit the couple, whom he on one occasion refers to as his "best friends".

1894 was another busy year for Alfred. In January, he made one of his biggest investments ever – a factory to produce weapons in Karlskoga in Sweden, AB Bofors-Gullspång (Bofors in Värmland). The opportunities offered by his laboratory in San Remo were limited. In Karlskoga, he would have plenty of room to experiment without the public authorities intervening, as they had done in France. His plan was to experiment with semi-smokeless gunpowder, projectile missiles and canons. The 61-year old also made plans for the Björkborn mansion, which was located close by the factory site. During a few months, he had furnished a beautiful home there, hiring a French kitchen staff (he was not fond of

Swedish cuisine) and acquiring three new horses - Orloff stallions, in the words of the town people of Karlskoga rechristened Nobel's "Urluffare". [346] Soon he was spending the better part of the summer season in Björkborn. His plan was to settle down here when he retired.

Speaking of contradictions: While Alfred was well underway with the investigation of diverse types of conflict resolution models, he was also making his largest ever investment in production for the military: A weapons factory. Why did he continue with inventions for military purpose? By now he was a wealthy man. He had no need to continue inventing or even, strictly speaking, work at all. With his extensive literary, artistic, and philanthropic interests, he had enough to keep him occupied for the rest of his days. For that matter, he could have enjoyed life at the beach in San Remo, reading poetry, as Bertha had suggested.

Alfred had chosen a career as an inventor of explosives. Having grown up with a father who worked in the technical military industry as well as working himself with explosives since he was a teenager, changing course might not be an easy matter. Personally, he stated that it was first and foremost the *technical* aspects of the inventions that aroused his curiosity. The American engineer Samuel C. Florman explains the joy of making technological discoveries in this way: "The art of engineering's nature has been misunderstood. Analysis, rationality, materialism and practical creativity do not exclude emotional satisfaction; they are to the contrary shortcuts to such satisfaction ... at the heart of engineering activity there lies existential joy." [347]

Was it "existential joy" that Alfred experienced during the hours he spent among different apparatuses, cans of powder and oils in the laboratory? Was he simply put, just having fun? In conversation with a colleague, Alfred is reported to have said: "Well, as you know, we are handling extremely diabolical inventions. But as technical problems they are so challenging - financial and commercial considerations aside - and due to that alone, so interesting."

Most certainly he was competitive. When he invested in Bofors, he wrote to his assistant Ragnar Sohlman: "It will be lively in Bofors, as soon as we have put into practice some of the ongoing new discoveries. It would be great fun to see old Sweden as a weapons rival to Germany and England." [348]

Play, curiosity, competitive instinct - the motives may have been many. When Alfred on one occasion was asked about his attitude towards weapons technology, he used the arguments about the benefits of a terror balance. He expressed that he saw no contradiction between the development of military explosives and peace work. [349] To a famous French arms manufacturer he reportedly said: "Let Damocles' sword hang over each head, gentlemen, and you will be witnesses to a miracle - all wars will be done away with if the weapon is called bacteriology." [350]

The biographer Erik Bergengren summarizes Nobel's attitude as follows: "Behind the inventor's work with explosives and semi-smokeless gunpowder there was always a sincere wish to make war impossible by improving the technology in these fields." [351]

Orchestrates Alfred's support

While Alfred made plans for his factory at Bofors-Gullspång, "Goethe's fly" continued to buzz around her benefactor. Would he attend the next peace congress? Did he want to read a letter she had received from Bjørnstjerne Bjørnson? The winged words from the peace advocate in the north would certainly strengthen his belief in the cause! [352]

In 1895, the Austrian peace activist witnessed another success: The establishment of the Hungarian peace association. It had proved to be *too* great a challenge for the Austrian peace association to function as a mouthpiece for both Austria and Hungary. Neither the Hungarians nor the Bohemians felt affiliation with the central organization in Vienna. Bertha travelled to Budapest and gave a lecture, which was successful and inspired the foundation of a Hungarian organization. The famous Hungarian poet Mór Jókai became the leader. Obviously proud, she mentions this in a letter to Alfred. She ascribes the success to her being able to unite the parties, which again was due to a "certain prestige that I have for the moment," as she puts it. At the very end, she gives a hint: "If I had the means to take action today, I would achieve joyous and unexpected results." [353]

And Alfred finds expression for his loyalty: "I will make a thousand florins available to your Hungarian committee." [354] However, his donation would not be used exactly as he had intended. Bertha is quick to write back and suggests where Alfred's support should go:

Yes, it is through my own initiative and with the moral and financial support of the society in Vienna that the association in Budapest was started, but now it is independent of us, and in addition – it is *rich*, Hungarian bankers have contributed a great deal...*My* society on the other hand, is lacking resources, as is the International Peace Agency in Bern, which is the center of the peace movement and needs funds to prepare the conference. [355]

What was Alfred's reaction to this?

After a couple of weeks his reply arrives: "Understood! I will send the sum of 1000 florins to your friends of peace and you can transfer half to the agency in Bern." [356]

"Goethe's fly" had her way again.

A double-edged sword

Bertha's letters sometimes disclose that she was uncertain about Alfred's reasons for supporting her peace work. Was it just out of friendship? Or was it because he had begun to *believe* in the peace cause?

Like many women who were in the public eye, she had to struggle to be taken seriously. Bertha knew that she benefited from her charisma and charm, something she called it "a double-edged sword". On the one hand, she was conscious and proud of it, on the other hand, she wanted her *work* rather than her person to be in the spotlight. In her appearance and conduct, the author of the grisly *Lay Down Your Arms!*, a novel which often was called "unfeminine" because of its descriptions of war and bloodbath, was considered to be highly attractive. [357] Bertha often became the center of attention among the participants at peace congresses and in different social situations. However: Did people gather around her because they took her work seriously, or because she in addition to being a world-famous author, was an attractive woman who could also adorn herself with the title of baroness?

Some of her letters express her feelings of unease about this. For example, when she replies to a letter from Bartholomäus Carneri, in which he lets her know that he had "hesitated" when she asked if he wanted to be a member of the Austrian peace society, but that in the end he gave in, "won over less by the cause in itself than by your personal charm." [358] In a lengthy reply, he was given his just deserts: "What separates us two is faith," she writes, emphasizing that only someone who helped her, not because he or she was "won over by personal charm", but because of a belief in "the possibility and the necessity of the battle for peace", could truly be an ally. [359]

Was Alfred Nobel a true ally? Did he contribute because he believed in "the possibility and the necessity of the battle for peace"? From time to time Bertha questions his motives. In the fall of 1895, Alfred writes: "Dear baroness and friend. I have received two letters from you who are so busy. I am taking very diligent care of these two manuscripts written by such a charming author." [360] In her reply, Bertha puts him duly in his place: "Dear monsieur and friend. No, my letters are not asking to be 'carefully taken care of as manuscripts written by a charming author' – they hope to awaken an echo of sympathy, not for the author, but for *the work* which is so dear to her." (Bertha's emphasis) [361]

Over and over again, she encourages her benefactor to *believe* in the peace work. Was this "the wonderful thing" she hoped would happen?

The year 1900 – a milestone?

Bertha was not the type to succumb to pondering and neither did she have time for it. The turn of the century was only a few years away. The road forward was straight - towards world peace! However, many pieces had to fall into place if an "international peace regime" was to be reached before 1900. It was simply a matter of rolling up one's sleeves and getting to work.

The turn of a century has always had something magical about it. Many people had high expectations about the beginning of the 20th century, because the end of the 19th century had brought so many changes. With a view over the garden of Harmannsdorf, where the autumn leaves fell from the trees, Bertha was full of faith that the peace cause soon would experience a new season. She let the words dance across the paper: "In the same way we envision that on New Year's Eve we will become a new human being - the threshold to the 20th century can also be crossed by a new humanity. Not a humanity that is transformed, that has become like angels, but quite simply, a humanity that has freed itself from a barbarity which has long since become intolerable."

She continued to see connections between the great advancements of this period and the cause closest to her heart: "When one has done away with torture, why not with war? I concede that stupid and cruel people still exist - but goodness and intelligence will prevail in the end." [362] Most Western countries had begun to abandon the use of torture during the 19th century and slavery had been abolished as well.

Bertha would return to the beginning of the 20th century as a milestone: If one reached 1900 without another great war breaking out in Europe, a new system could be introduced, where right would come before might: An international mechanism which ensured that conflicts would be resolved through arbitration. [363] If only the pacifists worked energetically enough, the turn of the century would be the occasion of the "official conference for the pacification of Europe."

She was most likely referring to a peace conference that was to be arranged for all the governments of Europe in Paris the year 1900. The world exposition in that year could offer the right framework for "the peace regime's entrance", she wrote to Alfred. However, to reach this milestone, the peace movement's efforts would have to "take on the form of a hurricane" and "virtually drown governments with information, press articles, public statements, and more!" [364] Berthas metaphors were powerful, reflecting her faith, which was unshakable.

But she needed Alfred's support in this.

The intensity of her letters increases. It had been internationally agreed that the English Prime Minister William Gladstone's proposal for a permanent European court of arbitration would be investigated in further detail, she writes to him. And soon yet another victory: An arbitration agreement between the USA and Great Britain in the Venezuela - question (1895-97). [365] It had the support of Gladstone and was promoted through the peace conferences. [366] Visibly proud of this, Bertha sends Alfred an article from *Neue Freie Presse*: "What a victory!" she writes, with her usual conviction, "and I *know* that it's thanks to the efforts of our federation!" [367]

Also, the Danish government created headlines when it gave its support to the Peace Bureau in Bern: "It is a great step forward, a peace budget - that is something new. People are starting to view our institutions as synonymous with 'public utility value'". [368] In 1895, the number of peace associations had reached a new record. All the 654 from 12 countries were now members of IPB, *The International Peace Bureau* in Bern. They still experienced defeats, but despite Italy's occupation of Eritrea and the war between China and Japan which broke out in 1893 and was still going on, "freedom, reason and goodness would triumph in the end!" [369]

Not everyone shared her enthusiasm. When Bertha went to a festival in Nice, she met by chance Juliette Adam, whose salon she had visited in Paris in 1886. She immediately invited the editor to a lecture about peace, whereupon Adam replied: "Absolutely not! I am for war!" [370]

Adam was still hoping for a war of revenge between France and Germany. However, it was a hope that faded with every passing year.

"What we have given, you and I, will survive"

Bertha continued her campaign towards Alfred. In a long letter, she compares herself to the Swiss Henri Dunant, the founder of the Red Cross and of the Geneva Convention. [371] To make him understand the importance of his support, she lets him know that an important reason why Dunant succeeded in founding the Red Cross was that he came from a well-off business family, and had personally paid for the publication of his book *A Memory of Solferino* (1862). In this work, he gives an account of the sufferings he witnessed during the bloody battle of Solferino in 1859, where the Frenchmen and Sardinians beat the Austrians. The book brought him international recognition and prompted the creation of the Red Cross.

To do so, Dunant had sacrificed his fortune, she writes, but to sacrifice a fortune, you first had to *have* one, after all, one had to be able to write and dedicate oneself to the work and not, like herself "spend eleven months every year in solitude in the countryside to work on novels so she could finance her existence." [372]

That same year (1896), Bertha was hard at work writing novels again – a sign of her depleted finances. But the writing proved heavy going. The pacifist was a fervent soul who could work around the clock when she was passionate about something. But when she needed to do things she disliked, it was cumbersome. The hurried nature of her writing took its toll on the quality of her books, which received increasingly negative reviews. [373] Was she beginning to worry that she might have to spend the rest of her life writing books that did not matter?

By now her appeals to Alfred were urgent. But were they really necessary? Hadn't he already made it clear to her already that in his will he would set up a fund for the awarding of prizes which would also benefit peace workers? Yes, but later he had not mentioned it with a single word in his letters. Bertha did not in fact know for sure if the endowment was secured. A letter she wrote in the spring of 1896, indicates as much: "You have written to me once that you are allocating a large endowment to the peace cause. Yes, please do, I am asking you *seriously*! Regardless of whether I am here, what we have given, you and I, will survive." (Bertha's emphasis) [374]

Nobel's final will

While Alfred's health was ailing, he continued to maintain his busy schedule. Once more he saw his "flowergirl". In September 1894, he travelled to Vienna where Sofie lived with her daughter Gretchen. The visit was a success. "I saw that you were in better health than ever before and cannot understand why you complain so much," he wrote to her upon his return. [375] In the same letter, he let her know that he would include an annual allowance for her in his will. This was the last time ever Alfred saw his "flower girl".

On November 27, 1895, he signed the third and last version of his will. The wording was much clearer than in the previous draft: A fund was to be established, the interest of which was to be divided into five equal parts. These parts were to be given "in the form of prizes to those who, during the preceding year, shall have conferred the greatest benefit to mankind" within the fields of Physics, Chemistry, Physiology or Medicine, Literature and Peace. [376] The prizes were to be awarded annually and in the form of a monetary prize to the person who most deserved it, independent of nationality.

The section on peace specifies that the prize should go "to the person who shall have done the most or the best work for fraternity between nations, for the abolition or reduction of standing armies and for the holding and promotion of peace congresses." [377]

Thus, disarmament and peace conferences, which Bertha fought for, were included in the final formulation.

"Goethe's fly" had gotten her way one last time.

Nobel as playwright: "Sad as hell"

"I've written a play for the theatre, a tragic one, make no mistake, and as sad as hell," Alfred wrote to his nephew Ludvig in March 1896. [378]

The contradictory aspects of his personality were still there. The ink had scarcely dried on the last version of his will before he set to work on a new document, written in darker ink. In his official will, he had included a utopian dimension, the hope of a better world in which the natural sciences and new inventions could lead humanity forward and literature play an "idealistic" part. In the play *Nemesis*, written during the last year of his life, the dark and contradictory forces in him were released. Alfred's "second will" in literary form is far from being in tune with the ideals of evolutionary optimism: Violence is the most important ingredient of the prose tragedy.

He wrote the four-act play while he was bedridden. Early in 1896, the doctors ordered complete bed rest. At home in San Remo, Alfred followed his habitual practice of wrapping wet towels around his head, lying in bed, reading or writing when he was well enough to do so. He did not put down his pen until he had finished in March 1896. Finally, he had succeeded in completing a literary project. Everything else he had written as an adult had been drafts. Up until then most of what he had written had been poetry.

To Bertha he writes: "Because I haven't had the opportunity to take part in more serious activities during my illness, I have written a tragedy." [379] She, with her former experience from the stage and love for the theatre, responds with immediate enthusiasm: "Beatrice Cenci? The subject is dramatic. I am very excited." Her letter is bubbling over with curiosity: How many acts had Alfred written? Just one? (Alfred had in his modesty written a "tiny" play). Where was he planning to stage it? At the Burgtheater in Vienna, they might be interested in a new Scandinavian drama. "I am almost sure to have it accepted by a theatre in Vienna: the directors there have several times asked me to give them a drama – they think that my name on the poster will arouse people's curiosity even as a translator," she continues, apparently seeing herself in the role as the play's translator. She asks him to send her a copy of the manuscript. She even has suggestions for which actresses could play the main character. [380] The letter is full of ideas from the professional writer to the amateur. First and foremost, she supports the project: "I am sure that it's well written; I haven't forgotten the beauty and zeal of the verses you showed me in Paris." [381]

Had Bertha known the contents of his tragedy, she might have been more guarded in her enthusiasm. *Nemesis* was something quite different from the vulnerable and melodious verses he had shown her when they first met in Paris.

Vengeance

In Greek mythology, *Nemesis* is the goddess of divine retribution against those who succumb to *hubris* (arrogance before the gods). Individuals who rise too high are knocked down and conceit is punished. The theme of revenge is also prominent in Nobel's drama, which was based on a story from reality: The tragic fate of the young Italian noblewoman Beatrice Cenci (1577–1599), who was abused by her tyrannical father, Francesco Cenci, and executed when she sought vengeance. According to the legend, her wandering ghost appears every year on the date of her beheading, on the bridge to Castel Sant'Angelo in Rome, carrying her decapitated head.

Many authors have been concerned with her fate. In 1819, Percy Bysshe Shelley produced a moving description of Beatrice's fate in the five-act drama in verse, *Cenci*. [382] Had Alfred been influenced by the drama of one of his favorite poets? Regardless, he treats the subject "completely different than Shelley," he writes to Bertha, so it will "hardly shock a rigorous public". [383] In his next letter to her, he emphasizes that "the most offensive scenes have been toned down as the old Cenci begins by explaining to Beatrice that she in reality is not his daughter." [384]

Although Alfred had made the play somewhat less offensive by removing the incest theme, his version was nevertheless just as brutal as Shelley's. Already during the opening scene, the reader understands where it is heading: The 18-year old Beatrice is tricked by her stepfather, Count Cenci, to drink a "love potion" made by a witch following a recipe from the stepfather. The drink makes her wild with longing and an easy prey for the Count. They have intercourse, and when the innocent girl awakens, she is transformed into "a murderous angel with black wings". Possessed by the desire for revenge, she runs to the priest Guerra and offers him her body if he will torture and kill her stepfather. Guerra concedes. The play ends with the assassins burying her stepfather alive. Thus, Beatrice gets her revenge.

Alfred was approaching the end of his life when he wrote *Nemesis*. Why did he write it? Nobel's motives for writing the play may be complex and have been the subject to thorough analysis. [385] Was it an expression of feelings of being exploited, a desire to avenge himself on those who had sought to take advantage of him financially? Or regrets for his relationship with Sofie Hess, which he in many ways felt to be unworthy? Or a punishment for inventing the world's strongest explosive and making himself rich on an invention which also led to lives being lost?

Some have read the play as a critique of capitalist society. Others hold that Nobel wasn't too serious about the theme – he was just trying to learn to master the drama form. [386] There are dozens of possible interpretations, but about one thing there is little doubt: the play's universe is full of suffering. *Nemesis'* star-studded heavens are "inhabited by millions of worlds, where human beings, not different from our kind, sin and are punished, suffer and sigh." [387]

Some of its form and content, like the surrealistic and dreamlike scenes, give associations to August Strindberg's expressionistic *A Dream Play (Ett drömspel, 1901)*, which also has sin and suffering as themes, although Nobel's rape drama is darker than Strindberg's child of pain. He had read several of his compatriot's works, and may have been influenced by his dark melancholy. The two Swedes were living in Paris at the same time but there is little indication that they ever met. [388]

Several Nobel biographers have pointed out that, formally speaking, *Nemesis* is one of the weakest things Nobel had written and that the characters are one-dimensional. [389] All copies of the play, apart from three, were maculated after his death by his family. Most likely due to fear that the public image of the inventor would suffer from its publication.

Controversial

In the spring of 1896, Alfred and Bertha continue their dialogue about *Nemesis*. He takes her suggestion to stage it in Vienna seriously. In his next letter, he tells her about the challenges he envisions about staging it. [390] Would one take the risk in the Catholic Austria of staging a play that criticizes the clergy? In the play, men of science are lauded, such as Giordano Bruno, Galileo Galilei and Leonardo da Vinci. Perhaps he thought that the play's critique of the church's abuse of power would appeal to the anti-clerical champion of peace.

He also lets her know that the play is written in Swedish, pointing out that "somebody must translate it into German." [391] "In Swedish? I thought you had written it in French..." was Bertha's immediate response in a brief letter only a week later. [392] One can detect a touch of disappointment – if the play was in Swedish, naturally she wouldn't be able to translate it. Was Alfred hoping that she would find a Swedish-German translator for his play?

This was the last time the play is mentioned in their letters. It seems as if the project became too complicated. The plans for a collaboration on a staging evaporated.

Perhaps it was just as well that Bertha never had the chance to read the manuscript. The brutal ingredients of the play would hardly have been to the taste of the humanitarian optimist, who previously had let him know she thought that August Strindberg's *The Defense of a Fool* was "hideous". [393] *Nemesis* was even darker than Strindberg's disillusioned wedding drama. However, she knew him well enough to know that he struggled with the darker forces inside himself. A few weeks later, she wrote to him: "Oh, how you detest human beings! And still there are so many who are *good* and it is for *their* sake that one must change the world because the future belongs to them." (Bertha's emphasis) [394]

Illness and publication problems

She continues to inspire Alfred and tempt him to get more involved in the worthy cause. The same year (1896), she tries to get him to join her on what she describes as a "tour for peace":

> Travel with me, either to Berlin, or to Paris - where I can hold conferences and speak to people in positions of power – and you will see, as Dunant has succeeded in uniting a conference in Geneva where all of the powers attended - we will succeed in assembling a diplomatic conference for pacification and disarmament and an institution for an international court of arbitration. [395]

However, Alfred was far from being in any condition to travel anywhere. Over the next few months, he fell gravely ill. This time it was his heart. In the fall of 1896, he went to see a famous heart specialist in Paris. A letter he wrote shows that the man who had spent his entire life working with the explosive nitroglycerine retained his gallows humor also during this period of his life:

> Because of my heart problems I must stay in Paris for a few more days, until the doctors I am consulting, manage to clarify how I am to be treated. It may sound a bit ironic that it is being recommended that I ingest nitroglycerine. [396] They call it

'trinktin' so as not to frighten away the apothecaries and customers. [397]

Alfred had completed his will. He had also written a final, reconciliatory letter to Sofie Hess, where he recommends that she marry the Captain von Kapivar. [398]

He still had something left undone: *Nemesis*, would he be able to find someone to read the play and publish it, maybe even help him stage it? The contact with Bertha had led nowhere. In the summer of 1896, Alfred sends the manuscript to Josefina Weggergrund, a Swedish author and editor, whose daughter was married to his nephew Ludvig. But Josefine disappoints him – she does not comment on the contents of the play, she just corrects his spelling! [399] Was there really no one who was educated and sensitive enough and could read and comment upon *Nemesis?* Nobel's third attempt was the Norwegian Ragnhild Strøm, married to his assistant Ragnar Sohlman. Could she read the drama and perhaps translate it into Norwegian for him? The young engineer Sohlman was surprised about this inquiry to his wife. [400] But neither this attempt succeeded. For reasons unknown, Ragnhild Strøm did not read the play.

During his stay in Paris in the fall of 1896, the sick and run-down Alfred decided to go for the simplest solution – to have the play typed out by a young office assistant and to publish it in Swedish. [401] But he needed someone to proofread it before it went to press!

He contacts the young Swedish priest Nathan Söderblom, who was a pastor in the Swedish church in Paris. [402] The liberal minister had already met Alfred – who had a reputation of being a benefactor among the Swedes in Paris. Now the wealthy businessman asks the poor pastor for a favor: It was a matter of a recently written work. It would be delivered for typesetting at a reputable printer in Paris. Did the pastor know a Swede who could proofread it?

"Well now," the pastor replied, "my wife."

So, finally, Alfred had someone read and comment upon his text:

Anna Söderblom, a pastor's wife!

The sources say nothing about what she thought of Alfred's brutal tragedy. But at last he managed to deliver his *Nemesis* to the printers on November 7, 1896, only a few weeks before he passed away. [403]

The last compliment

A few months have passed since Bertha had heard from him. In a letter written in November 1896, she asks if he is well. Or is it that he is no longer interested in her "life's work?" She wishes so much that he begins to *believe* in the cause! "Nobody can force love. Oh, I would like so much to bring out your love - not for my insignificant person, but for the great cause I am serving and which is so worthy of your enthusiasm. You, who are so fond of the progressive ideas for social advancement!" she continues. [404]

There was no reason to worry. Alfred had long since included a prize for the cause in his will. And in his last letter to Bertha, written from Paris on November 21, 1896, where he was consulting with doctors for his heart problems, he gave her his unconditional recognition, in tune with his usual sense of irony:

Chère Baronne et amie, 'am I well' – no, unfortunately, I am not; I am still consulting with doctors... I, who possess no heart in the figurative sense, I own one in the physiological sense, and I feel it as well. But enough about me and my small miseries. I am delighted to see that the peace movement is winning ground. It is due to the civilization of the masses and particularly the opponents of prejudices and darkness (*'chasse-préjugés et chasse-ténèbres'*), among which you hold a high rank. That is your noble title (*'Ce sont vos titres de noblesse'*). Heartily yours, Alfred Nobel. [405]

Bertha, who in her youth wasn't accepted into the high nobility's circles because she was lacking the right number of ancestors with blue blood, was now "ennobled" by her Swedish benefactor. A "noble title" given for her commitment and efforts, a title she had not been born to, but had achieved through her own work and belief in "the possibility and the necessity of the battle for peace." [406]

Alfred's last letter to Bertha was signed less than three weeks before he passed away in his home in San Remo on December 10, 1896, alone, but for the company of two servants.

Chapter 9

"And the winner is..." - First female prize recipient

A disputed will

Several thousand people lined the streets when Alfred Nobel was followed to his final resting place in Stockholm on December 30, 1896. Many compatriots wanted to pay their last respects to the great inventor and entrepreneur, who lived the life of a recluse. The funeral procession included forty carriages, four of them full of funeral wreaths. The ceremony was held in the oldest church in Stockholm, Storkyrkan (Stockholm Cathedral), and was led by Nobel's friend, Pastor Nathan Söderblom. [407] Nobel was interred in Nya Kyrkogården, today the Norra begravningsplatsen - a major cemetery of Metropolitan Stockholm. He was cremated according to his own wish.

After his death, several weeks passed before the contents of his will were made public. In January 1897, the newspapers announced that Alfred Nobel had left more than 35 million crowns to recipients other than his family. Nobel's will, written in his own hand, became the subject of a lot of attention on the part of both the Swedish and foreign press. The Swedish King Oscar II was particularly worried that the money should disappear from the country, as Alfred had written that the prizes were to be awarded irrespective of nationality.

There were several further complications. The king was unpleasantly surprised about Nobel's decision that the peace prize was to be awarded "by a committee of five people, to be appointed by the Norwegian parliament." He thought the inventor had been "unpatriotic". At the time, the relations between Norway and Sweden were tense. In addition, King Oscar feared that the Norwegian parliament would use the prize money for anti-Swedish ends! Members of the Swedish government were also concerned that the issue would serve to fuel greater friction between the two countries.

The peace prize was the only prize that would not be handed out by Sweden. Why did Nobel choose Norway for this honor? He does not explain this. Perhaps Nobel thought it was reasonable that Norway, still in union with Sweden, also should have the honor of awarding one prize. As a nation of little significance in terms of foreign policy, Norway was to a greater extent neutral. Maybe he also had been influenced by Bjørnstjerne Bjørnson, the Norwegian champion of the peace cause, whom he admired? Norwegian parliamentarians had shown an interest in international mediation and arbitration issues, and had become quite active in the work of the Inter-Parliamentary Union. [408] This might also have influenced Nobel to want to acknowledge the Norwegians as compared with the politically more aggressive Swedes.

Otherwise, the will was vague on details, with little specific information on how the prizes were to be awarded. The implementation of it caused many controversies and considerable headaches, especially as Nobel did not use a lawyer. Some of his relatives were reluctant to see the money go out of the family. The heirs of Alfred's brother Robert Nobel decided to file a suit to contest the will. [409]

In the end, Nobel's wishes were realized. This was largely thanks to the efforts of the executors Ragnar Sohlman and Rudolf Lilljequist, another of his engineers, as well as his nephew, Emanuel Nobel. They were all committed to making Nobel's will come true. With time they overcame the obstacles, and the execution of the will could commence. In 1897, the Norwegian Nobel Committee was established. [410] It took another three years before the basic rules for the Nobel foundation, which administers the fund, were adopted on June 29, 1900.

The year after, in 1901, the first Nobel prizes were handed out.

Grand expectations

Bertha followed the process with excitement. When she learned about the wording of the will in January 1897, she wrote happily in her diary that a prize "shall be awarded to those who have done the most for the peace cause. I am incredibly happy about this recognition of and support for the cause...everyone in the building is congratulating me. Did not sleep much due to excitement!" [411]

Three days later, she proudly wrote to her colleague Arthur Hermann Fried: "The Nobel Foundation? Well, I think it is grand, grand, and am all the prouder because *I* was the one who introduced Nobel to the movement and suggested that he do something important for it..." [412]

As work for disarmament and peace congresses were specifically mentioned in the will, many believed that Bertha would receive the peace prize as one of the first recipients. When she walked in the streets of Vienna, people would stop to congratulate her. In a letter to Carneri, she wrote: "I know very well that Nobel who was my friend *wanted* to give me the prize. If he had only made it simpler and clearer." [413]

However, as it took some time before the execution of the will was carried out, Bertha soon got other things on her mind. In August of 1898, the Russian Czar Nicholas II stirred up a lot of attention when he presented his peace manifesto, where he, among other things, expressed that he saw it as his duty to "stop these never-ending armaments, and to search for means to stop the evil that threatens the entire world." [414] Bertha placed hope in the young czar, and found his peace manifesto "the most splendid peace document that was ever issued... a new page of history was turned." [415] Sadly, the "Czar of Peace" would soon disappoint when he began to practice a violent and authoritarian policy in the conflict with Finland, which was escalating in 1899.

Of more lasting importance was the First Hague Peace

Conference the same year, in fact convened on the initiative of the Czar. The leaders of 59 of the world's sovereign States were represented and peace activists from all over Europe, the United States, Mexico, China and Japan streamed into The Hague from May 18 to June 29. One of the major results of the conference was to establish the Permanent Court of Arbitration – the world's leading body for the resolution of international disputes by arbitration. [416]

It was only with difficulty that Bertha made it to the conference: After writing three letters she finally managed to convince Theodor Herzl, the feature editor of the *Neue Freie Presse*, to pay for her travel and accommodation when he commissioned her to write for his new paper *Die Welt*. She was one of the most active pacifists behind the scenes, doing the press and information work. [417] Her diary about her experiences during her stay reveals that she was very disappointed with the involvement of the press.

To get funding was always a challenge, and receiving the Nobel prize would make her work so much easier. However, in 1901, the Nobel committee decided that the first peace prize should be shared between Henry Dunant, the founder of the Red Cross and the Frenchman Frédéric Passy, who among other things took part in founding the Inter-Parliamentary Union. Bertha was disappointed, although she supported and respected the work of the winners, especially Dunant, who had become a friend of hers.

Death of Arthur

The year after, her disappointment would pale in the shadow of an even greater loss: On December 10, 1902 (coincidentally the same date as the death of Alfred Nobel), her beloved Arthur died in his sleep, after a period of illness. His health had deteriorated in the last few years. The cause of death was probably tuberculosis, due to an infection that Bertha believed he contracted during their stay in Georgia. Her husband lived to be only 52 years old.

Bertha was devastated. The notes in her diary from the following months are incoherent. Her sole consolation and encouragement during this time was a loving letter that Arthur had left her: "Thank you. You have made me so happy. There have never been any bad feelings between us ...We have both done what we could to move the world forward. Keep your chin up! Don't lose hope! You must continue your work for peace as long as your allotted time on this earth lasts!" These were her beloved husband's final words to her. [418]

"And despite everything: his love for me was faithful to the end. 'Boulotte' he called out while he was dying – and not "Marie Louise". That should be a consolation and a satisfaction to me," she wrote in her diary after sitting by Arthur's deathbed. [419]

The widow tried to continue her work, but had a tough time at it. To distract herself, she accepted an invitation from Prince Albert of Monaco to open a peace institute in Monte Carlo. There she spent some free time in the beautiful garden in warm, luxurious surroundings: "There is an abundance of beauty here. Whether it stills all longing?? Oh no – you must be *two* to enjoy the beauty, and my second me is now ashes," she wrote in her diary and added: "The only thing that matters, which really makes a person happy, is love. Only love, love alone." [420]

The baroness would wear a mourning veil for the rest of her life. In 1902, the Harmannsdorf estate was auctioned because of over-indebtedness and she eventually moved into a new apartment near the Ring, at Zedlitzgasse 7, Vienna. In her study, directly behind her desk, hung a gigantic portrait of Arthur, decorated with palms and white roses, almost like an altar.

After her husband's death, it was only her work that she lived and breathed for. Bertha now had one aim in life: "Not to be an old pensioner in the village. Have something to say in the world." [421] She worked hard, and continued to write articles, give lectures and recruit people to peace work. For the opening of the Inter-Parliamentary Union's conference in Vienna in 1903, the 60-year-old lady wrote a 25-page article during a single day. She drew a lot of support from her pacifist friends, not least from Alfred Hermann Fried, who had become an important ally for her.

Did it lift her spirits somewhat during this challenging time to know that she had been named the most important woman of the era by the *Berliner Tageblatt*? In a reader's survey printed in the paper in May 1903, Bertha was at the top of the list, ahead of both Carmen Sylva and Sarah Bernhardt. The results were as follows:

Bertha von Suttner – 156 votes
Carmen Sylva – 142 votes
Sarah Bernhardt – 139 votes
Eleonora Duse – 132 votes
Marie von Ebner-Eschenbach – 71 votes. [422]

A test of patience

The years passed by without the Nobel Committee deciding to honor the now famous Austrian peace champion. The second peace prize (1902) was shared by Élie Ducommun, president of The International Peace Bureau in Bern and Charles Albert Godat, leader of The Inter-Parliamentary Bureau in the same city. In 1903, the third peace prize went to William Randal Cremer, who among other things had been the initiator behind the establishment of the Inter-Parliamentary Union. Bertha was disappointed, although she supported and respected several of the candidates. However, her disappointment was mitigated by pacifists all over Europe who now went out and publicly supported her candidacy. They were beginning to view her as an unjustly treated victim of the Norwegian Nobel Committee.

In 1904, the Institute of International Law, an amalgamation of experts on international law founded in Belgium in 1873, received the peace prize, among other things for its work in promoting international arbitration. Then, unexpectedly, a helping hand came from the north when Bjørnstjerne Bjørnson intervened. That same year, the national poet wrote a long statement in support of Bertha von Suttner which was printed in *Berliner Tageblatt*. [423] Here he went as far as to threaten to withdraw from the Nobel Committee, where he was a member, if the Austrian peace activist was not awarded the prize. He also sent a formal letter to the Committee with the same message. [424] Nobel's nephew Emmanuel also publicly declared his support for Bertha, stating among other things, that his uncle had said to him, after having read one of her letters: "I want to do something great for Bertha von Suttner and the peace cause." Subsequently, Emmanuel offered to pay her expenses for a trip to the USA, where she was invited to the peace congress in Boston in 1904.

Bertha decided to go, and the trip was an enormous success. The peace activist travelled across the USA and held lectures, spoke in churches and at schools, for filled-to-capacity auditoriums. Her optimistic attitude hit home with the Americans, who were wildly enthusiastic about her. For them she represented the old Europe. With her striking appearance and dignified attitude, she created an impression of royalty. As Fried observed: "If there were a throne behind her, one would not hesitate for a second in believing that she was a queen." [425] About her trip, she wrote in her diary: "It seems as if I am more well-known there than in Vienna." [426]

The USA now became for her the great hope for the peace movement. She felt that the American citizens had a special role to play in promoting peace. One of the highlights was a meeting with President Roosevelt in the White House on October 7. Roosevelt was optimistic about the peace movement and said to her: "Believe me, world peace will come because it must come, but it will come step by step." [427] During her visit, she also met newspaper king Joseph Pulitzer, whose paper, *The World*, supported the peace movement, and Carl Schurz.

Back in Europe, the baroness continued writing and talking about peace. She went on a long lecture tour through Germany in the autumn of 1905, receiving applause everywhere. While she was staying in Wiesbaden, she finally received the long yearned-for telegram from Christiania: the year's Nobel peace prize was hers.

"A sleepless night − strange: instead of joy, it is also accompanied by sorrow. But it is still wonderful," she wrote in her diary. [428]

Christiania, April 1906

In April 1906, Bertha travelled to Christiania to receive the prize, as she had been ill in December of the preceding year. The award ceremony took place in the Hals Brothers Concert Hall, because the crowd that was expected would be too numerous for the recently opened Nobel Institute.

A gasp went through the packed auditorium when Bjørnstjerne Bjørnson led her in. The baroness was dressed in an elegant black suit and the veil of mourning she had worn since her husband's death. King Haakon VII, the first king of Norway after the 1905 dissolution of the union with Sweden, sat in the first row. Her acceptance speech was entitled: "On the evolution of the peace movement". [429] Bertha had the audience in the palm of her hand from the first instant. When she spoke, she spoke slowly and softly. In her speech, she gave Alfred Nobel full recognition for the significance of his role in the work of the peace movement. She wisely avoided touching upon the recent dissolution of the union between Sweden and Norway, but she did comment upon one thing – she said that it was not a coincidence that Nobel had chosen the Norwegian Parliament to be responsible for the peace prize. The session concluded with thunderous applause.

The next few days the 62-year-old's schedule was tight. Already the day after, she had an audience with the king. Another highlight was a great women's festivity in honor of the first woman to win the prize. There was a choir singing to her honor, a ladies' orchestra, peace hymns, long poems, and congratulatory speeches – one ovation after the other. Subsequently, there was a dinner with the prime minister, with music and joint singing. "These Norwegians – how they can sing" she wrote enthusiastically to Fried, "one would never experience something like it in Central Europe!" [430]

After her visit in Christiania, the prize winner travelled to Sweden where she gave lectures in Stockholm, Göteborg and Uppsala with a huge press corps on her heels. Many women's associations organized receptions in her honor. Then she went to Copenhagen, where she had an audience with the Danish royal couple. There were banquets, bouquets of flowers, congratulatory speeches...Everywhere she went, tribute was paid to her.

When Bertha returned to Vienna, she was strengthened by the recognition the prize had brought her.

Epilogue

A guiding star

World peace did not come in the year 1900, as Bertha and the most optimistic members of the peace movement had hoped for. Instead, in 1914, "the lights were turned off", as the English foreign minister Edward Grey expressed it when the First World War broke out.

The first female Nobel prize winner continued her peace-work vigorously until the end of her life. She also participated in the Second Hague Peace Conference of 1907, where she contributed to the public debate in the (so-called) "Courrier de la Conférence de la Paix". The journal, edited by the British journalist William Stead, dealt exclusively with the events of the peace conference.

Her last major effort was in 1912, when she once again went on an extensive lecture-tour to the USA, speaking in front of over 20 000 people in total. In a letter to Fried, the 69-year-old called the seven-month tour "a last crusade for the cause". [431] Bertha spoke in churches, schools and big lecture halls to packed audiences. She was especially celebrated by the American women's clubs. As usual, the trip was a success. While travelling, she continued to write her political reviews for the *Friedenswarte*. At the end of her tour, she met Andrew Carnegie, who afterwards wrote her a letter, promising her a pension for the rest of her life.

Back in Europe, she despaired over the development she witnessed during the final years of her life and tried to warn against it. In the spring of 1913, she ran into the young Austrian author Stefan Zweig on the street in Vienna. Zweig belonged to the young generation of Viennese authors who had only a limited interest in the political development. A new poem from the author

Rainer Maria Rilke or a Burgtheater premiere was far more interesting than any political event. "Why don't you young people do something?" the baroness cried, according to Zweig, "it concerns you most of all! Fight back, get together! Don't always leave everything to a few old women nobody listens to."

Not until it was too late, did Zweig take her warning seriously. A few years later, he wrote regretfully in a letter to a friend: "I believe, like yourself that this war could have been prevented, and that the *only* reason that this didn't happen is that we did not fight hard enough against it while there was still time. Sometimes I can see the good Bertha von Suttner in front of me, and she is saying, the way she did: 'I know that you see me as a fool, I pray to God that you are right.'" [432]

In August of 1913, the baroness spoke at the International Peace Congress at The Hague where she was greatly honored as the "generalissimo" of the peace movement. Despite her declining health, Bertha continued to work hard during the last year of her life.

The peace champion was spared having to experience war breaking out. After a period of illness, Bertha von Suttner died in her sleep at home in Vienna on June 21, 1914, just one week before the Austrian-Hungarian heir to the throne Franz Ferdinand was shot and killed in Sarajevo. [433] She was 71 years old.

Were her efforts then in vain? No. In the aftermath of the First World War, a lot of the work commenced by Bertha and her colleagues was carried on. Several heads of state and politicians were inspired by the early peace movement's work. President Woodrow Wilson was influenced by the movement in developing his proposal for the League of Nations. The Inter-Parliamentary Union continued to meet after the war. Many of the members later worked actively as their respective countries' representatives to the League of Nations. In the work for disarmament, people were still inspired by the early peace movement's work. The Permanent Court of Arbitration in The Hague, established in 1899, was involved in many cases after 1914.

In particular, Bertha von Suttner's novel *Lay Down Your Arms!*

continued and still continues to be a source of inspiration. A book permeated with the author's belief that change is possible if one believes in it and fights for it.

And every year, on December 10, we witness what is perhaps the most visible result of Bertha's influence when the Nobel Peace Prize is awarded.

Towards the end of her life, Bertha would think back to the time when she answered Alfred's advert as one of the countless times she did something she "shouldn't", according to the customs of the time. Later, when a journalist pointed this out to her, her comment was: "Oh well. One shouldn't answer adverts – that is a rule. But all the same - what if I hadn't answered Nobel's advert?" [434]

Would the Nobel peace prize have existed if Bertha had not responded to the job vacancy advert from a strange gentleman in Paris in 1875? It is impossible to know for certain, but it is most likely the prize would have been very different. The correspondence between Alfred and Bertha documents how she influenced him to respect the work of the peace congresses and disarmament work, and subsequently he included these criteria in his will. The consequence is that annually, we witness an award ceremony that may offer courage and inspiration to people all over the world. As Bertha expressed it:

In this way, a guiding star will remain in the sky. Time after time and year after year, the clouds that cover it will be chased away. The name of the star is human happiness. And yes, this happiness will and must arrive. And after his death, Alfred Nobel is guiding our eyes towards this star, so we can say to future generations: be noble, and you will find happiness. [435]

A chronology

1833 October 21. Alfred Bernhard Nobel is born at Norrlandsgatan 9, a townhouse located in an outlying district of Stockholm. He is the third child of Immanuel and Andriette (née Ahlsell) Nobel. The same year Immanuel goes bankrupt.

1842 The family moves to St. Petersburg. Immanuel Nobel relocates to build up a machine shop which supplies among other things land mines for the Russian government.

1843 June 9. Bertha Sophia Felicita, born Countess Kinsky von Chinic und Tettau, is born in Prague. Her 75-year old father, Field Marshal Franz Joseph von Kinsky, dies before she is born. Her 25-year old mother, Sophie, moves with Bertha and her brother Arthur to their guardian Friederich Fürstenberg in Brno, Moravia.

1850 17 years of age, Alfred Nobel goes abroad for studies in the USA, France, Italy and Germany. In Paris, he meets the famous chemist Th. J. Pelouze, who introduces him to the explosive nitro-glycerine.

1856 Immanuel Nobel's machine shop in St. Petersburg goes bankrupt after the Crimean War. He moves back to Stockholm with Andriette. Alfred and his brothers stay behind in St. Petersburg and continue experimenting with explosive oils.

1859 The war between Austria - Italy. The Battle of Solferino with its horrendous human losses.

1861 18 years of age, Bertha attends her debut ball which is a fiasco. Afterwards, she is engaged to the 52-year old baron Gustav Heine-Gelnern, but soon after she breaks the engagement.

1863 Alfred moves back to Stockholm and continues the experiments with nitro-glycerine. The same year he produces a promising mixture of black powder which he markets as blasting oil. This is the first of his 355 patents.

1864 The war between Austria - Prussia and Denmark. Bertha meets Ekaterina Dadiani, Princess of Mingrelia, at the Hoburg v.d. Höhe spa. Alfred's youngest brother Emil dies in an explosion accident in their laboratory.

1865 Alfred moves to Germany and starts a dynamite factory in Krümmel outside of Hamburg. Bertha begins to study singing at Gilbert-Louis Duprez's singing academy in Paris.

1866 The war between Austria and Prussia. Alfred travels to the USA and starts the US Blasting Company.

1867 Alfred works to improve the safety of the blasting oil. He mixes nitro-glycerine and kieselguhr, a light porous clay-like earth type, designs the dough for the sticks, develops a detonator and gives the invention the name *dynamite* (Greek for "power"). The same year he receives the patent for the formula.

1870 The French-German war.

1873 30 years of age, Bertha accepts a position as governess with the family of Baron Karl Gundaccar von Suttners. Here she falls in love with the family's youngest son, Arthur. At the age of 40, Alfred buys a house on the Avenue Malakoff in Paris.

1875 Alfred invents the blasting gelatin, or gelignite, for which he receives a patent the following year. Bertha replies to Alfred's advert for a secretary and travels to Paris. One week later she returns to Vienna and her fiancé Baron Arthur Gundaccar von Suttner.

1876 Alfred meets Sofie Hess, with whom he initiates a romantic relationship. Bertha and Arthur marry and move to the province of Mingrelia in Georgia and settle near Ekaterina Dadiani. The same year, Alfred's brother Robert starts an oil business in the Baku region.

1880 Alfred establishes Dynamite Nobel by merging the Italian and Swiss companies. Sofie Hess moves to Paris and settles down near Alfred. In Georgia, Bertha and Arthur begin to write articles for German and Austrian newspapers.

1883 Bertha's first book, *A Soul's Inventory,* is published.

1885 Bertha and Arthur return to Austria as established writers. They move into the von Suttner's family estate, Harmannsdorf, close to the village of Eggenburg.

1886 Bertha writes *The Machine Age.* The same year, she travels to Paris with Arthur. Alfred Nobel introduces them in the salon of Madame Juliette Adam. Bertha learns about The International Arbitration and Peace Association, founded in London by Hodgson Pratt. Alfred establishes the Nobel-Dynamite Trust Co (London, UK).

1889 Bertha completes the anti-war novel *Lay Down Your Arms!*, which is published that same year. The book becomes an immediate success. The same year the first universal peace congress is held.

1890 Alfred sells his invention ballistite to the Italians and moves to San Remo.

1891 Alfred Nobel breaks off his relationship with Sofie Hess when she becomes pregnant with someone else. Subsequently, he moves from Paris to San Remo. Bertha and her Austrian peace society take part in the peace congress in Rome. Bertha becomes first female member of the Inter-Parliamentary Union.

1892 Alfred and Bertha meet for the third time in Bern during the annual international peace congress. The same year, Bertha starts the peace magazine *Lay Down Your Arms!* together with Alfred Hermann Fried.

1893 Alfred writes the first draft of his will.

1894 Alfred invests in a weapon factory in Bofors and buys the estate Björkborn in Karlskoga, Sweden.

1895 Alfred writes the final draft of his will, which includes a prize for the one who "has worked the most for fraternity between nations, for the abolition or reduction of standing armies and for the holding and promotion of peace congresses."

1896 Alfred writes the tragedy *Nemesis.* On December 10, he passes away in San Remo.

1898 Nobel's will is made public and draws a great deal of attention. Because of a lawsuit from certain members of his family, it takes some time before it is approved.

1899 The First Hague Peace Conference takes place in June and leads to the establishment of The Permanent Court of Arbitration.

1900 The Nobel Foundation is established.

1901 The first Nobel Peace Prize is awarded by the Norwegian parliament to Henry Dunant, founder of the Red Cross and Frédéric Passy, who took part in laying the foundation for the Inter-Parliamentary Union.

1902 The second Peace Prize is awarded to Élie Ducommun, president of the International Peace Bureau in Bern and Charles Albert Godat, head of the Inter-Parliamentary Bureau in the same city. Arthur von Suttner passes away.

1903 The third Peace Prize goes to William Randal Cremer, the founder of the Inter-Parliamentary Union. Pacifists all over Europe are upset that Bertha von Suttner has not received the prize yet.

1904 The Institute of International Law receives the Peace Prize for its work in promoting international arbitration. Bjørnstjerne Bjørnson writes to the Nobel Committee and threatens to withdraw if Bertha is not awarded the peace prize soon. She travels to the USA on an extensive lecture tour.

1905 June 7. The Norwegian Parliament declares secession from Sweden. The president of the parliament, Jørgen Løvland, opens the Nobel Institute. Bertha finally receives the Peace Prize, but is unable to travel to Norway that year.

1906 Bertha travels to Christiania in April to accept the peace prize. Bjørnstjerne Bjørnson presents the first female recipient of the prize.

1914 Bertha continues her peace work until the end of her life. On June 21, a week before the two gunshots in Sarajevo, she dies in her home in Vienna.

Notes

[1] Palmowski, Jan (1997, 2003, 2004). *A Dictionary of Contemporary World History. From 1900 to the present day.* Oxford University Press, p. 472: "The Nobel Peace Prize. The world's most prestigious prize, awarded for the 'preservation of peace'."

[2] Hamann, Brigitte (1996). *Bertha von Suttner. A life for Peace.* Originally: Hamann, Brigitte (1986): *Bertha von Suttner. Ein Leben für den Frieden.* Syracuse, NY og München.

[3] Suttner, Bertha von (1910). *Memoirs of Bertha von Suttner: The Records of an Eventful Life.* Boston, Ginn.

[4] The originals of this unique source material are to be found either in the private Alfred Nobel archive, kept in the Swedish National Archive (Stockholm), or in the Bertha von Suttner collection in the library of the United Nations (Geneva). They are complementary as a combined sequence, but neither series is complete.

[5] Biedermann, Edelgard (2001). *Chère Baronne et Amie - Cher monsieur et ami. Der Briefwechsel zwischen Alfred Nobel und Bertha von Suttner.* All quotations from these letters have been translated by me from the original, unless otherwise stated.

[6] According to Lee Gutkind, American writer and the founder of the literary magazine *Creative Nonfiction*, creative non-fiction is simply "true stories well told". Barbara Lounsberry, American writer and Professor in English, lists four constitutive characteristics of the genre:
1. Documentable subject matter from the real world.
2. Exhaustive research to establish the credibility of the narrative.
3. "The Scene" (describing and revivifying the context of events).
4. Fine writing: a literary prose style.

[7] Biedermann, Edelgard (2001). *Chère Baronne et amie - Cher monsieur et ami. Der Briefwechsel zwischen Alfred Nobel und Bertha von Suttner.* Georg Olms Verlag, Hildesheim, p. 75 ff.

[8] Suttner, Bertha von (1910). *Memoirs of Bertha von Suttner: The Records of an Eventful Life.* Authorized translation [of the *Memoiren*]. 2 vols. Boston, Ginn, p. 205.

[9] Alfred Nobel in a letter to Miss Sophie Ahlström, who applied for his secretarial post in 1895. Pauli, Hertha (1957). *Cry of the heart. The story of Bertha von Suttner.* New York, Ives Washburn, p. 148.

[10] *Sou:* One of several coins formerly used in France, worth a small amount.

[11] Fant, Kenne (1991). *Alfred Bernhard Nobel.* Nordstedts, Stockholm, p. 134.

[12] Sohlman, Ragnar (1983). *Ett testamente. Hur Alfred Nobels dröm blev virkelighet.* Stockholm, Atlantis, p. 81.

[13] Letter from Ludvig Nobel to Alfred, Dec. 24, 1875. Biedermann (2001), p. 212.

[14] *Bildung* refers to the German tradition of self-cultivation (as related to the German word for: creation, image, shape), wherein philosophy and education are linked in a manner that refers to a process of both personal and cultural maturation.

[15] Von Suttner (1910), Vol. I, p. 207.

[16] The expression is found in Rundquist, Angela (1989). *Blått Blod och Liljevita Händer, En etnologisk studie av aristokratiska kvinnor 1850-1900*. Stockholm, Carlssons. (Blue Blood and Lily-white Hands. An ethnological study of aristocratic women 1850-1900). The term "blue blood" (*sangre azul*) had Spanish origin: Compared to the Moors, the Visigoth aristocracy had light skin which allowed the veins to show.

[17] Rundquist (1989), p. 197.

[18] The church's name in English is St Mary-of-the-Snows.

[19] Ulrich Kinsky is an example of a well-known Kinsky rebel: He was one of the noblemen who participated in the event which is known as "The defenestration of Prague" in 1618. This historical event was a trigger to the Czech rebellion against the Emperor, and hence to the Thirty Years' War. Read more about this in Hamann, Brigitte (1996). *Bertha von Suttner: A Life for Peace*. Syracuse, NY: Syracuse University Press, p. 1 ff.

[20] See pictures of the Kinsky brothers in Hamann (1996), p. 164.

[21] Immermann, Karl Leberecht (1840). *Düsseldorfer Anfänge, Werk*. Berlin und Stuttgart, Verlag von W. Spemann (1887), p. 127 ff.

[22] Rundquist (1989), p. 197.

[23] Schück H and R. Sohlman (1926). *Alfred Nobel och hans släkt*. Uppsala, Almqvist & Wiksells Boktryckeri AB, p. 238.

[24] Pauli (1957), p. 113.

[25] Inland Revenue record describes Immanuel as "penniless" and his taxable occupation as "artist". Quote from the IR protocols. Fant (1991), p. 22.

[26] Lundin- Strindberg (1882). *Gamla Stockholm*. Stockholm, Seilgmann. Quoted in Fant (1991), p. 29.

[27] Nobel senior writes in a letter to his brother-in-law Ludvig Ahlsell: "My dear, hard-working Alfred is highly thought of by both his parents and his brothers for being knowledgeable as well as an indefatigable worker, none of which can be replaced." Fant (1991), p. 30.

[28] The information about Nobel's library is from Erlandsson, Åke (2002). *Alfred Nobels Bibliotek*. Stockholm, Bokforlaget Atlantis, p. 22 ff.

[29] Erlandsson (2002), p. 117.

[30] A letter from Juliette Drouet, a French actress and Victor Hugo's lover since 1833, urges Alfred to remember that he is a much appreciated guest at their table. The Nobel archive, National Archive, Stockholm.

[31] Some of Bertha's other favorite authors were Sand, Balzac and Dumas and, among the playwrights, Corneille, Racine, Molière and Dumas. During her youth, she also read philosophy, including Kant, Schopenhauer, Strauss, Feuerbach, Pascal and Comte, and took an interest in the natural sciences and history as well. To learn more about her studies as a young woman, see Vol. 1 of her *Memoirs*, p. 57-66.

[32] At the end of his life in 1895, Alfred catalogued his scientific and literary projects. The category "literature and prose" contains 14 works, which include drafts for novels, plays, and most predominantly, poetry. The list demonstrates that even late in his life he had several literary projects in his thoughts. For further reading, see Erlandsson, Åke (2002). *Alfred Nobels bibliotek: en bibliografi*. Stockholm, Atlantis.

[33] Robert Nobel in a letter to his fiancée Pauline from St Petersburg, 4 December 1859. Erlandsson, Åke (ed. 2006). *Dikter/Poems av Alfred Nobel*. Stockholm, Bokförlaget Atlantis, p. 12.

[34] It was customary to divide long narrative poems into cantos, as in Shelley's *The Revolt of Islam* or Byron's *Childe Harold*, and Nobel's heading presumably indicates that

he intended to continue with Canto II, III, etc. Despite its length, it seems the poem was never concluded. Erlandsson (2006), p. 23. The quotes from Nobel's poems *Canto I* and *Ett Fantasiens Offer* in this book are from Erlandsson's work (2006).

[35] Possibly written in the second half of the 1870s. Erlandsson (2006), p. 42.

[36] Alfred in a letter to his brother Robert, 24.11.1868. Erlandsson (2006), p. 17.

[37] C. Lesingham Smith in a letter to Alfred Nobel dated November 1868. Erlandsson (2006), p. 17.

[38] *Paradise Lost*, epic poem by John Milton (1608-1674), first published in 1667. The poem is considered to be Milton's masterpiece and one of the central works of English literature. Themes are the angels' rebellion, creation, the fall from grace and exile from paradise. Milton wrote the poem in blank verse: Unrhymed iambic pentameter.

[39] Erlandsson (2006), p. 89.

[40] Von Suttner (1910), Vol. I, p. 208.

[41] Ibid., p. 207.

[42] The descriptions of her wanderings through Paris are inspired by Cora Sandel's descriptions of the streets of Paris from the beginning of the 1900s in her novel *Alberte og friheten*. Sandel, Cora (1931). *Alberte og friheten*. Oslo, Gyldendal Norsk Forlag.

[43] Bustle – an undergarment worn during the period 1860–1880 which had the effect of causing a woman's skirt to curve outward in an arc just below the small of the back. In its simplest form, the bustle was a small, stuffed cushion, while in more elaborate models it was made of a large frame that could be bent and shaped.

[44] Gustav von Heine-Gelder (1812-1886) was a German-Austrian publisher and founder of the journal *Das Fremdenblatt*.

[45] Rundquist (1989), p. 91.

[46] Von Suttner (1910), Vol. I, p. 209. ff.

[47] Passport description of Alfred Nobel displayed at the Nobel Museum, Stockholm.

[48] Pauli (1957), p. 193. The description belongs to Henry de Mosenthal, a famous British scholar and scientist who met Alfred in 1882. Nobel's later assistant Ragnar Sohlman described his employer as follows: "In his outward appearance, the impression Nobel made was one of nervousness. His movements were lively, his gait lightly tripping, his facial expressions changing, much like his conversation, which was at times peppered with original flights of fancy and spontaneous ideas." Fant, Kenne (1991), p. 12.

[49] Schück H. og Sohlman R. (1926). *Alfred Nobel och hans släkt*. Uppsala, Almqvist & Wiksells Boktryckeri AB, p. 221.

[50] R. L. Schoenwald. *Nineteenth Century Thought: The Discovery of Change* (New Jersey 1965). Quoted in Simensen, Jarle (1986). *Aschehougs verdenshistorie, Vol. 12, Vesten erobrer Verden 1870-1914*. Oslo, Aschehoug.

[51] Von Suttner (1910), Vol. I, p. 124.

[52] Zweig (1949), p. 53.

[53] Von Suttner (1910), Vol. I, p. 125.

[54] *The New York Times*, 4 May 1866. Strandh, Sigvard (1983). *Alfred Nobel. Mannen, Verket, Samtiden*. Stockholm, Natur och Kultur, p. 74.

[55] Brandell et al. (1983), p. 33.

[56] Von Suttner (1910), Vol. I, p. 210 ff.

[57] Ibid., p. 72.

[58] Retrieved from http://nobelprize.org/alfred_nobel/biographical/articles/erlandsson-Alfred Nobel - the Poet. Erlandsson, Åke (1998, May 18). Here one may read the entire poem and Erlendsson's concise presentation of everything Alfred has written in terms of

poetry.

[59] Bergengren (1960), p. 83. Most biographers believe that the Swedish girl worked as an apothecary's apprentice in Paris and that Alfred met her while he was studying with the chemist Pelouze.

[60] Von Suttner (1910), Vol. I, p. 208: "All I could do when I was alone was to cry or write home..."

[61] Fant (1991).

[62] Von Suttner (1910), Vol. I, p. 209.

[63] Ibid., p. 192.

[64] Hamann (1996), p. 19.

[65] Von Suttner (1910), Vol. I, p. 204.

[66] Ibid., p. 197.

[67] Von Suttner (1910), Vol. I, p. 210 ff.

[68] Strandh (1983), p. 151.

[69] Von Suttner (1910), Vol. I., p. 211.

[70] According to the biographer Brigitte Hamann, the couple was not wed in Gumpoldskirchen, but in St. Giles church in Gumpendorf. The event is not very well documented. According to Hamann, Bertha noted the wrong church in her diary, something which might demonstrate how much of a hurry the couple were in to get married, and how little importance she assigned to religion. Hamann (1996), p. 27.

[71] Readers who are interested in learning more about the Dadiani Dynasty may consult the website of The National Parliamentary Library of Georgia: http://dadiani.si.edu/dadianipalace.html#top

[72] Von Suttner (1910), Vol. I, p.105 ff.

[73] Hamann (1996), p. 27.

[74] Von Suttner (1910), Vol. I, p. 218.

[75] Hamsun, Knut (1903). I Æventyrland. Oplevet og drømt i Kaukasien. Oslo, Gyldendal.

[76] The journey is described in its entirety in von Suttner (1910), Vol. I, p. 219 ff.

[77] Von Suttner (1910), Vol. I, p. 219 ff.

[78] Ibid., p. 225.

[79] Von Suttner (1910), Vol. I, p. 258.

[80] Hamsun, Knut (1903). Dronning Tamara. Skuespil i tre Akter. Oslo, Gyldendal.

[81] Von Suttner (1910), Vol. I, p. 228.

[82] Ibid., p. 210 ff.

[83] Only a few years later, after having read Tolstoy's "Christianism and patriotism", Bertha acquired a more balanced view of this historical event. In this work, Tolstoy argues that the so-called "liberation" of the Slavic brothers, was merely a pretext used by the Russians to justify striking back at the Turks. Von Suttner (1910), Vol. I, p. 231.

[84] Von Suttner (1910), Vol. I, p. 72.

[85] Ibid., p. 234.

[86] Ibid., p. 250.

[87] Hamann (1996), p. 34.

[88] Ibid., p. 35.

[89] Tolstoy (1977), p. 16

[90] Hamann (1996), p. 35.

[91] Von Suttner (1910), Vol. I, p. 235 ff.

[92] Quoted in a letter to Irma Troll-Borostyáni, February 20, 1888. Hamann (1996), p. 37.

[93] Bertha in a self-portrait for Neue Illustrierte Zeitung, 07.09.1884. Hamann (1996), p.

40.

[94] Von Suttner (1883). *Inventory of a soul,* p. 119. Quoted in Hamann (1996), p. 41.

[95] Alfred in a letter to Bertha from April 28,1883. Biedermann (2001), p. 76.

[96] Erlandsson, Åke (2006), p. 31.

[97] Erlandsson, Åke (2002), p. 10.

[98] Most biographers (e.g. Sohlman, Fant and Evlanoff) believe that Sofie Hess worked in a flower-shop, but according to Sjöman she worked in a confectionary. Sjöman, Vilgot. (1995). *Mitt hjärtebarn. De länge hemlighållna breven mellan ALFRED NOBEL och hans älskerinna SOFIE HESS.* Stockholm: Natur och Kultur.

[99] My main source for the description of Alfred Nobel's first meeting with Sofie Hess is Evlanoff, Michael and Fluor, Marjorie (1969). *Alfred Nobel: The Loneliest Millionaire.* Los Angeles, W. Ritchie Press. Evlanoff was a friend of Nobel's relatives.

[100] Sjöman (1995), p. 27.

[101] Ibid., p. 185.

[102] Ibid., p. 110.

[103] Erlandsson (2002), p. 38.

[104] George Brandes in a letter to Bertha von Suttner, quoted in Hamann (1996), p. 231.

[105] The poem is available in English to read at this website: http://sacred-texts.com/asia/mps/index.htm

[106] Hamann (1996), p. 45.

[107] Ibid., p. 45.

[108] Von Suttner (1910), Vol. I, p. 276 ff.

[109] The description of the couple's study belongs to their friend Alfred Fried who came to visit. Hamann (1996), p. 47.

[110] Alfred in a letter to Bertha,17.08.1885. Biedermann (2001), p. 77.

[111] Alfred in a letter to Sofie Hess, 20.09.1884. Sohlman (1983), p. 149.

[112] Strandh (1983), p. 226.

[113] Sohlman (1950), p. 111.

[114] Alfred in a letter to Sofie, 27.09.1878. Sohlman (1983), p. 94.

[115] Alfred in a letter to Sofie, 20.09.1884. Sjöman (1995), p. 180.

[116] Meticulously and carefully prepared, "The Troll" is entered as follows in his accounts:
Hats The Troll 300 francs
To The Troll by post 3,000
Gloves The Troll 42 francs and myself 3 70 francs
Housekeeping 3.080 francs, wine bill, The Troll 930 francs
The Troll: sparkling sapphire earrings 3, 000 francs.

[117] "An outfit has been ordered from Moret – in shade a bit lighter than navy blue. But Moret did not have a beautiful collection and I would therefore advise against ordering a lot from him ... At Louvre I purchased an abundance of gloves, veils and scarves that I have sent to Meissl's Hotel in Vienna. It should be there by Wednesday..." Alfred in a letter to Sofie, 20.09.1884. Sohlman, Ragnar (1983): *Ett testamente. Hur Alfred Nobels dröm blev verklighet.* Bokförlaget Atlantis, Stockholm, p. 149. The letters between Alfred and Sofie are collected in Sjöman, Vilgot (1995). *Mitt hjärtebarn. De länge hemlighållna breven mellan Alfred Nobel och hans älskerinna Sofie Hess.* p. 95 ff.

[118] The description of Sofie's flat in Paris is by Ragnar Sohlman, Alfred Nobel's assistant and friend late in his life. Sohlman (1983), p.88

[119] Sjöman (1995), p. 364.

[120] Alfred in a letter to Sofie, 20.09.1884. Sohlman (1983), p. 106.

[121] Alfred in a letter to Bertha, 17. 08.1885. Biedermann (2001), p. 77.

[122] Sohlman (1983), p. 46. "Nivlheim", Norse for *Niflheim*, in Norse mythology, the deepest part of Sheol, the place of the dead.

[123] Hamann (1996), p. 48.

[124] Bertha's emphasis in a letter to Carneri, 05.01.1890. Hamann (1996), p. 48.

[125] Alnæs, Karsten (2005). *Historien om Europa. 1800-1900.* Vol. 3, p. 183.

[126] There was little happiness to be found in the pompous baroque chambers of Hofburg or at the majestic *Lustschloss* Schönbrunn, where the emperor lived. His wife, the beautiful, but morbidly depressed Elisabeth, with whom he had lived in joyless matrimony, was murdered by an anarchist in Geneva. His son, Crown Prince Rudolf, committed suicide. The latter's brother, the Arch Duke Maximilian, was shot and killed in Mexico. Although his family was plagued by accidents and deaths, Franz Joseph was impervious and continued his daily, duty-bound work.

[127] Von Suttner (1888). *Schriftsteller-Roman,* p. 272 ff. in Hamann (1996), p. 49.

[128] "Despite the perfume that shimmered around her, despite the jewels she was loaded down with and the costly laces, flounces and fabrics, this 'lady' now seems to have long since become historic, like an unhappy and pitiable helpless creature", Zweig (1949), p. 67.

[129] Hamann (1996), p. 262.

[130] Von Suttner, *High Life* (1886), p. 73. Hamann (1996), p. 262.

[131] Ibid., p. 210 ff.. Hamann (1996), p. 50.

[132] Von Suttner (1910), Vol. I, p. 213.

[133] In the novel *Die von Hohenstein*, the German author Friederich von Spielhagen makes fun of the aristocratic women's laziness and compares them to the hardworking women of the working class. The author gives vivid descriptions of the efforts the noblewomen make to avoid getting dirt under their fingernails, flour on their noses or sticky bread dough on their palms. Their hands were to be white, but their attitudes were not equally pure. Quite to the contrary – in von Spielhagen's work, women of the aristocracy were depicted as virtual devils. Spielhagen, Friederich von (1864). *Die von Hohenstein*, Berlin.

[134] Von Suttner (1910), Vol. I, p. 275 ff.

[135] Several of Bertha's contemporary Austrian authors spent time in Paris in this period, such as Max Nordeau, Rainer Maria Rilke and Stefan Zweig. Bjøl, Erling (1979). *Den tapte tid. Vår tids kulturhistorie 1890-1914.* Oslo, Cappelen, p. 97 ff.

[136] Von Suttner (1910), p. 278.

[137] Bertha in a letter to Alfred, Biedermann (2001), p.183.

[138] Von Suttner, "Erinnerungen an Alfred Nobel", in NFP (*Neue Freie Presse*), Jan. 12, 1897. Hamann (1996), p. 57.

[139] Von Suttner (1910), Vol 1, p. 278.

[140] Tägil in Brandell et al. (1983), p. 25 ff.

[141] Erlandsson (2002). p. 36.

[142] Alfred Nobel began buying Scandinavian literature at a relatively late stage in his life. Among other works, his book collection included a collection of Scandinavian authors who came into the spotlight in Paris in the late 1880s. Some, such as Bjørnson and Strindberg, had lived there for extended periods of time and some of their works had been translated into French. In addition, Alfred had acquired a relatively complete collection of the most important contemporary Norwegian authors of the day.

[143] See Brandell in Brandell et. al. (1983), p. 77.

[144] For further reading about the French salons, see Roger Price (1987). *A Social History of Nineteenth-Century France*. Holmes & Meier Pub, p. 97 f.

[145] Von Suttner (1910), Vol. I, p. 280 f.

[146] The best known of her novels is *Païenne* (1883).

[147] Von Suttner (1910), Vol.1, p. 280 ff.

[148] Ibid., p. 281.

[149] Von Suttner. *High Life* (1886), p. 140, quoted in Hamann (1996), p. 60.

[150] Hamann (1996), p. 282 ff.

[151] The French Academy, founded in 1636, is France's official authority on the usage, vocabulary and grammar of the French language. Membership is considered to be one of the country's greatest honors.

[152] Von Suttner (1910), Vol. I, p. 283 f.

[153] Von Suttner (1889). *Die Waffen nieder. Collected Works*, Vol. 11 (Dresden, date unavailable), p. 64, quoted in Hamann (1996), p. 58.

[154] Von Suttner (1910), Vol. I p. 280 ff.

[155] *Memoirs*, 3 ff., in Hamann (1996), p. 61.

[156] Von Suttner. *The Machine Age*, p. 277 ff.

[157] Von Suttner (1910), Vol. I, p. 294.

[158] The complete title, in the original German, is *Die Waffen nieder. Eine Lebensgeschichte.* (Lay down Your Arms. The story of a life), 1889.

[159] *Lay Down Your Arms!* is considered to be the most powerful antiwar novel in German until the publication of *Im Westen Nicht Neues* (*All Quiet on the Western Front*, 1929) by Erich Maria Remarque.

[160] Von Suttner (1910), Vol. I, p. 315.

[161] Von Suttner, Bertha (1892). *Lay Down Your Arms: The Autobiography of Martha von Tilling*. Authorized translation [of Die Waffen nieder]. London, Longmans, 1892, p. 187.

[162] Ibid., p. 220 ff.

[163] Ibid., p. 45.

[164] Ibid., p. 62 ff.

[165] Ibid., p. 287.

[166] Von Suttner (1910), Vol. I, p. 297.

[167] Hamann (1996), p. 70.

[168] Von Suttner (1910), Vol. I, p. 297.

[169] Alfred Nobel, letter to Bertha von Suttner, November 24, 1889. Biedermann (2001), p. 85.

[170] Recorded in shorthand at the Austrian Council of State [Austrian Reichsrat], April 18, 1890, in Hamann (1996), p. 72.

[171] Carneri in *Neue Freie Presse*, March 15, 1890. Hamann (1996), p. 71.

[172] Reutter and Rüffer, *Peace Women* (2004), p. 21.

[173] Letter from Tolstoy, Hamann (1996), p. 72.

[174] Bertha von Suttner, *Krieg und Frieden* (War and Peace), a lecture given in Munich, February 5, 1900. Hamann (1996), p. 73.

[175] Felix Salten. *Die Suttner (zum 70. Geburstag)*. Press clipping, United Nations Library Genève, Suttner - Open Collections in Hamann (1996), p. 79.

[176] Some twentieth century commentators have considered the book "devoid of great literary qualities". The biographer Beatrix Kempf wrote that it was "certainly no masterpiece", others have pointed out its "aesthetic shortcomings". Read more about this

[177] Ibid. p. 75 ff.

[178] For more about this, see Angela Rundquist (1989). *Blått blod och liljevita händer. En etnologisk studie av aristokratiska kvinnor 1850-1900 (Blue Blood and Lily-white Hands. An ethnological study of aristocratic women 1850-1900)*. Stockholm, Carlsson.

[179] Hamann (1996), p. 264 ff.

[180] Bertha von Suttner in a letter to Bartholomäus von Carneri, September 11, 1890. Hamann (1996), p. 74.

[181] Alfred in a letter to Sofie, April 1890. Biedermann (2001), p. 88.

[182] The letter continues as follows: "It is by the way wrong of you to shout: *Lay Down Your Arms*, when you use them yourself and more so, as your own weapons - your captivating style and elevated ideas - carry and will carry further and quite differently than those of Lebellerne, Nordenfeldterne, Bangerne and all the others' bloody tools." Alfred in a letter to Bertha, 01.04. 1890. Biedermann (2001), p. 88.

[183] Alfred in a letter to Bertha, 24.11.1889. Biedermann (2001), p. 85.

[184] Reviews from *Aftonbladet* and *Stockholms Dagblad*, December 21, 1890, have been translated in Biedermann (2001), p. 89.

[185] Erlandsson (2002), p. 34.

[186] Bertha's works that were found in Alfred's library at the Björkborn manor in Värmland after his death: *Ein schlechter Mensch* (1884), *Ein Manuskript* (1885), *Daniela Dormes* (1886), *Die Tiefinnersten* (1893) and *Vor dem Gewitter* (1894). *Inventarium einer Seele* and *Das Maschinenzeitalter* were missing, as well as the German edition of *Die Waffen nieder!* Bertha's letter to Alfred of 27.10.1892 states that she sent him a German edition of the novel *Die Waffen nieder!* Biedermann (2001), p. 82.

[187] Alfred in a letter to James Thorne in Strandh (1983), p. 158.

[188] Sohlman (1950), p. 109.

[189] Sjöman, Vilgot (2001). *Vem älskar Alfred Nobel?* Stockholm: Natur och Kultur. p. 317.

[190] Juliette Adam to Alfred Nobel, 17 April 1888. Sjöman (1995), p. 318.

[191] Alfred in a letter to Sofie, 09.04.1888. Sjöman (1995), p. 221.

[192] Both the German and French commanders used the explosive during the war in 1870-71 to remove blockades and fortifications and to blow up bridges. Dynamite was also the first explosive used by terrorists. For more about this, see Tägil in Brandell et al. (1983), p. 20 ff.

[193] Sjöman (1995), p. 363.

[194] For more about Sofie Hess' family background, see Sjöman (1995), p. 49 ff.

[195] Sjöman (1995), p. 42.

[196] Alfred in a letter to Bertha, 06.11.1888. Biedermann (2001), p. 83. Alfred is probably referring to the canon experiments in Sevran, a commune in the northeastern suburbs of Paris.

[197] Von Suttner (1910), vol. I, p. 189.

[198] Von Suttner (1910), vol. I, p. 232.

[199] See Halvdan Koht's report on Bertha von Suttner as a Nobel Peace Prize candidate in The Norwegian Stortings Nobel Committee report on the Nobel Peace Prize IV, 1904, The Nobel Institute Library, p. 53.

[200] Biedermann (2001), p. 104.
[201] Shakespeare. *Henry the Fifth*, Act 5, scene 2:
"What rub or what impediment there is
Why that the naked, poor, and mangled peace,
Dear nurse of arts, plenties, and joyful births,
Should not in this best garden of the world,
Our fertile France, put up her lovely visage"
[202] Hamann (1996), p. 80.
[203] Some of the internationally active founders of the movement during this time were Frédéric Passy of France, Hodgson Pratt of Great Britain, Christopher von Egidy of Germany, Élie Ducommon and Albert Gobat of Switzerland, Ernesto Moneta of Italy, Fredrik Bajer of Denmark, Carel Asser of the Netherlands, Henri la Fontaine of Belgium, Klas P. Arnoldsson of Sweden and Christian Lous Lange of Norway.
[204] Letter to author Hermann Rollett, 20.08.89, Stadtbibliothek in Wien, in Hamann (1996), p. 79.
[205] Von Suttner (1910), vol. I, p. 313.
[206] Fried, Alfred Hermann. *BvS for Her 70th Birthday. Neue Freie Presse*, 09.06.1913 in Hamann (1996), p. 80.
[207] Alonso, Harriet Hyman (1993). *Peace as a Women's Issue. A History of the U.S. Movement for World Peace and Women's Rights.* Syracuse University Press, p. 25.
[208] In most Western countries, universal suffrage was expanded to include women during the first two decades of the 20th century, New Zealand was first in 1893, followed by Australia in 1902, Finland in 1906, Denmark in 1915, Great Britain and Sweden in 1918 and Germany in 1919. In France, women did not have the right to vote until in 1944 and in Switzerland in 1971. In Norway, women were granted restricted voting rights in 1909 and universal suffrage was introduced in 1913. Alonso (1993), p. 25.
[209] *Det Norske Fredsblad* nr. 3–4, 1896, p. 5 in Rønning (2005), p. 32.
[210] William Ladd in Alonso (1993).
[211] Hamann (1996), p. 80.
[212] Alfred in a letter to Bertha, 14.09.91. Biedermann (2001), p. 90.
[213] *L'art pour l'art*: This slogan "Art for Art's Sake" was coined by the French philosopher and politician Victor Cousin in 1836, as an expression of the idea that an artwork is to be judged only on the basis of art's own laws. The work shall be independent of the random moral, religious or social tendencies of any given period.
[214] Bertha in a letter to Alfred, 24.10.1891. Biedermann (2001), p. 91.
[215] Alfred in a letter to Bertha, 31.10.1891. Biedermann (2001), p. 92.
[216] To read more about this idea, see Tägil in Brandell et al. (1983), p. 36.
[217] Bertha in a letter to Carneri, 02.10. 1891. Hamann (1996), p. 93.
[218] This inter-parliamentary institution was established in 1889 by Frédéric Passy (France) and William Randal Cremer (United Kingdom) as the first permanent forum for political multilateral negotiations. Its headquarters are currently located in Geneva, Switzerland.
[219] Bertha in a letter to Alfred, 04.11.1891. Biedermann (2001), p. 93.
[220] Alfred in a letter to Bertha, 24.11.1889. Biedermann (2001), p. 85.
[221] Hamann (1996), p. 91.
[222] *Mittheilungen der österreichischen Gesellschaft der Friedensfreunde*, (1892) 14, in Hamann (1996), p. 91.
[223] Bertha in a letter to Alfred, 06.02.1892. Biedermann (2001), p. 99.

[224] Von Suttner (1910), vol. I, p. 289.

[225] The conferences she attended included the Inter-Parliamentary Conference in Bern in 1892, the Peace Congress in Chicago in 1893 and in The Hague in 1894, the Inter-Parliamentary Conference in Brussels in 1895 and the Peace Congress in Budapest in 1896, the Inter-Parliamentary Conference in Budapest that same year and in Hamburg in 1887.

[226] The description comes from her close colleague A.H. Fried. *Persönlichkeiten: Bertha von Suttner* (Berlin, n.d.), 20 ff. in Hamann (1996), p. 293.

[227] About the letters: A total of 24 letters from Alfred to Bertha and 70 letters from Bertha to Alfred have been preserved. Most of the letters were written between 1888 and 1896. Starting in 1888, Alfred wrote to Bertha every year and on a regular basis. Of Alfred's preserved letters, there were on average three letters per year; of Berthas letters to Alfred, the first preserved letters were from 1891, when she wrote four letters to the inventor. After 1892 (the same year as their third meeting in Bern), the number of letters from Bertha undergoes an explosive growth: she wrote between six and ten letters a year until 1896, the last year of Alfred's life, when she wrote 30 letters to the inventor. While Alfred wrote from various locations, mostly Paris, Berthas letters were almost without exception written from the Harmannsdorf estate. Some were written on the stationary of Öesterreichischen Gesellschaft der Friedensfreunde (The Austrian Peace Society) in Vienna. To read more about this, see Biedermann (2001).

[228] Alfred wrote 216 letters to Sofie Hess during his life. See Sjöman (1995).

[229] Sjöman (1995), p. 95 ff.

[230] The observation was made by Ragnar Sohlman after reading Alfred's correspondence with Sofie Hess. Sohlman (1983), p. 112.

[231] Sjöman (1995), p. 113.

[232] Sjöman (2001), p. 298. Sjöman refers to the letter to the Swedish Sophie Ahlström, with whom Alfred attended the play.

[233] Alfred in a letter to Bertha, 28.04.1883. Biedermann (2001), p. 76.

[234] More about this in Erlandsson (2006), p. 48.

[235] Erlandsson (2006), p. 98-99.

[236] Undated letter in German to Sofie Hess from unknown man in Sjöman (1995), p. 63.

[237] Von Suttner (1910), vol. II, p. 151.

[238] A. H. Fried. *Persönlichkeiten: Bertha von Suttner* (Berlin, n.d.), p. 7, in Hamann (1996), p. 169.

[239] Diary, June 1, 1898 in Hamann (1996), p. 171.

[240] Decades later, Adolf Hitler, a citizen of Vienna from 1907 to 1913, saw Lueger as an inspiration for his own view on Jews. The populist and anti-Semitic politics of Lueger's Christian Social Party were sometimes viewed as a model for Hitler's Nazism. See Fareed Zacharia's book, *The Future of Freedom: Illiberal Democracy at Home and Abroad*. Norton (2007).

[241] Bertha in a letter to Alfred 30.04.1896. Biedermann (2001), p. 181.

[242] Hamann (1996), p. 105.

[243] Bertha in a letter to Carneri, 01.02.1892. Hamann (1996), p. 100.

[244] Bertha in a letter to Alfred, 16.04.1892. Biedermann (2001), p. 103.

[245] Alfred in a letter to Bertha, 27.12.1891. Biedermann (2001), p. 98.

[246] Hamann (1996), p. 90.

[247] Biedermann (2001), p. 103.

[248] Von Suttner (1910), vol. II, p. 160.

[249] See for example Bertha Goldmann's letter to Alfred Nobel, 08.02.1891, in Sjöman (1995), p. 294.

[250] Alfred in a letter to Sofie, 10.02.1891, Sjöman (1995), p. 295.

[251] Sofie in letters to Alfred, 01.2. 1891, 14.2.1891, 30.3.1891. Sjöman (1995), p. 294-295, and p. 297.

[252] Bertha in a letter to Alfred, 06.02.1892. Biedermann (2001).

[253] From Norway, the President of the Norwegian Storting, Viggo Ullmann, attended.

[254] Bertha presented this proposal together with the Italian peace champion Ernesto Teodoro Moneta and the Englishman James Capper (Hamann 1996), p. 255 ff.

[255] Hamann (1996), p. 60.

[256] This point is explored more in depth in Lughofer, Johann Georg, "Bertha von Suttner. A Prototypical European Writer", *Letter Journal for Linguistics and Literary Studies*, issue: 09/ 2011, on www.ceeol.com.

[257] "But what has been the condition of the world since that day the seamless robe [of Pax Romana] first suffered mutilation by the claws of avarice, we can read - would that we could not also see! O human race! what tempests must need toss thee, what treasure be thrown into the sea, what shipwrecks must be endured, so long as thou, like a beast of many heads, strivest after diverse ends! Thou art sick in either intellect, and sick likewise in thy affection. Thou healest not thy high understanding by argument irrefutable, nor thy lower by the countenance of experience. Nor dost thou heal thy affection by the sweetness of divine persuasion, when the voice of the Holy Spirit breathes upon thee, "Behold, how good and how pleasant it is for brethren to dwell together in unity!" (Alighieri, Dante (1312-13). *De Monarchia*. 16:1).

[258] Ginsberg, Roy H. (2010). Demystifying the European Union: The Enduring Logic of Regional Integration, p. 61. Lanham: Rowman & Littlefield.

[259] Emeric Crucé made his ideas known to the world in his work *Le Nouveau Cynée ou Discours d'Estat* (*The New Cyneas, or a Discourse on the State*,1623).

[260] In *Lay Down Your Arms!*, the author summarizes the ideas of Charles-Irénée Castel Saint-Pierre and some other earlier thinkers on the subject of European unity.

[261] A call for European Unity also appeared in the form of an essay written by the British Quaker and philosopher William Penn (1644-1718). He argued that a European Parliament was needed for states to settle their disputes peacefully.

[262] Kant's ideas are discussed in Grace Roosevelts essay "A Brief History of the Quest for Peace" in *Pacifism and Just War Theory in Europe from the 16th to the 20th Centuries*, Global Policy Forum, 1999, p. 4 ff.

[263] Victor Hugo's full address can be found at this website: http://www.gavroche.org/vhugo/peacecongress.shtml. The following quote is taken from Cortright, David (2008). *Peace: A History of Movements and Ideas*. Cambridge, Cambridge University Press, p. 35.

[264] Bertha presented this proposal together with the Italian peace champion Ernesto Teodoro Moneta and the Englishman James Capper. Hamann (1996), p. 255 ff.

[265] For further reading about Alfred Nobel's cooperation with industrialists and professors at ETH (Eidgenössische Technische Hochschule) in the period 1890–1891, see for example Strandh in Brandell et al. (1983), p. 94 ff.

[266] Von Suttner (1910), vol. I, p. 429 ff.

[267] Letter from M. A Rieffel, the Austrian peace association's treasurer in Alfred Nobel's archive, Stockholm. E II: 2; dated 5th September 1892. Biedermann (2001), p. 110.

[268] The conversation is quoted in von Suttner (1910), vol. 1, p. 435 ff.

[269] Von Suttner (1910), vol. I, p. 435 ff.

[270] Von Suttner (1910), vol. I, p. 209 ff.

[271] Von Suttner (1910), vol. I, p. 277 ff.

[272] Alfred in a letter, 05.09.1892. Schück and Sohlman (1926), p. 221.

[273] Pauli, Herta (1947). *Alfred Nobel. Dynamite King - Architect of Peace*. London: Nicholson & Watson, p. 230.

[274] Alfred also mentions the idea of a moratorium in a letter to Bertha 31.10.1891, Biedermann (2001), p. 92.

[275] Alfred in a letter to Bey, 05.09.1892. Schück and Sohlman (1926), p. 221.

[276] Alfred in a letter to Bertha, 06.11.1892. Biedermann (2001), p. 115.

[277] Bertha in a letter to Alfred, 24.12.1892. Biedermann (2001), p. 118.

[278] The English edition was published by Longmans & Co. in London.

[279] Bertha in a letter to Alfred, 24.12.1892. Biedermann (2001), p. 119.

[280] Bertha in a letter to Alfred Hermann Fried, 02.01.1892. Hamann (1996), p. 94.

[281] Bjørnson had mentioned to her that he was toying with the idea of starting a journal that resembled *Revue du Monde;* "a journal *with* all the biggest names and contributions to freedom, legislation, against war and despots of all kinds." Bjørnstjerne Bjørnson in a letter to Bertha von Suttner, Paris 14.01.1901. Keel, A. (1986-1987). (ed.) Bjørnstjerne Bjørnsons Briefwechsel mit Deutschen. Basel: Helbing & Lichtenhahn.

[282] Von Suttner (1910), vol. I, p. 179.

[283] Fridtjof Nansen's lecture in Vienna, May 7, 1898 quoted in *Neue Freie Presse,* Hamann (1996), p. 97.

[284] Hamann (1996), p. 97.

[285] Hamann (1996), p. 127.

[286] Hamann (1996), p. 94.

[287] Alfred in a letter to Bertha, 07.01.1893. Biedermann (2001), p. 122.

[288] Alfred in a letter to Bertha, 07.01.1893. Biedermann (2001). The Nobel-biographer Hertha E. Pauli believes this conflict resolution model was Alfred's best suggestion, and even better than the formulation he would write in his final testament. See Pauli (1947). *Alfred Nobel. Dynamite King - Architect of Peace*. p. 240 ff.

[289] Bertha in a letter to Alfred 21.01.1893. Biedermann (2001), p.124.

[290] In *Memoirs* (1910) she has copied letters from peace activists and authors such as Johann von Bloch, D'Estournelles de Constant, Hodgson Pratt, Elie Ducommun, Henri Dunant, Leo Tolstoy, Frédéric Passy and Prince Albert I. See Von Suttner (1910), vol. II, p. 245 ff.

[291] Von Suttner (1910), vol. II, p. 37 ff.

[292] "...Can you send me a few lines that I can print in my monthly publication?" Bertha in a letter to Bjørnstjerne Bjørnson in *Briefwechsel mit Deutschen*, p. 247.

[293] Bertha was curious about the development of the peace issue in Norway. When a few years later she met the Norwegian feminist Randi Blehr (married to Member of Parliament and four-time Prime Minister Otto Blehr), she asked whether it was really the case as she had heard that the relation between Norway and Sweden could be compared to the relation between two "quarrelsome siblings"? "No," was Mrs. Blehr's reply, "the relation is rather like a marriage where the man has everything and the woman has no voice, and in keeping with the modern ideas of our times, it cannot be a happy marriage. In this union, Norway has been given the role of a wife without authority and what she wants is what every woman with an awareness of equal rights wants in a marriage - the right to her own personality." Von Suttner (1910), vol. II, p 328-329.

[294] The magazine he had in mind was *Kvinners Blad* and the editor was the Danish Rigmor Stampe. September edition, 1898. Letter from Bjørnson to von Suttner, 17.08.98. Keel, A. (1986-87). (ed.). *Bjørnstjerne Bjørnsons Briefwechsel mit Deutschen.*

[295] While the peace palace was under construction, all nations were asked to contribute building materials, and Norway contributed granite from Heggedal.

[296] Von Suttner (1910), vol. I, p. 219.

[297] Bertha in a letter to Alfred 12.08.94. Biedermann (2001), p. 146.

[298] Bertha in a letter to Alfred 07.02.96. Biedermann (2001), p. 168. The invention received a great deal of attention and Røntgen would receive the Nobel Prize in physics for it a few years later (1901).

[299] Alfred in a letter to Bertha, 13.07.93. Biedermann (2001), p. 137.

[300] Von Suttner (1910), vol. I, p. 499 ff.

[301] Bertha in a letter to Alfred 08.02.1893. Biedermann (2001), p. 125. See also the subsequent letter of 10.02.1893 and "undated", p. 126 and 127.

[302] Bertha in a letter to Alfred 21.06.1893. Biedermann (2001), p. 135.

[303] Bramstead (1964), p. 48 ff.

[304] Bertha in a letter to Alfred 28.04.1893. Biedermann (2001), p. 129.

[305] The estate was not sold until after Arthur' death in 1902.

[306] Alfred in a letter to Bertha 17.05.93. Biedermann (2001), p. 131.

[307] Alfred in a letter to Bertha 15.06.93. Biedermann (2001), p. 134.

[308] Bertha in a letter to Alfred 21.06.1893. Biedermann, (2001), p. 135.

[309] Bertha in a letter to Alfred 17.07.1893. Biedermann, (2001), p. 137.

[310] Bertha in a letter to Alfred 12.01.1896. Biedermann (2001), p.163.

[311] Bertha in a letter to Alfred 28.04.93. Biedermann (2001), p. 129.

[312] Bertha in a letter to Alfred 11.04.94. Biedermann (2001), p.142.

[313] Bertha in a letter to Alfred 07.06.1893, 21.06, 1893, 06.07, 1893, and 12.01.1896. Biedermann (2001), p.132, 135,136, and 165.

[314] Bertha in a letter to Alfred 29.10.1895. Biedermann (2001), p. 160.

[315] See photograph of Alfred Nobel by the bridge in Dolce Aqua (Taggia) in Brandell et al., p. 22.

[316] Bergengren, Erik (1960), p. 180.

[317] Sohlman, Ragnar (1983). *Et testamente*, p. 31. Alfred Nobel named the young engineer Ragnar Sohlmann as executor of his will and the latter has written about this process and the years as Nobel's assistant.

[318] Bertha in a letter to Alfred 06.02.1892. Biedermann (2001), p. 99.

[319] Alfred in a letter to Bertha, 07.01.1893. Biedermann (2001), p. 122. The letter is written in French and the wording of this part is: "Je voudrais par testament disposer d'une partie de ma fortune en prix à distribuer tous les cinq ans (disons six fois en tout car si dans trente ans on n'aura pas réussi à réformer le système actuel il faudra retourner carrément à la barbarie) à celui ou celle qui aura fait le plus grand pas d'avancement à la pacification de l'Europe."

[320] Tägil in Brandell et al. p. 42 ff.

[321] Sohlman (1983), p. 112. See also Tägil in Brandell et al. (1983), p. 42 ff.

[322] Tägil in Brandell et al. (1983), p. 42. Schück describes Nobel's other drafts as somewhat "messy". Tägil's comment is that Alfred's insecurity at times appears "striking".

[323] Alfred in a farewell letter to Bey, written 18 August, 1892. Schück og Solman (1926), p. 227.

[324] Tägil in Brandell et al. (1983), p. 38.

[325] There are about 60 letters, brochures and newspaper clippings from Gregoire Aristarchi Bey to Alfred Nobel from between 1891-1892 in the Nobel Archives in Stockholm. Read more about this in Brandell (1903), p. 45.

[326] The first time Bertha von Suttner's name is mentioned in the letter to Bey is when Nobel rejects Bey's suggestion that he purchase his own "publication" as a means of disseminating peace information throughout the world: "If I had had the least bit of faith in this type of propaganda, I would instead have contacted Madame von Suttner, who edits a publication in this genre. In my opinion, however, it does not amount to anything but throwing money out the window." Letter to Bey 18 August 1892. Schück og Sohlman (1926), p. 227.

[327] Alfred in a letter to Bertha 06.11.1892. Biedermann (2001), p. 115.

[328] Gunnar Eriksson in Brandell et al. (1983), p. 9 ff.

[329] Grimberg, Carl (1987), p. 141.

[330] Bertha in a letter to Alfred 23.09.1894. Biedermann (2001), p. 148-149.

[331] Bertha in a letter to Alfred 26.05.1894. Biedermann (2001), p. 144.

[332] For a general overview of the different directions of the peace movement and thoughts about peace, see: The Oxford International Encyclopedia of Peace, Nigel & Young (ed.). Oxford University Press, 2010, 4 volumes.

[333] Rønning (2005), p. 12.

[334] In Norway, the most important conflict was between those who wanted to defend themselves against a potential attack from an outside power, and those who were consistent pacifists. The background for this was Norway's right to defend itself against a potential attack from Sweden. This conflict completely paralyzed the Norwegian peace association for a period. The Norwegian historian and politician Halvdan Koht clearly emphasized his point of view when he called conscientious objectors "infatuated idealists", a statement which provoked a heated uproar. The disagreements were many, but the one idea the parties could agree upon was that of arbitration.

[335] Rønning (2005), p. 60.

[336] Tolstoy in a letter dated 28.08.1901, quoted in von Suttner (1910), vol. II, p. 372.

[337] Tolstoy's ideas of non-violent resistance would have great significance for later peace activists such as Mahatma Gandhi (1869-1948), who led the Indian nationalist movement against British rule and who was internationally recognized among other things for his doctrine of non-violence as a means of political and social resistance.

[338] Tolstoy, Leo (1984). The Kingdom of God is Within You. Lincoln, University of Nebraska Press.

[339] Bertha in a letter to Alfred Fried 06.01.1910. Hamann (1996), p. 254.

[340] Rønning (2005), p. 5.

[341] The Polish-German Marxist politician Rosa Luxemburg (1871-1919) was among those who believed that the most important thing was the struggle against capitalism. According to Luxemburg, Poland's independence was only possible through a revolution in Germany, Austria and Russia. Being one of the founders of the Spartacus League (a Marxist revolutionary movement organized in Germany during World War I in 1915), she was shot in connection with the failed Spartacist uprising in Berlin in January 1919.

[342] Von Suttner. Das Machinenzeitalter (The Machine Age), 3rd ed., p. 137, quoted in Hamann (1996), p. 257.

[343] Virginia Woolf (1938). Three Guineas 1938 (New York, Harvest,1966), p. 84 ff. Woolf's essay is written in response to a letter from a male member of an anti-war society, asking her for her reply to the question "How in your opinion are we to prevent war?" An

unusual letter, according to Woolf - since when before has an educated man asked a woman how in her opinion war can be prevented? *Three Guineas* is a complex essay. Woolf seldom gives unambiguous answers. Basically, she criticizes the existing structure of education and the professions, showing how they encourage attitudes that may lead to fascism. She writes that most men, also those who are highly educated, are inclined to vote *for* war, if they are asked. This causes her to ask the question: What kind of education can teach men to denounce war?

Woolf's first guinea goes to changing the patriarchal education system, so that education becomes more humanitarian. Here she is thinking along the same lines as Bertha von Suttner. The second guinea she gives to the education of educated men's daughters. As the most important thing for a girl was to make a good marriage, girls were still encouraged to be accommodating, supporting men's values and opinions, and refraining from voicing any opinions which could provoke them. Girls must therefore receive education just like boys, so they can learn to think independently. Woolf imagined, for example, a new kind of college that avoids teaching the tools of domination and pugnacity: "an experimental college, an adventurous college...It should teach...the art of understanding other people's lives and minds...The teachers should be drawn from the good livers as well as from the good thinkers." The third guinea shall according to Woolf go more generally "to protect culture and intellectual liberty."

[344] Bertha in a letter to Alfred, 21.01.1893. Biedermann (2001), p.124.

[345] From 1892, Bertha writes Alfred at least ten letters a year. For an overview, see Biedermann (2001), p. 203.

[346] The next year Alfred received a distinguished visitor on September 18, 1895, King Oscar II came to visit the workshops and have lunch with Nobel in the mansion of Björkborn decorated for the occasion.

[347] Samuel C. Florman describes the existential pleasures of the art of engineering in his work in *The Civilized Engineer*. New York, St. Martin's Press, (1988).

[348] Sven Tägil in Brandell et al. (1983), p. 29.

[349] Nobel also expressed the view, popular in the 19th century, that a scientist is not responsible for how his invention is used. This responsibility is in the hands of politicians and decision-makers.

[350] Tägil in Brandell et al. (1983). p. 33.

[351] Bergengren, Erik (1960), p. 85.

[352] We know that Alfred Nobel was fond of Bjørnstjerne Bjørnson from letters he wrote to his assistant Ragnar Sohlman, married to Norwegian Ragnhild Strøm. In a letter to Sohlman, Nobel wrote: "Tell your kind wife that I am in love, not with Bjørnson, but with his writing." Brandell et al. (1983), p. 71.

[353] Bertha in a letter to Alfred, 12.01.1896. Biedermann (2001), p. 163.

[354] Alfred in a letter to Bertha 18.02.1896. Biedermann (2001), p. 169.

[355] Bertha in a letter to Alfred, 27.02.1896. Biedermann (2001), p. 170.

[356] Alfred in a letter to Bertha, 18.03.1896. Biedermann (2001), p. 174.

[357] Compared to other 19th century women authors who were considered unconventional, such as George Sand (pseudonym for Louise Aurore Dudevant, 1804-1876), Bertha did not challenge the prevailing perception of femininity. Sand, as an example, lived provocatively and always appeared in public dressed in men's clothing and with a cigar in her mouth. She had several lovers (famous men such as Musset and Chopin), drank and smoked. Bertha, on the other hand, lived a traditional life in a monogamous marriage, and she seldom touched alcohol and never smoked.

[358] Bartholomäus von Carneri in a letter to Bertha von Suttner, 05.03.1896. Von Suttner (1910), vol. II, p. 98.

[359] Bertha von Suttner in a letter to Carneri 10.03.1896. Von Suttner (1910), vol. II, p. 101.

[360] Alfred in a letter to Bertha, 21.09.1895. Biedermann (2001), p. 157.

[361] Bertha in a letter to Alfred, 26.09.1895. Biedermann (2001), p. 159.

[362] Bertha in a letter to Alfred, 17.07.1893. Biedermann (2001), p. 137.

[363] Bertha in a letter to Alfred, 12.08.1894. Biedermann (2001), p. 148. This was a goal the peace movement aimed to attain, perhaps the most important goal of all, in that the permanent international court of arbitration would be established in The Hague in 1899.

[364] Bertha in a letter to Alfred, 28.10.1894. Biedermann (2001), p. 150.

[365] A number of arbitration agreements were formed during the final years before the turn of the century. In the Norwegian peace newsletter *Det Norske Fredsblad*, the friends of peace could read about the many, small victories the fight for arbitration had won during recent years. Since 1815, more than 100 cases of international arbitration were registered, of which almost 70 decisions were made in the final decades before the turn of the century. *Det Norske Fredsblad*, no. 16-17, 1895, p. 3 in Rønning (2005), p. 41.

[366] The Americans and the British had for several years been arguing about a parcel of land located between Venezuela and the British-owned Guyana. Great Britain finally gave in to the American demands after an arbitral tribunal made a ruling.

[367] Bertha in a letter to Alfred, 15.11.1896. Biedermann (2001), p. 189.

[368] Bertha in a letter to Alfred, 11.04.1894. Biedermann (2001), p. 142.

[369] Bertha in a letter to Alfred, 07.02.96. Biedermann (2001), p. 168.

[370] Pauli (1957), p. 182.

[371] Dunant was for several years a contributor to Bertha's magazine *Lay Down Your Arms*. He was proposed as a candidate for the first peace prize. His candidacy prevailed, largely thanks to the German high school teacher Rudolf Müller and the Norwegian military physician Hans Daae. At the first award's ceremony in 1901, the Nobel peace prize was shared between Henry Dunant and Frédéric Passy.

[372] Bertha in a letter to Alfred, 12.01.1896. Biedermann (2001), p. 164.

[373] The same year (1896), the novel *Poor and Lonely (Arm und Einsam)* was published. The themes were a repetition: Sentimental love stories from the daily life of a family from the nobility of lesser means.

[374] Bertha in a letter to Alfred, 28.03.1896. Biedermann (2001), p. 179.

[375] Alfred in a letter to Sofie ,12.09.1894. Sjömann (1995), p. 337.

[376] In addition, Sveriges Riksbank (Sweden's central bank) established The Sveriges Riksbank Prize in Economic Sciences in Memory of Alfred Nobel in 1968.

[377] "...The whole of my remaining realizable estate shall be dealt with in the following way: the capital, invested in safe securities by my executors, shall constitute a fund, the interest on which shall be annually distributed in the form of prizes to those who, during the preceding year, shall have conferred the greatest benefit to mankind. The said interest shall be divided into five equal parts, which shall be apportioned as follows: one part to the person who shall have made the most important discovery or invention within the field of physics; one part to the person who shall have made the most important chemical discovery or improvement; one part to the person who shall have made the most important discovery within the domain of physiology or medicine; one part to the person who shall have produced in the field of literature the most outstanding work in an ideal direction; and one part to the person who shall have done the most or the best work for fraternity

between nations, for the abolition or reduction of standing armies and for the holding and promotion of peace congresses". For the full text of Alfred Nobel's will, see: https://www.nobelprize.org/alfred_nobel/will/will-full.html

[378] Fant (1991), p. 312.

[379] Alfred in a letter to Bertha 18.03.1896. Biedermann (2001), p. 175.

[380] Adèle Sandrock had recently played Rebekka West in Ibsen's "Rosmersholm" at the Burgtheater in Vienna. Bertha suggests that she could play Beatrice, the main character. Bertha in a letter to Alfred 23.03.1896. Biedermann (2001), p. 176.

[381] Bertha in a letter to Alfred 23.03.1896. Biedermann (2001), p. 176.

[382] Percy Bysshe Shelley's verse drama *The Cenci: A Tragedy in Five Acts*, published spring 1820 by C. & J. Ollier, London, 1819.

[383] Alfred in a letter to Bertha, 18.03.1896. Biedermann (2001), p. 174.

[384] Alfred in a letter to Bertha, 30.03.1896. Biedermann (2001), p. 179.

[385] For a thorough analysis of the drama *Nemesis*, see *Vem älskar Alfred Nobel?* (2001) by the Swedish writer and filmmaker Vilgot Sjöman.

[386] In addition to Shelley's drama from 1819, Beatrice Cenci was the subject of a number of literary and musical works during the 1800s, such as *Les Cenci*, a short story by Stendhal (1837), *Béatrix Cenci*, a verse drama (1839), by Polish poet, Juliusz Słowacki, *Béatrix Cenci* by Astolphe de Custine (1853), *Beatrice Cenci*, a novel by Francesco Domenico Guerrazzi (1854), "Beatrice Cenci (In a City Shop-Window)" a poem by Sarah Piatt, American poet (1871).

[387] Sjöman (2001), p. 79.

[388] Erlandsson (2002), p. 45.

[389] See for example Sjöman (2001), p. 72.

[390] Alfred in a letter to Bertha, 06.04.1896. Biedermann (2001), p. 180.

[391] Alfred in a letter to Bertha,18.03.1896. Biedermann (2001), p. 175.

[392] Bertha in a letter to Alfred, 06.04. 1896. Biedermann (2001), p. 180.

[393] Bertha in a letter to Alfred, 12.08.1894. Biedermann (2001), p. 146.

[394] Bertha in a letter to Alfred, 03.06.1896. Biedermann (2001), p. 184.

[395] Bertha in a letter to Alfred, 12.01.1896. Biedermann (2001), p. 163.

[396] Nitro-glycerine is also used for medical purposes.

[397] Letter in Schück og Sohlman (1926), p. 247.

[398] Alfred in his last letter to Sofie, 07.03.1895: "Dear Sofie, is it true that your white knight wants to wed you? Then he is acting not only properly but wisely. However, you must then renounce a large portion of your vanity and many foolish ideas. But when all is said and done, you are at least a sincere little person of feeling and that also is of great value. I even believe that you are not wholly without conscience, as long as Praterstrasse [her family] stays a thousand kilometres away. Yours sincerely, Alfred Nobel." Sohlman (1983), p. 115.

[399] In Alfred's next letter one detects a bit of disappointment: "critique on the other hand should always be welcome – the sharper, the better. You have only skimmed through it." Alfred Nobel in a letter to Josefina Wettergrund, 6. August 1896, B 1: 10 Kopibok XXIV in Sjöman (2001), p. 128.

[400] Sohlman (1983), p. 52.

[401] Alfred contacts a Swedish business man, Ch. Waerns, whose young office assistant took care of the typing of the drama. "I am having my little "Nemesis" printed here (in Paris). In my next letter, I will get back to the question about what I owe you and the young gentleman in your office who was kind enough to help me..." Alfred Nobel to Herr

Ch. Waern. Paris 07.11.1896. Kopibok XXIV Opubl. in Sjöman (2001), p. 130.

[402] Nathan Söderblom. *Alfred Nobel och fredssaken*, 11 desember, 1930, in Nathan Söderblom's collection *C Manuskript* 1930 2 September – December. Handskrift- och musikavdelingen, Uppsala Universitetsbibliotek. Opubl., in Sjöman (2001), p. 135. Söderblom also characterized Nobel as one of "the strangest people I have met", both a "benefactor" and a person full of "bizarre ideas".

[403] After Nobel's death the drama was ignored, probably because it did not fit in with Alfred's image as Sweden's great "benefactor". In fact, most copies of *Nemesis* were shredded, only three copies were preserved. In the Nobel anniversary publication it was written that "this only printed work from Nobel's pen should undoubtedly give the public the wrong impression of him." See Sjöman (1995), p. 182.

[404] Bertha in a letter to Alfred, 12.11.1896. Biedermann (2001), p. 188.

[405] Alfred in a letter to Bertha, 21.11.1896. Biedermann (2001), p. 191. The original of this last letter from Alfred to Bertha does not exist, only a copy of it in Von Suttner (1910), vol. II, p. 141.

[406] Bertha in a letter to Bartholomeus von Carneri, 10.03.1896. Von Suttner (1910), vol. II, p. 101.

[407] Nathan Söderblom received the Nobel Peace Prize in 1930 for his ecumenical peace work.

[408] In the work of the Inter-Parliamentary Union, the Norwegian historian and political scientist Christian Lous Lange played a major role. In 1909, he became secretary-general of the Union.

[409] The main argument of Nobel's relatives was that no residence was established in Sweden. France considered Nobel a resident even though he had homes all over Europe and died in Italy. His assistant Ragnar Sohlman had to rescue Nobel's stocks and financial papers out of various French banks and take them back home to Sweden.

[410] The members of the first Norwegian Nobel committee (1901-1906) were Jørgen Løvland (chairman), John Lund, Bjørnstjerne Bjørnson, Johannes Steen and Hans Jacob Horst.

[411] Diary, Jan. 4th, 1897, in Hamann (1996), p. 198.

[412] In a letter to Fried, Jan 9, 1897, Hamann (1996), p. 329.

[413] In a letter to Carneri, December 12, 1897, Hamann (1996), p. 201

[414] More about the tzar's peace manifesto in Stråth, Bo (2015). *Europe's Utopias of Peace, 1815, 1919, 1951*, part of the series "Europe's Legacy in the Modern World". Bloomsbury Publishing PLC.

[415] Diary, August 29, 1898, Hamann (1996), p. 138.

[416] Three additional conventions were produced at the conference in The Hague; the Convention for the Pacific Settlement of International Disputes ["Convention I (1899)"]; the Convention with Respect to the Laws and Customs of War by Land ["Convention II (1899)"]; and the Convention for the Adaptation to Maritime Warfare of the Principles of the Geneva Convention ["Convention III (1899)"].

[417] In addition to William Stead, Jan Gottlieb Bloch, Alfred Hermann Fried and Nikolai Novikov.

[418] Arthur in a letter to Bertha, quoted in Von Suttner (1910), vol. II , p. 398.

[419] Diary, April 11, 1903, in Hamann (1996), p. 182.

[420] Diary, Feb. 21, 1903, in Hamann (1996), p. 180.

[421] Diary, July 5, 1903, in Hamann (1996), p. 183.

[422] *Berliner Tageblatt*, May 7, 1903, in Hamann (1996), p. 183.

[423] Bjørnstjerne Bjørnson in *Berliner Tageblatt*, December 11, 1904.

[424] Bjørnstjerne Bjørnson in a letter to Det norske Stortings Nobelkomité, 02.11.1904, letter no. 1 in folder BB 927 A, at NBO (National Library of Norway, Oslo). Bjørnson himself was on leave from the Nobel committee that year, since he lived in Rome.

[425] A. H. Fried. *Personlichkeiten: Bertha von Suttner* (Berlin, n.d.), p. 14, in Hamann (1996), p. 293.

[426] Diary, April. 14, 1903, in Hamann (1996), p. 208.

[427] *Neue Badische Landeszeitung*, Dec. 2, 1904, Lecture report, Hamann, p. 208.

[428] Diary, Dec. 1, 1905, in Hamann (1996), p. 211.

[429] Bertha von Suttner's whole acceptance speech may be read here: http://www.nobelprize.org/nobel_prizes/peace/laureates/1905/suttner-lecture.html.

[430] Letter to Fried, April 26, 1906, in Hamann (1996), p. 214.

[431] Bertha in a letter to Alfred Hermann Fried, May 20, 1912 in Hamann p. 292.

[432] Stefan Zweig in *Die Welt von Gestern*, Hamburg, 1965, p. 194 in Hamann (1996), p. 300.

[433] The cause of death was most likely stomach cancer. In her diary, during the last months of her life, Bertha spoke of nausea and violent stomach disorders, in addition to the longer periods of tiredness. In accordance with her wishes, her body was cremated at Gotha and her ashes left there in the columbarium.

[434] Diary, July 14, 1906, in Hamann (1996), p. 21.

[435] Von Suttner (1910), vol. II, p. 144.

Literature

Alnæs, K. (2005). *Historien om Europa. 1800-1900. Bind 3. Oppbrudd.* Oslo: Gyldendal.

Alonso, H. H. (1993). *Peace as a Women's Issue. A History of the U.S. Movement for World Peace and Women's Rights.* Syracuse, NY: Syracuse University Press.

Anonymous. (2005). *En kvinne i Berlin. Dagboknotater fra 20. april til 22. juni 1945.* Oslo: Damm.

Abrams, I. (1988). *The Nobel Peace Prize and the Laureates. An Illustrated Biographical History, 1901-1987.* Boston: G.K. Hall.

Abrams, I. (1993). The Odd Couple. *Scanorama, 23(11)*, pp. 52-56.

Ahlander, D. S. (2000). *Alfred Nobel. Från fattiglapp till Nobelpris.* Stockholm: Bokförlaget Natur och Kultur.

Austen, J. (2003). *Stolthet og fordom.* (Translated by Merete Alfsen). Oslo: Aschehoug forlag.

Barash, D. P. (2000). *Approaches to Peace. A Reader in Peace Studies.* Oxford: Oxford University Press.

Bellamy, A.J. (2006). *Just Wars. From Cicero to Iraq.* Cambridge: Polity Press.

Beller, S. (2006). *A Concise History of Austria.* Cambridge: Cambridge University Press.

Bergengren, E. (1960). *Alfred Nobel.* Stockholm: Geber.

Biedermann, E. (2001). *Chère Baronne et Amie - Cher monsieur et amie. Der Briefwechsel zwischen Alfred Nobel und Bertha von Suttner.* Hildesheim: Georg Olms Verlag.

Bjøl, E. (1979). *Den tapte tid. Vår tids kulturhistorie 1890-1914.* Oslo: Cappelen.

Bjørke, H. (1989). *Bertha von Suttner: I kamp mot våpnene.* Oslo: Folkereisning mot krig.

Bjørnson, B. & Keel. A. (1986). Bjørnstjerne Bjørnsons Briefwechsel mit Deutschen. T. 1 : 1859-1898. Basel: Helbing & Lichtenhahn.
http://univofoslo.worldcat.org/title/bjrnstjerne-bjrnsons-briefwechsel-mit-deutschen/oclc/16501589 (Accessed 30.03.2017).

Boissel, P. (2004). *Grand-Hôtel, Café de la Paix. Two centuries of Parisian Life.* Paris : Éditions Italiques.

Bomann-Larsen. T. (2004). *Folket. Haakon & Maud II.* Oslo: Cappelen.

Bramsted, E.K. (1964). *Aristocracy and the Middle-Classes in Germany. Social types in German literature, 1830-1900.* Chicago: University of Chicago Press.

Brandell, G., Browaldh, T., Eriksson, G., Strandh, S. & Tägil, S. (1983). *Nobel och hans tid. Fem essayer.* Stockholm: Atlantis.

Bromark, S. & Tretvoll, H. F. (2009). *Sigurd Evensmo. Alene blant de mange. En biografi.* Oslo: Cappelen Damm.

Bury, J.P.T (1949). *France 1814-1940.* Reading: Cox & Wyman, Ltd.

Christiansen, R. (2004). *Romantic Affinities. Portraits from an Age 1780-1830.* London: Random House.

Cortright, D. (2008). *Peace: A History of Movements and Ideas.* Cambridge: Cambridge University Press.

Dahlbäck, K. (1994). *Ändå tycks allt vara osagt. August Strindberg som brevskrivare.* Stockholm: Natur och Kultur.

Dahl, S. (2008). *Wien og Weimar. Østerrikske modernister og tyske klassikere og romantikere.* Oslo: Bokvennen.

Darwin, C. (date not given). *The Origin of Species. By means of natural selection or the preservation of favoured races in the struggle for life.* [On the Origin of Species (1859)] Publisher: John Murray.

Dennett, D. C. (1995). *Darwin's Dangerous Idea. Evolution and the Meanings of Life.* London: Penguin Books.

Downie, D. (2005). *Paris, Paris. Journey into the City of Light.* Transatlantic Press.

Egeland, M. (2000). *Hvem bestemmer over livet? Biografien som historisk og litterær genre.* Oslo: Universitetsforlaget.

Engelstad, I. & Øverland, J. (1981). *Frihet til å skrive. Artikler om kvinnelitteratur fra Amalie Skram til Cecilie Løveid.* Oslo: Pax Forlag.

Erlandsson, Å. (2002). *Alfred Nobels bibliotek. En bibliografi.* Stockholm: Bokförlaget Atlantis.

Erlandsson, Å. (ed.). (2006). *Dikter/Poems av Alfred Nobel.* Stockholm: Bokförlaget Atlantis.

Evlanoff, M. & Fluor, M. (1969). *Alfred Nobel. The Loneliest Millionaire.* Los Angeles: The Ward Ritchie Press.

Fant, K. (1991). *Alfred Bernhard Nobel.* Stockholm: Nordstedts.

Felder, D. (1991). *How to Work for Peace.* Tallahassee: Florida A & M University Press.

Fidjestøl, A. (2007). *Eit halvt liv. Ein biografi om Per Sivle.* Oslo: Det Norske Samlaget.

Figueiredo, I. de (2007). *Henrik Ibsen. Masken.* Oslo: Aschehoug & Co.

Finsland, A. (1948). *Bjørnstjerne Bjørnson og fredssaken inntil 1900.* Oslo: Gyldendal forlag.

Flaubert, G. (1946). *Hjertets skole.* (Translated by av Eva Skodvin). Oslo: Ekko forlag.

Funder, A. (2003). *Stasiland. Stories from Behind the Berlin Wall.* London: Granta Books.

Frängsmyr, T. (1996). *Alfred Nobel.* Stockholm: Swedish Institute.

Galtung, J. (1975). *Peace: Research. Education. Action. Essays in Peace Research,* vol. I. København: Christian Ejlers' Forlag.

Greer, T. H. & Lewis, G. (2005). *A Brief History of the Western World.* Belmont, CA: Thomson Wadsworth.

Grimberg, C. (1987). *Menneskenes liv og historie 17. Tyrkia, Østerrike og Preussen. Den franske revolusjon.* (Translated by Bernhard Hagtvedt). Oslo: Cappelen Damm.

Hamann, B. (1986). *Bertha von Suttner. Ein Leben für den Frieden.* München: Piper.

Hamann, B. (1996). *Bertha von Suttner. A life for Peace.* (Translated by Ann Dubsky). Syracuse, NY: Syracuse University Press.

Hamsun, Knut (1903). *I Æventyrland. Oplevet og drømt i Kaukasien.* Oslo. Gyldendal.

Hamsun, Knut (1903). *Dronning Tamara. Skuespil i tre Akter.* Oslo. Gyldendal.

Harle, V. (ed.). (1989). *Studies in the History of European Peace Ideas.* Tampere Peace Research Institute Research Reports, No. 37, Finland.

Heffermehl, F. (2008). *Nobels Vilje.* Oslo: Vidarforlaget.

Hemingway, E. (1930). *Farvel til Våpnene.* (Translated by Herman Wildenvey). Oslo: Gyldendal forlag.

Hogenhuis-Seliverstoff, A. (2002). *Juliette Adam (1836- 1936) l'instigatrice.* Paris: L'Harmattan.

Howard, M. (2002). *The Invention of Peace and the Reinvention of War.* London: Profile Books ltd.

Johannisson, K. (2010). *Melankolske rom. Om angst, lede og sårbarhet gjennom tidene.*

(Translated by Monica Aasprong). Oslo: Cappelen Damm.

Jonassen, M. (2007). *De overlevende. 19 norske kvinner og menn forteller om sine liv i Hitlers fangeleirer.* Oslo: Cappelen Damm.

Jorfald, U. (1962). *Bertha von Suttner og Nobels fredspris.* Oslo: Bokcentralen.

Jørgensen, J. C. (2005). *Om breve. Ni essays om brevformen i hverdagen, litteraturen og journalistikken.* København: Museum Tusculanum Press.

Kaltefleiter, W. & Pfalzgraff, R.L. (1985). *The Peace Movements in Europe & The United States.* London: Croom Helm.

Keel, A. (1999). *Bjørnstjerne Bjørnson. En biografi 1880-1920.* Oslo: Gyldendal.

Kempf, B. (1964). *Bertha von Suttner. Das Lebensbild einer grossen Frau. Schriftstellerin. Politikerin. Journalistin.* Wien: Österreichischer Bundesverlag.

Klinge, M. (1985). *Borgerskapets brytningstid. Cappelens Verdenshistorie,* bind. 14. Oslo: Cappelen.

Koht, H. (1906). *Freds-tanken i Noregs-sogo. Noreg i den samfolkelege rettsvoksteren.* Oslo: Det Norske Samlaget.

Larsson, U. (2008). *Alfred Nobel. Networks of Innovation.* Stockholm: Archives of The Nobel Museum (Gumanistika).

Leira, H. (2002). *Internasjonal idealisme og Norge. Utenrikspolitisk tenkning fra Justus Lipsius til Halvdan Koht.* (Hovedoppgave i statsvitenskap, Universitetet i Oslo).

Leira, H. (2004). "Hele vort Folk er naturlige og fødte Fredsvenner". Norsk fredstenkning fram til 1906. *Historisk tidsskrift,* bind 83, s. 153-180. Oslo: Universitetsforlaget.

Linden, W.H. van der (1987). *The International Peace Movement 1815-1874.* Amsterdam: Tilleul Publications.

Luft, D. S. (2003). *Eros and Inwardness in Vienna. Weininger, Musil, Doderer.* Chicago: The University of Chicago Press.

Lughofer, J. G. (2011). Bertha von Suttner. A Prototypical European Writer. *Letter Journal for Linguistics and Literary Studies,* Vol. 09, pp.186-209.

Mak, G. (2004). *Europa. En reise gjennom det 20. århundret.* Oslo: Cappelen Damm.

Montefiore, S. S. (2003). *Stalin. Den Røde Tsarens Hoff.* (Translated by Jorunn Carlsen og Arne-Carsten Carlsen). Oslo: Cappelen.

Moynahan, B. (2007). *The French Century, An Illustrated History of Modern France.* Paris: Flammarion.

Munthe, A. (1935). *Boken om San Michele.* Stockholm: Åhlén & Åkerlund.

Nash, R. H. (1969). *Ideas of History. Vol 1: Speculative approaches to history.* New York: E.P. Dutton & Co., Inc.

Neiberg, M. S. (2001). *Warfare in World History.* London and New York: Routledge.

Nisbet, R. (1994). *History of the Idea of Progress.* New Brunswick, NJ: Transaction Publishers.

Obama, B. (2006). *The Audacity of Hope: thoughts on reclaiming the American dream.* New York: Three Rivers Press.

Palmer, R.R., Colton J. & Kramer L. (2007). *A History of the Modern World.* New York: McGraw-Hill.

Palmowski, J. (2003). *A Dictionary of Contemporary World History. From 1900 to the Present Day.* Oxford: Oxford University Press.

Pauli, H. (1947). *Alfred Nobel: Dynamite King, Architect of Peace.* London: Nicholson & Watson.

Pauli, H. (1957). *Cry of the heart. The story of Bertha von Suttner.* New York: Ives Washburn.

Made in the USA
Columbia, SC
03 November 2023

25394556R00124